8 SIMPLE RULES

FOR MARRYING MY DAUGHTER

and Other Reasonable Advice from
the Father of the Bride
(Not That Anyone Is Paying Attention)

W. BRUCE CAMERON

A Fireside Book
PUBLISHED BY SIMON & SCHUSTER
NEW YORK   LONDON   TORONTO   SYDNEY

Fireside
A Division of Simon & Schuster, Inc.
1230 Avenue of the Americas
New York, NY 10020

First Fireside hardcover edition April 2008

Fireside and colophon are registered trademarks of Simon &
Schuster, Inc.

For information about special discounts for bulk purchases, please
contact Simon & Schuster Special Sales at 1-800-456-6798 or
business@simonandschuster.com.

Designed by Mary Austin Speaker

Manufactured in the United States of America

10   9   8   7   6   5   4   3   2   1

Library of Congress Cataloging-in-Publication Data
Cameron, W. Bruce.
   8 simple rules for marrying my daughter / by W. Bruce Cameron.
      p. cm.
   1. Weddings—Humor. I. Title. II. Title: Eight simple rules for
marrying my daughter.
   PN6231.W37C36 2008
   814'.6—dc22

                                        2007040861

ISBN-13: 978-1-4165-5891-0
ISBN-10:   1-4165-5891-8

For Georgia Lee and Chelsea

ACKNOWLEDGMENTS

I f you're reading this, I'm indebted to you for supporting my writing, and would thank you by name except then my book would be nothing but a list of names, which I'm pretty sure my editor wouldn't be happy with. So in addition to you, dear reader, I would like to thank the following individuals for all they have done for me.

Thank you, John Temple, editor, publisher, and president of the *Rocky Mountain News*, the fine newspaper that gave me my first break by publishing my humor column, and Maria Cote, my current editor and gardening counselor.

My column is now carried in something like fifty newspapers, thanks to the efforts of Richard Newcombe and his staff at Creators Syndicate, particularly my editor Anthony Zurcher. Thanks to Oliver North for introducing me to Richard.

When Diane Reverand left the business I despaired that I would ever again have such a talented editor, but then Trish Todd stepped in and made writing this book a joyful and easy process, a rare thing in this business.

Thanks, Trish, and thanks to my agent Scott Miller at Trident Media, for putting me together with Trish.

Besides Scott, I am also blessed with the most dedicated and honest representatives in the business. Thank you, Gary Loder at The Gersh Agency, for sticking with me on the roller-coaster ride, and to Lauren Lloyd for joining the ride at precisely its scariest moment, and to Amy Schiffman at Gersh for believing in this project. Thank you, Melissa Campbell, for your connections at Gersh!

Thanks, Steve Younger and Hayes Michael, for protecting my back against those who would stab it.

Thanks, Bob Bridges, for being my volunteer fireman and protecting me from self-immolation.

Thank you, Rhona Raskin, for being an early adopter of Cameron Humor, and for introducing me to the concept of genius in comedy.

Thanks, Lisa Craig, for designing and maintaining the Web site at www.wbrucecameron.com. It is still one of the most professional author sites on the Internet, and if you don't believe me, go look at it for yourself.

Thanks to Aaron, Susan, Diane, Gary, Holly, Ari, Brian, and Katherine: my buddies on the WGA publicity committee. Look you guys, free publicity! The tuxedo I'm wearing on the cover of the hardcover version of this book was provided by Mr. Tuxedo in West Los Angeles, whose owner Hagop Terzian gave me both guidance and a special break on price so I wouldn't look as if I were going to prom in 1978.

Thanks to Oprah Winfrey for having me on her show and making me (as far as I can determine) the first humor writer to have a book excerpted in *O, The Oprah Magazine*. I'd buy you a car but someone said you already have one.

Thanks to Jennifer Altabef—your friendship means so much to me.

Thanks to Kurt Hamilton for letting me have the corner office.

Thanks to James Armstrong for caring more about the truth than the money.

Thanks to Claire LaZebnik for appreciating my Madness, to Margaret Nagel for trying to help me during this Lifetime, and to Annabelle Gurwitch for getting me Fired.

Thank you to the Robert Benchley Society for giving me the Robert Benchley Award for humor and for buying me lunch, and to Dave Barry for standing in judgment of me.

Thanks to Geoff Jennings for trying to fix the book business, or at least my part of it.

Thanks to my parents for their loving support and their DNA, both of which I couldn't live without.

Thanks to Amy and Julie for being my older sisters.

Thanks to Tom Rooker for all of his help and for moving in next door and for waiting until he did to do so.

My three children let me write about them in my column without complaint, even though I make up stuff about them sometimes, like just now when I said "without complaint." I appreciate it.

Thanks to Big Al, Evie, Ted, Maria, Jakob, Maya, and Ethan for being willing to share their genius with me. Thanks Jen for getting that I got it.

Danny Schmitz and Bob Krakower have invested themselves in my future, and so far their return on that investment has been worse than buying Enron at ninety dollars a share. Thanks, guys, for not dumping the stock.

Thanks to Sudy Hurst for putting me in league with the juniors.

Thanks to Tim Bete for offering a taste of Dayton.

And thanks to those true friends who have been so solidly in support of me: Samantha Dunn, Diane Driscoll, Rick and Sylvia Baker, Suzette Standring, Bill Timmeus, Marlene Stevens, Markie Post, Marcia Wallace, Norma Vela, Julie Cypher, Gavin MacLeod, Robert Haught, Andrew Gunn, Leslie Rockiter, Amy Steftenagle, Stephanie Miller, Jane and Gary Wilson, John McDonnell, Patrick Flannagan, Jaynee Brown, Dave Lieber, David Leinberger, for heaven's sake that's enough. The only way a writer can have the courage or at least the delusions to keep going is with the encouragement of his friends and I know I've neglected to list most of them here.

So I'll stop after thanking one more person: Cathryn Michon, my partner in business and in life, without whom I would write nothing because what would be the point? Thank you, Cathryn, for everything.

CONTENTS

INTRODUCTION

A father's job is to protect his daughters from dangerous things, like puberty. This isn't easy, because the daughters don't want to be protected—in fact, when they get to be teenagers, "dangerous" somehow becomes synonymous with "attractive."

When they were little, they were frightened there were monsters in their closets, and wanted you to check. Then they got older, and you worry there might be boys in there, and they scream at you that you have no right to look in the closet, it is their private property! (Even though it is in the home that you pay for.) When they were small, they wanted the light left on so they could sleep, but now they want to sit in the living room with the lights turned off (and their boyfriends presumably turned on), and they get annoyed when you noisily flip on all the lights so you can better see the shotgun you are cleaning. Back when they were young, they wore cute little T-shirts and shorts—and as teenagers they appear to be wearing *exactly the same clothes,* outfits so tiny on their alarmingly developed bodies you feel the need to wrap a quilt around them, or maybe spray them with insulation.

You used to be the most important male figure in

their lives, and now they regard you as if you are something growing on the shower curtain. You've been replaced by a slinking, sniveling succession of slackers who stare at your daughters with ill-disguised desire.

Boys.

The first time a boy comes over to see your daughter, your instinct is to ask him to leave your property and your planet. Unfortunately, even if you get rid of this one, others will soon follow—people have been irresponsibly breeding boys for a long time, and why this isn't prevented by the Geneva Convention, you'll never understand. Other than convening an emergency session of the UN Security Council, there are few practical solutions available to you, though basketball player Charles Barkley had an interesting take on what to do about the boys sniffing around his daughter: "I figure if I kill the first one, word will get out."

My response to the viral spread of teenage boys was to write the *8 Simple Rules for Dating My Teenage Daughter*, which ultimately became an ABC television show starring the late John Ritter. (Example—Rule One: If you pull into my driveway and honk, you'd better be delivering a package, because you're sure as heck not picking anything up.)

These 8 Simple Rules, posted on their bedroom doors when my daughters refused the idea of wearing T-shirts with the rules printed on the back, worked about as well as you could expect, which is to say, not at all. My daughters continued to behave in ways I can only describe as FBF (forbidden by father) until they finally became old enough to admit I was right along. (I suppose I should reveal that though they were old enough to make this humble admission, they didn't actually do so.)

Then they moved out, somehow thinking this would mean an end to FBF activities, which is absurd. My job to protect my daughters will not end until I've had my first autopsy. The fact that the forbidden activities are no longer occurring in my own living room is not at all relevant, though I do appreciate having more space on my couch.

Which brings us to the subject of this book: marriage.

Now, I am not against my daughters getting married and having children—far from it, I can't *wait* until they have teenage daughters of their own!

> (Now Grown) Former Teenage Daughter: *Can you believe it? When I told my daughter she was grounded, she screamed that she hated me and locked herself in the bedroom!*

> Father: *Really? I can't imagine.*

> Former Teenage Daughter: *Then she snuck out her bedroom window!*

> Father: *(helpless laughter)*

Yet as much as I am looking forward to having the above conversation, I am against my daughters marrying too young, too hastily, or too soon for me to get used to the idea that a "son"-in-law is suddenly going to be part of my permanent family. Why can't we wait a few years, until we're all, say, retired?

I think we can all agree that the world runs better when we learn from our fathers. When it comes to love, I've had a series of problems finding someone who truly appreciates just how wonderful I am, which has led to a couple of relationship disasters, including a divorce. Now I realize that my wonderfulness is best doled out in small doses, or maybe even just kept completely to myself. With my glorious male wonderfulness thus in check, I've managed to find and keep a steady girlfriend for a couple of years, though she's just off a nasty breakup herself, so we're both proceeding with caution. This is called "learning from our mistakes," and my daughters, both still in their twenties, strike me as too young to have made an adequate number of mistakes from which to learn, though when it comes to boys, I've done my best to prevent them from making mistakes, and I don't care if this *is* paradoxical. What is it they say? Life begins at forty! What a perfect age for my daughters to start contemplating getting married!

Unfortunately, you can't issue an FBF against biology—I know, because I've tried. Despite the fact that your daughter is still your little girl, when she looks in the mirror, she sees a full-grown women, one she apparently feels is ready to get married to some loser.

Or not! Maybe he's not a loser! One of your jobs is to find this out—just because he refuses to watch *America's Most Wanted* doesn't mean he's afraid he'll see his face on it. Just because he asks you how things are going at work doesn't mean he's mentally tabulating your net worth because he's planning to steal your money and sack your village. Just because he kisses your daughter doesn't mean he's an alien being, intending to impregnate her with a creature that will burst out of her chest and destroy mankind.*

On the other hand, all three of the above are reasonable suspicions that should be investigated via polygraph and liver biopsy, and if he refuses, he should not be marrying your daughter. (Yet if you think about it, isn't agreeing to a polygraph exactly what someone would do if he were guilty?)

Then, entirely separate from the topic of marriage is the

---

lien, Twentieth Century-Fox, 1979

subject of the *wedding*. You'll find that during the planning and execution of this complex ritual, your advice and counsel are very much appreciated by you.

Just as *8 Simple Rules for Dating My Teenage Daughter* is an owner's manual for any parent whose little girl has transformed overnight into little monster, this book, *8 Simple Rules for Marrying My Daughter*, is also a how-to guide. How to handle all the joyous events in your future: your daughter's engagement, wedding, marriage, and requests for loans. How to cure your daughter of Bridemania (you'll need a Bible, a crucifix, and some holy water). How to deal with your future son-in-law in a way that's friendly and yet still totally intimidating.

Whether your daughter is years and years away from getting married (as I still insist mine should be) or has recently had someone propose, in these pages you'll find the answers to your questions, like:

- It's the happiest time of her life—so why is everybody crying?
- Shopping for a wedding gown—how can something so boring be so frightening?
- What's the difference between the traditional and nontraditional wedding? (Traditionally, the father of the bride pays for both.)
- The wedding theme song—should we use the music from *Mission: Impossible?*

Oddly, the whole earth-shattering series of events begins not with the father, but with a man to whom you've probably given little thought or notice: the prospective groom-to-be.

ONE

~

There Are 8 Simple Rules for Marrying My Daughter

"Groom" as a noun means "man who will marry my daughter." "Groom" as a verb means "monkeys eating lice off each other." The challenge for a father is to accept the reality of the former without fixating on a mental image of the latter.

Usually, the news that one of the boys who has been hanging around eating all the food in the house has somehow morphed into a fiancé comes as a big shock to the father, who had no idea things were this serious because the only clue anyone gave him was that his daughter mentioned that her relationship was "very, very serious" and that they "might get married." How come nobody ever tells him anything?

In ancient times, the boy gave a clear sign to a father of his intentions by offering a gift of respect, like a donkey or a fiefdom. In today's world, this very practical system has fallen to the wayside. (Though to be truthful, I don't really want a donkey. A sports car would be nice, however. And a fiefdom would still be okay.)

It was also a practice for the father to pay a dowry to the

1

groom—sort of like paying ransom, except that the kidnapper got to keep her! This is pretty baffling until you consider that in ancient times, girls often married in their teens: There are moments when a father would quite frankly pay anything to get someone else to take responsibility for his teenage daughter. The practice of giving a dowry has evolved into the tradition of having the father pay for the wedding. (Though I have to say, if you're ever afforded the opportunity to fulfill your obligation with nothing more than a couple of goats, do it!)

Now the father finds himself playing catch-up. The daughter seems sure this guy is "the one," but what does she know? Every single other man in her life has turned out to be a loser—otherwise, they'd still be in her life. With that kind of track record, how can she be trusted to get it right this time?

Who is this guy, anyway? He could be anything—a thief, a con artist, a member of Congress. Just because he's clever enough to burrow into the family doesn't mean he belongs there, any more than a prairie-dog village belongs in the front yard.

Only a father can administer the type of interrogation and investigation necessary under these circumstances— oddly, no one else thinks it even matters.

THE FATHER IS ALWAYS RIGHT—IF YOU DON'T BELIEVE IT, JUST ASK HIM

Is anyone good enough to marry your daughter?

No!

This isn't to say that you don't want your daughter to be happy. Some of the best moments of your life involve your daughter being happy (like, for example, on Father's Day, when she would give you gifts and make you dinner. Why can't every day be like that?) In fact, that's the point. You want her to be happy, but what are the odds that this guy, selected at what feels like random, can make her so? He's not making *you* happy, that's for sure!

Be careful how you phrase your comments and questions: You might come off sounding unfriendly, even hostile—which is exactly what you want.

Key to protecting your daughter is establishing that you're the boss. You make the rules, including:

8 Simple Rules for Marrying My Daughter

Rule #1

If you neglected to ask my permission before you proposed to my daughter, don't worry about it, you can make it up to me by making sure your wedding is both beautiful and to a different woman.

Rule #2

There are many, many men your age in this world, but there is only one woman who is my daughter. She is unique. You, on the other hand, can be replaced at any time.

Rule #3

My whole life, it has been my job to make my daughter happy. Now it will be your job. My job will be to make sure you do your job. And don't think that just because my daughter has picked you, it means you meet my personal standards for what is good for her. I haven't made up my mind yet, and will be evaluating you over a time period known as "forever."

Rule #4

You may be wondering how to address me: Dad? Bruce? Mr. Cameron? Let's end the awkwardness. For the time being, I suggest you stick with "sir." Sample phrases to help you become accustomed to this term: "May I wash your car for you today, sir?" "Are there any tasks that I can do around the house while you watch the ballgame, sir?" "Is there anything I can do to make your life better, sir?"

Rule #5

I may be old-fashioned, but I believe that any man who wishes to marry my daughter should have a good job and a successful career. I'm not saying you need to be the sole source of income, but I am saying if you don't take care of my daughter, *I* will take care of *you*.

Rule #6

You do not have a legal contract with my daughter; she can break off the engagement if she wants and there is nothing you can do about it except change your name and move out of the country. The same goes for you: I would not want you marrying my daughter if you do not truly feel you are the right man for her, nor, if you break it off, would I want you marrying anybody else. Ever.

Rule #7

You may, in a very male episode of last-minute panic, decide that you need to sow some wild oats right before the wedding. Let's define our roles: If you are the sower, I will be your reaper.

Rule #8

The vows you will be taking commit you to be faithful to my daughter "'til death do you part." Please know if you break your vows, I'll immediately exercise the second part of the contract.

THE SON-IN-LAW: YOU'RE NOT LOSING A DAUGHTER, YOU'RE GAINING A DEBTOR

With a biological son, it is generally recognized that as the parent, what you say is law. (At least, this is generally recognized among parents.) With a son-in-law, however, the chain of command isn't as clear. Whatever you say to the man who is married to your daughter is, in essence, said to both of them. And as we've seen, she doesn't always do what you tell her, or she wouldn't have gone out with this guy in the first place. So you can issue a reasonable directive ("Please do not come within fifty yards of my daughter"), he'll ask your daughter about it, and she will utter some irresponsible response like "Don't pay any attention to my father." It's as if the guy is walking around with his own appeals court in his pocket.

The relationship between father and son-in-law is therefore fraught with tension and is probably best avoided altogether. Isn't it true that in some societies the daughters never get married and have children but rather devote their years to making sure their fathers are happy? (I recognize that societies adopting this admirable practice will eventually be, well, extinct, but what do you care? By the time it occurs to everyone that not having babies means no one is left to pay Social Security, you'll be extinct yourself.)

So okay, maybe it's not true, but that's no reason not to try it.

In other societies, marriages are arranged by the head of the household. (I know this one is true.) There are people, called "women," who don't think this system is a good idea, and people, called "fathers" who think it is pretty sensible. The upside to the system is that you can pick your own son-in-law, like maybe the new starting quarterback for the Denver Broncos. The downside is that you can never be sure that the Broncos will make the playoffs.

But even if your son-in-law is the greatest guy in the world (after yourself) and invites you to sit on the team bench whenever the Broncos have a home game, the relationship is still a difficult one. Let's face it, he is the man you *know* is sleeping with your daughter. With every other guy, you've been able to look at their relationship with a certain amount of benign denial, even if they traveled to Europe on vacation and stayed in the same hotel room the whole time. (Lots of people in Europe don't sleep together. Queen Elizabeth and Prince Philip, for example.) You spent most of her childhood protecting her from male predators and now all of a sudden you're sending her home with one. (That's how it feels, anyway.) He's now involved in decisions affecting your daughter's life that don't seem like they should be any of his business—like where she is going to live, for example. Obviously, your daughter should live close enough to her father so that it is practical to bake him a pie. There's no justification for him suddenly announcing that he and *your* daughter are moving to Miami, even if he did get traded to the Dolphins.

Also, as the head man in the family, your statements of fact have always been treated as unchallengeable truth or at least completely ignored. A son-in-law, however, is another man, and men like to argue the facts. So when you begin lecturing him on how in some societies the father is tended to like a king by his daughters, he'll look at you and say, "What society? Where?" And then you'll be forced to change the subject.

"How come you threw that interception in that game against Kansas City?" you'll ask accusingly. That'll shut him up.

With your son-in-law interjecting his so-called legitimate questions into your proclamations, your daughter will begin to think of you as less than perfect, undermining your authority. If fathers everywhere lose authority, it will lead to a breakdown of the family, causing a collapse in the world order, leading to looting and burning. Therefore, it is only logical that if your daughter gets married, the world will come to an end.

"How is that logical?" your son-in-law will challenge.

See how irritating this is?

The conclusion to all this is simple: The worst system is where the daughter gets to pick the man she'll marry, though the one where the father gets to pick is worst, too.

MY DAUGHTER'S PROPOSED GROOM

For the past several years, my daughters have been doing what I suppose you could call "test dating"—finding young men to bring to me to see if I approved, the way a cat will bring home a dead bird. (I'm not sure this is how they would characterize their actions, but clearly that's the underlying intent.) My daughters were worried that I'd be unfriendly and insulting, but for the most part, I've been very kind and accepting of these chuckleheads.

The fact that I'm willing to participate in this exercise at all goes to show what a wonderful father I've become. I know what we're doing here, we're practicing for the Big Game—

that day, ten or twenty years from now, when we'll all agree that one of these men is acceptable as a husband, subject to my veto. My gentle and helpful criticisms of the test candidates provide loving guidance to my daughters as they refine their selection criteria.

"Loving guidance!" Samantha, my older daughter, hoots. Now in her mid-twenties, Sam's a tall brunette who inherited my natural athletic ability but stubbornly maintains that her sports trophies came from her efforts and not her dad's DNA. She manages the operations for a large venture-capital firm, and I suppose you would say that the label "competitive personality" applies to her the way "competitive environment" applies to hockey. She often pretends to think I'm wrong when we argue about something, but then later will reconsider the conversation and call me back with more arguments.

Fortunately, my younger daughter, Valerie, is not yet of the age where I have to worry about her getting married. Out of college and in her early twenties, Valerie has too many jobs to find the time to even date somebody. Last time I checked, she was selling natural hypoallergenic beauty products made from, I don't know, bird spit and snake sweat; she was manufacturing clothing made from organic fibers and cow poop; she was teaching Sanskrit to the homeless; and she was taking extension classes in Ancient Religions Nobody Knows About. Her boyfriend of the moment, named Moldy or Mulchy or something, is one of those crunchy neo-eco types, who looks like he is expressing his political beliefs by biodegrading within his clothing. The two of them seem to have little in common except a cheerful belief that we are all doomed.

I also have a son, but he won't be getting married any time soon, either. He's in college, totally focused on depleting my cash assets. He speaks seriously of medical school, and I suppose having a doctor in the family will extend my life expectancy to the point where I can pay off his student loans. People say he reminds them of me, probably because he is young and good-looking.

Which brings us to Geoff, my older daughter's current boyfriend. He's handsome, hardworking, and respectful, so naturally he makes me very suspicious.

Her previous slacker boyfriends never volunteered to help around the house, but Geoff is always willing to lend a hand, which naturally makes me very suspicious. Why's he trying so hard to please me—what is he trying to cover up?

Usually the guys she brings over avoid my eyes and mumble in response to my casual questions about their probation officer. Geoff always chats with me about things he knows I'm interested in, which naturally makes me very suspicious. Why's he trying so hard to suck up to me?

I don't voice my concerns to my daughter, though, because as a loving father I'm sensitive to the fact that if I do so, he might not help me clean out the garage.

When Geoff shows up at my home one afternoon saying he "needs to talk" to me, he seems nervous, as if he is planning to say he can't come over this weekend to work on the garage. If that's the case, I decide, I'll be charitable. It's enough that he offered in the first place, I'll tell him, so we'll just pick a weekend that works for him. Besides, I've been putting off cleaning out the garage since the thing was built. What's another week?

I invite Geoff in and am surprised when he accepts my offer of a beer—normally he doesn't drink much. I soberly pour myself an iced tea, mentally calculating in my head that I'm owed a beer later.

"How's work, Mr. Cameron?" Geoff asks. I explain where

I am with my various projects, taking care to avoid using the words "completely stalled." It takes a while to avoid saying that, and while I talk I notice that Geoff's eyes seem distant, which is odd in and of itself—normally we both find what I say to be fascinating.

Yet I am totally unprepared for what he says when I wrap up my presentation and ask him if he has any questions for me.

"The thing is, Mr. Cameron, I'm here because, you know . . ." He gulps the last of his beer. "I'm here to ask your permission to marry your daughter. To ask her to marry me. To propose marriage."

I blink at the evasive and unclear language. "Excuse me?"

"I'm asking for your daughter's hand in marriage."

"Her hand?" I sputter.

"Well." He grins. "I guess all of her. Yes, sir. I want to marry Sam."

Now, I have always believed in the tradition where the man asks for the father's permission to marry the daughter and the father says no. But he looks so sincere, and so in need of another beer, that I stifle my immediate reaction— besides, I don't have a loaded weapon nearby, anyway.

In a way, the fact that he wants to make Sam his wife is a compliment, testimony to what a wonderful woman my daughter has become because of my parenting, so to reject him out of hand would be uncaring. He is saying, in essence, that he wants to become my son-in-law, something that I might be willing to entertain in a few years. Several years. Many, many years.

"George," I start to say, searching for the right words.

"Geoff," he corrects.

"Geoff," I agree. "Don't you think this is rushing things

a bit? You barely know her. A man and a woman should be together for at least a year or two before they even discuss marriage."

"We've been dating five years."

I'm thunderstruck. Five years! Why on earth have we waited until *now* to clean out the garage? "Are you sure it's been that long?"

"Yes, five years last month, actually."

"Well . . . don't you think that if you have taken *five years*, maybe you're just not sure?" I counter.

Clearly, this is not something that he'd considered. He opens his mouth, then closes it.

"Plus, I know things are not going well for you at work right now," I say.

"I just got promoted."

"Sure, promoted, but who knows what that really means?" I say shrewdly. "With job instability, with you waffling over this issue for five years, I think maybe you should reconsider, don't you? What do you say we go out to the garage and talk about it."

"But," he says, "I love your daughter. She means the world to me. I want to be married to her."

I know what you're thinking—same thing I thought. No fair! He cleverly lured me into the open with his light weaponry—"we've dated for five years"—and now has opened up on me with heavy artillery. What's a father to say to something like "I love your daughter, she means the world to me?"

I stare at Geoff, bewildered. For the first time, I consider just how gutsy it is for him to come over here and talk to me, man-to-man, drinking a manly beverage and asking permission to take one of my most precious possessions away from me.

I also consider that they aren't actually my possessions at

all, my daughters. They are free-willed women who haven't really done what I wanted since they turned two years old. I can say no, here, and then maybe attempt some other reasonable measures to prevent them from getting married, such as trying to obtain a restraining order or a mob hit, but in the end I know that any man with the courage to enter my house and ask my permission to take my daughter's hand in marriage will have the courage to go around me if I try to stop it.

Which brings me to the final question. Why try to stop it? I instinctively want to protect my daughter from hurt. Marriage can be hard. A man can seem normal enough, but then as time goes by either develop or reveal significant problems—and if your daughter is married to him, they become *her* problems. All of these are good reasons to want to end this whole thing right here. Nobody but a father understands this—we just want the best for our daughters, and when they get married, determining what's best passes out of our control.

I always knew this moment would come—the first time I thought about it was when we saw the sonogram and the doctor proclaimed we were going to have a girl. But there hasn't been enough time between then and now! I'm not ready!

And that's what I'm about to tell him—forget it, I'm not ready, come back never. But then, totally unbidden, an image of my daughter slips into my head, not as she appeared in the sonogram, when she looked to me like a potato in a microwave, but just yesterday, when I happened to stop by her office and saw her in a conference room, running a meeting with her staff. She looked like a grown-up.

My little girl is all grown up.

A lump building in my throat, I stick out my hand for

Geoff to shake, grinning a little at the surprised look in his eyes. I guess he thought I'd say no.

"Okay," I tell him. "Of course."

THE DEGREES OF THE THIRD DEGREE

Once the father has accepted the future son-in-law, he should let the young man know that (a) he's welcomed into the family and will be loved like a son, and (b) he can still be shot. The message is, "If you hurt my little girl, I will kill you," though some fathers might prefer to temper the statement and say "murder you," or "slit your throat," or "drive over you with my SUV and set your corpse on fire."

To reinforce the message, the father will usually gather his male relatives and friends and subject the son-in-law-to-be to a friendly interrogation. I call this form of intimidation the "Running of the Groom." The father's buddies subject the would-be groom to the third degree, asking hostile questions and making veiled threats, and the son-in-law gets the message and never does anything to harm the daughter and maybe gets gone while the going's good. That's the theory, anyway.

For Geoff's Running of the Groom, I assembled a few of my friends and we went over to my neighbor Tom's house. Tom is my buddy and has a really nice bass boat that he bought for himself over his wife's objections, who said it was an expensive luxury because he probably would never have time to use it. He likes to invite his friends to come over and sit in the boat in his garage and tell them the story of how his wife Emily said he absolutely shouldn't buy it and he hung up the phone and signed the contract right there, showing her who is boss. He loves that story, though he gets a little glum when someone asks why the boat is in the garage, because he's been too busy to take it out on the water yet.

Tom is about five years younger than I am and works for a manufacturer as the vice president of affability, or some such. As I understand it, he has a bunch of salespeople who call him and tell him they've sold stuff, and he tells them they've done a good job. I don't really know what they're selling and sometimes I'm convinced Tom doesn't, either.

Tom doesn't work out as much as I did that one time, and I know from experience that he doesn't watch what he eats because Emily, a nurse, often works nights and so Tom and I frequently have dinner together. Tom is a good cook if you're into foods that manage to somehow be both delicious and fattening. And I'm a good friend—often I'll take the leftovers to my house to spare him the temptation of pumping up his cholesterol with, say, barbecue ribs. So Tom's a little heavy around the stomach, but very good-natured and willing to take a lot of kidding about his paunch and kid back that I've got the same waistline, ha ha.

Besides Tom and myself, I had my cousin Ward. Ward weighs about as much as one of Tom's dinners—a pasty, spindly guy who I figured would nonetheless be intimidating because he sold life insurance.

We decided to hold the Running of the Groom in Tom's boat to further put Geoff off balance. Tom slipped on his captain's hat to lend authority to the proceedings, though I vetoed the idea of us all wearing life jackets.

"Nice boat, you get to take it out much?" Geoff asked, settling down into one of the new seats. Tom gave him a dark look.

Cousin Ward cleared his throat and jumped right into it. "So Geoff . . . that's your real name, right? Geoff?" Tom and I gave Ward an admiring look, because neither one of us had thought to ask that question.

"Yes. Short for Geoffrey."

"Likely story," Tom snorted.

"Last name?" Ward pressed doggedly. I noticed he was filling in some kind of form.

"King."

"So Sam's name will be King?" Ward continued.

That one startled me. My daughter would be changing her last name. She wouldn't even be in my family anymore! I took a deep, shaky breath, eyeing Mr. King. "Geoff, I'd like to hear from you a little bit about how you are planning to care for my daughter, and maybe someday grandchildren—in the event that things don't work out for you at your current employer."

"Like, what if your company goes out of business?" Tom challenged.

Geoff frowned. "The federal government?"

Ward wrote it down.

"Lots of federal agencies go out of business," I said, though I couldn't think of a single one in the history of the world.

"Probably not the Internal Revenue Service, though," Geoff observed.

"And are you planning to stay there your whole career?" I queried.

"Just until I get my CPA," he responded.

Cousin Ward leaned forward. "Are you really prepared for marriage? Do you feel you have adequate insurance?"

I shook my head in irritation. "What we're trying to say, Geoff, is that now you're going to be part of the family."

"Our family," Tom agreed.

Geoff raised his eyebrows. "Oh, I didn't realize; Tom, you're related?"

"Well, no," Tom admitted.

I felt that the Running of the Groom was sort of running

off track. The point of it was to make Geoff understand that we were accepting him, but if he screwed up, there would be hell to pay. Nearly all fathers try some sort of variation of this, but mine was going poorly because as allies I had selected a couple of idiots.

I gave Geoff a stern look. "What we're trying to say, Geoff, is that if you hurt my daughter, my little girl, in any way, you'll be answering to me."

Tom nodded solemnly. "And me."

"And me," Cousin Ward added.

There, that went perfectly. Geoff swallowed, getting the message.

"Here's my card," Cousin Ward said. "Give me a call, I'd like to review your insurance policies."

UNCOVERING THE DARK SECRET

I've always wondered how Eva Braun's family handled what I suppose I would call the "boyfriend situation."

> EVA: *Dad, I've met this guy, he's got a really good job, lots of people report to him, and he even wrote a book!*

> DAD: *Sounds like a nice guy.*

> EVA: *Well, yeah, except he's Hitler.*

Of course, the daughter might be blinded by love and reluctant to examine the true character of her fiancé.

> EVA: *Oh foo, how bad can the Nazis really be?*

Thus it is up to the father to uncover whatever dark secret the groom is hiding. To do this, the father should avoid direct interrogation and instead pose trick questions that catch the unwary groom off guard. Thus ensnared, he'll be exposed as completely unworthy to marry your daughter, and she will listen to absolutely everything you have to say from then on.

DARK SECRET CLEVER TRICK QUESTIONS	
DON'T ASK	ASK
So, are you Hitler?	Have you ever conducted an Anschluss?
Are you a serial killer?	Come on, don't you feel a little sorry for the Boston Strangler?
Are you gay?*	Tom's feeling frisky, want to see him dance in the nude?†
Are you an ex-con?	I thought I'd fix some dinner, would you prefer yours be served on a dented metal tray?
Are you an alien being from another planet sent to Earth to marry my daughter?	Hey, remember in the movie *Alien*, that thing that burst out of John Hurt's chest . . . pretty cute little baby, didn't you think?
Are you a gambler?	I'll lay you ten to one odds you're not going to go through with this wedding, what do you say?
Are you some sort of spy for a foreign government?	Hey, Tom's got some ultra top-secret information, want to take a look?

---

* You don't need to have anything against homosexuals to prefer your daughter not marry a gay man.

† I admit this one probably wouldn't work because I don't think anyone—gay or straight—would want to see Tom in the nude.

The best time to ask these questions is before the wedding. But even if you wait until afterward, if the groom fails to answer them correctly, you can have the marriage annulled, I'm pretty sure that's a rule.

Of course, Geoff's Running of the Groom didn't happen right away. I'm getting ahead of myself in my eagerness to support the thesis that the father has total and complete control, if people would only pay attention to him.

To back up, after Geoff tricked me into giving him permission to marry my daughter, he had to ask *her*, which I guess is technically part of the whole getting engaged process. And that, of course, was a complicated issue in and of itself.

TWO

❧

An Announcement of Earth-Shattering Proportions and That Is No Exaggeration

Women think getting engaged is a pretty important event.

> FATHER: *Did you hear? Space aliens have landed and they will cure all disease and bring about world peace.*

> DAUGHTER: *That's nothing, I have really big news. I got engaged!*

Men, on the other hand, tend to have more perspective.

> ENGAGED MAN: *So I was watching the game, Green Bay had it fourth and six, and they decide to go for it, and my fiancée—did I tell you I got engaged this weekend?—my fiancée asks me what play action pass means, so I say . . .*

> FRIEND: *Wait, hold on, man, hold on. Back up. Did I hear you correctly? Are you serious? Green Bay went for it on fourth and six?*

When a young man proposes to your daughter, she will scream at the same decibel level she would use if a serial killer were climbing in the kitchen window. If you are in the vicinity, you are to be forgiven if you grab the nearest weapon—say, a bowl of popcorn—and race in and beat your daughter's fiancé over the head with it.

Even when it turns out to be a big misunderstanding, making a beating the first official act you bestow upon your future son-in-law can help set just the right tone in your relationship. You can always claim that in some cultures, braining a new fiancé with a bowl of popcorn is the traditional way to welcome him into the family.* It can also deliver two important messages to the newly engaged couple: (1) If you scare me again with unexpected screaming or wedding expenses, I may wind up inflicting physical pain upon your fiancé, and (2) I am out of popcorn.

This beautiful tradition involving the popcorn bowl was related to me by my neighbor Tom, who encountered the ritual after he proposed to his wife Emily in her parent's kitchen. Tom's father-in-law welcomed him into the family with such enthusiasm, Tom had to go to the emergency room. Tom's father-in-law insists that he thought his daughter was being attacked and was only trying to protect her, but I've always maintained that if he had known that Tom was proposing marriage, the old man would have reacted the same way. Tom is just lucky that Emily's father was sitting in the living room eating popcorn out of a porcelain bowl and wasn't in there cracking walnuts.

My older daughter, Sam, moved out of my home several years ago, though to make sure I would always miss her,

---

* They're going to use the "it's tradition!" argument on you a lot, so there's no reason why you shouldn't employ the same tactics.

she borrowed all of my appliances. This means I am spared the initial bout of screaming, so that by the time she comes over to tell me the really big news her voice is already a little hoarse.

I am a loving father, so even though I am watching a game, I recognize that this is a big moment for my daughter and turn away from my television because I have TIVO.

"Dad, I have some wonderful, wonderful news," she announces formally. Her fiancé, Geoff, holds back, under-standing that now that he is engaged to my daughter he has virtually no say in anything to do with the rest of his life.

"Let me guess. You're going to return my blender," I spec-ulate. I exchange glances with Geoff—I suppose I could say, "Oh, Geoff proposed? Yeah, I know. Let's watch the game," but I realize I'm supposed to act like I'm surprised.

She's frowning. "Could you stand up? And maybe move over here?"

She leads me to the wall where we always stand together for group photographs of my daughters and me scolding my son for making goofy faces at the camera. Her right hand is cupped over her left hand as if she's hurt herself punching somebody.

"Did you get in a fight?"

"A what?"

"Why are you holding your hand funny, did you scrape your knuckles on somebody's chin?"

"No! Dad, please. Just listen."

"Sure. But if you hit someone in the teeth, you might get infected."

"I didn't hit anybody, but if you don't shut up, that's going to change," she tells me.

My daughter is strong and tough, but I doubt that if she took a swing at me she could actually hurt me unless sh made contact. I give her a condescending look to let her know I'm not taking her threat seriously, but I do shut up just in case she meant it.

"Okay." She takes a deep breath. "I have some wonderful, wonderful news."

"You said that already," I point out.

"Yes, but then you ruined it by making the blender joke."

"It wasn't a joke, I really miss my blender." It's true, I feel a tug in my heart whenever I see the blank spot on the kitchen counter where the little fellow used to sit.

"Dad!" It's a sharp tone she will use a lot in the ensuing months. "Please. Just listen."

"Okay."

"Dad . . ." She glances at Geoff to make sure he he's paying attention. "Geoff and I are engaged [SCREAM]! I'm going to be married [SCREAM]!"

Having gone through it, I can offer advice to anyone whose daughter has just announced she has gotten engaged, whether or not it comes as a big shock.

1. Always hug her immediately. This will prevent her from seeing the expression on your face.
2. She doesn't expect you to scream, because men can't really do that, but you should make some excited pronouncement. Things like "wahoo!" and "oh boy!" are probably better than "the hell you say!" or "someone just spat on my grave!"
3. You should shake the hand of the groom-to-be, maybe a drink or perhaps stitches if you've used the y popcorn-bowl welcome.

tomatically assume she's having a psychotic r an adverse reaction to some new medica- may really love this guy, and perhaps, with your wisdom, you can turn him into either a man you're proud to call your son-in-law or a block of cement in the East River.

5. You probably shouldn't turn the game back on until they've left, even if it's the playoffs (I learned this one from personal experience).

The First Person You Tell, and Then the Other First Persons You Tell

If an engagement can be viewed as a long series of crises leading up to one gigantic crisis, the first crisis to emerge will be how to inform everyone of the engagement. Naturally, when the bride sets out to inform a long list of people that she is betrothed, she has to start with someone. But the question is, who should that person be? It's very important that the bride first tell her very, very best friend, the person she is closest to in the whole world, because if she doesn't, that person will never speak to her again.

Fortunately, by swearing that person to secrecy ("I'm getting married [SCREAM]! You're the first person I've told, so please don't tell anyone else, I haven't even told my parents yet."), the bride can usually advise a dozen people that they are the "first to know." More than that, though, and she runs the risk that one of them will blab and bring down the whole conspiracy, and then she'll have to round up a bunch of new best friends in time for the wedding.

Watching all of this unfold before my eyes is as interesting as observing an earthworm migration, but the only alternative would be to leave my own home—my living room has become Wedding Central. Sam's mother Judy, my ex, lives out of town with her husband, a man I kindly think of as "the Fop." He works as a success in the profit business, and Judy does something for his company. Naturally, plans were made to have the mother of the bride parachute in as often as possible, but for the time being, it was up to me to host the bridal alert phone tree.

"Why don't we just hire a blimp," I joke, "and have it circle the city flashing the news to everyone that way?"

"Oh, Dad," my daughter replies, "could we?"

My older daughter tells me that her mother and I are in the "top twenty first to know," so I guess I should feel honored. She's forgetting that technically I knew before she did, but I decide not to point that out. It's one of the few things I can do for her for her wedding that doesn't cost me anything.

EVERYBODY KNOWS EVERYTHING, EXCEPT THE FATHER

It turns out that everyone in the world has advice to give a newly engaged bride-to-be. After listening to my daughter tell her friends and relatives that she was engaged [SCREAM] and after hearing them all say, "Here's the *one thing* you should know," I have compiled a list of what every newly engaged woman should know.

A List of the *One Thing* Every Newly Engaged Woman Should Know

---

Don't Get Married in June
Everyone wants to get married in June for some reason,* probably (this is my theory, anyway) because

---

* For the past several years, there have been more weddings in July than in June. My personal theory is that the brides still want to get married in June, but the weddings themselves are so complicated that they wind up running into sudden death overtime.

it's between the hockey and football seasons. If you get married in June, reception halls are booked, caterers are booked, even the ministers are booked, so it will be much more expensive.

Get Married in June

Not only is it the most romantic month to get married (though no one can say why or offer a better alternative to my hockey theory), but the entire wedding industry is geared toward that month, so everyone is prepared for weddings and all the products and services are on sale, competing for your dollar, so it will be cheaper.

Don't Set Your Wedding Date for a While

Experts say that it takes seven to twelve months† to properly plan a wedding, or about the amount of time Eisenhower took to plan D-Day. The difference, of course, is that your wedding involves a lot more people. If you set a date right away, you'll find yourself backed up against an artificially created deadline, and you'll wind up spending the weeks before the wedding in a dead panic. If you wait, take a look at how everything is coming together first, and then set a date, you'll have a much more comfortable deadline, and you'll wind up spending the weeks before the wedding in a dead panic. Besides, a lot of men get cold feet when they are rushed to pick a date right after proposing— better give the groom time to adjust.

---

† I read somewhere that the average engagement now lasts seventeen months, which, let's face it, is longer than the last four of Pamela Anderson's marriages combined.

Set Your Wedding Date Immediately

You can't even plan something simple like the liberation of France if you don't have a firm date to work from. Plus, the time to get your fiancé to commit to a date is now—don't give him an opportunity to wriggle off the hook! Strike while the iron is hot! Tora! Tora! Tora!

Consider Eloping

Okay, maybe I'm the only one to come up with this tip, but I still think it's a good one. Remember, I was all alone on the hockey theory, too, but I think we can all agree now that I was correct about that. If you elope, you'd save a lot of money! It could be exciting, you could go someplace fun and take your father along. Hawaii is nice. So's Jamaica. Also, in case you missed the point earlier, you could save a lot of money!

Don't Even Consider Eloping

It would break your friends' hearts. It would break your family's hearts. Any time you went to a big fancy wedding, it would break your own heart. It would break the heart of every issuer of every credit card your father has. Your father must be kidding about eloping. He's such a kidder. Not that funny, but a kidder.

Inform Your Father That the Average Wedding Costs $27,000 (Actual Figure)*

The sooner he finds out, the sooner he can look into ways to raise the money, like smuggling drugs or kid-

---

* Several industry sources use this figure, though I know if you are seeing it for the first time you feel like someone just hit you

napping for ransom. He needs time to get used to the shock and to make all of his so-called jokes, like maybe you don't need a limo, ha ha.

Don't Inform Your Father That the Average Wedding Costs $27,000

Who wants her wedding to be average?

THE RING OF FIRE

The most important element of the engagement process is the ring, which is the method by which the groom communicates to the bride that either (a) he had someone (female) help him pick it out, or (b) it needs to be returned for something else.

Engagement rings are considered magical, and everyone is supposed to gaze fondly at it and make excessively exaggerated compliments like, "Wow, that diamond is so big it looks like Michael Moore riding a moped." (That's the one I use; you're welcome to have it.) Your daughter will spend hours and hours dreamily staring at it when she should be doing other things, like watching where she is driving.

My college-ensconced son, Chris, found the whole ring thing unnerving, because when his girlfriend saw the engagement ring, she got a milky look in her eyes, and he began to worry that never again would he be able to get her a sweatshirt as a birthday present. He even went so far as to ask me to tell his sister not to talk about the wedding to his girlfriend.

---

on the head with a bowl of popcorn. How can this be? Has the whole world gone crazy? (The answer, as will be revealed in this book, is yes, when it comes to weddings, the whole world has gone crazy.

I knew *that* wouldn't work—I'd endured too much screaming. They *had* to talk about it, there was nothing else they *could* talk about. "Chris," I advised, searching for a delicate way to put it, "that's like asking a bunch of dogs not to sniff each others' butts."

"Yeah, but it's like now all she wants to talk about is weddings and stuff nobody cares about."

I gazed fondly at him, remembering a time when I, too, was this stupid.

"Son, the only people who don't want to talk about it are men, and when it comes to this topic, what we want doesn't matter."

The ring that Geoff's sister helped him pick out is certainly pretty. "My sister said you're supposed to spend three times your monthly income," he explains.

"A time like this is no time to show fiscal responsibility," I agree.

"Dad," my older daughter warns, holding the ring so that it catches the light and gives me LASIK surgery.

I grin conspiratorially at my other daughter, but she's oddly pensive, looking away. Apparently she has decided to abandon her father and join the wedding dark side, and the decision is bothering her. I can't blame her, really—Valerie's in her early twenties, a time when a woman's brain grows nostalgic for the teen years, when her relationship with her parents was much closer and financially dependent. Sam getting engaged means that the family is changing, but Valerie isn't changing with it. Seeing her sister's frenzied happiness probably makes her wish that she, too, could become insane.

My son, however, is my staunch ally. "This whole thing is ridiculous," he declares bitterly. Then, seeing his girlfriend's expression, he pales. "I don't mean weddings, I mean the, uh, the whole . . ."

All the women are staring at him with dead eyes, while my daughter's diamond traces a red light across his chest like an assassin's laser sight probing for his heart.

"The idea that any piece of jewelry can possibly capture love," he blurts desperately.

There's a brief moment while the women consider whether they like this or if they should rip him to bits with their claws. Finally a decision is made. "That's so romantic," his girlfriend sighs, laying her head on his shoulder.

I stare at him, dumbfounded. No wonder he has such a pretty girlfriend! When I was in college the most romantic thing I ever did was ask a date what she wanted on her pizza.

My son's look is smug, and I know what he's thinking: Nothing says "I love you" more than a nice-looking sweatshirt.

THE MARRIAGE PROPOSAL: A FRAME-BY-FRAME ANALYSIS

The number one question asked new brides-to-be by their female friends is "How did he propose?" followed by "Why's your dad lying on the floor making heart-attack noises?"

As with everything else having to do with weddings, there is an expectation among young people today that proposals will be elaborate and showy. It wasn't always so: Back when Tom and Emily got engaged, the conversation went something like this.

EMILY: *Would you mind taking out the trash?*

TOM: *You sure? Here, let me just compact it a little.* (STEPS INTO TRASH CAN, GRUNTING)

EMILY: *Just take it out, okay?*

TOM: *No, look, there's plenty of room.*

EMILY: *It smells awful.*

TOM: *Did your father clean some fish or something?*

EMILY: *I don't know what it is.*

TOM: *Great, it's all over my shoes.*

EMILY: *Would you just take it out?*

TOM: *Hand me something to wipe my shoes with, okay?*

EMILY: *Sure, I'll get a paper towel.* (TURNS AWAY)

TOM (TO HER BACK): *Hey, also, would you marry me?*

EMILY (WHIRLING): *What?*

TOM: *Yuck, it is seeping into my socks.*

EMILY: *What did you say to me?*

TOM: *I said the fish juice is seeping into my socks. Now I've got slimy fish feet.*

EMILY: *No, before that.*

TOM: *Oh. Yeah. Do you want to get married or something?* (EMILY SCREAMS)

EMILY'S FATHER (FROM THE NEXT ROOM): *I'll save you, Emily!*

As romantic as that sounds, it is apparently not enough for today's young women, who have come to expect that a marriage proposal will be at least as entertaining as an evening with Blue Man Group.

For example, one winter I witnessed a very exciting proposal. My children had taken me skiing because they enjoy seeing their father come face-to-face with hard-packed snow. They soon grew tired of helping me back up and abandoned me on the slopes. I was getting on a chairlift when the attendants stopped me, letting a man and a woman get on the chair ahead of me.

"Dude, hope it's okay," the chairlift attendant apologized. "The dude in the chair ahead of you is asking his lady to marry him with a message in the snow."

"Dude," I responded, impressed.

"Dude." He nodded, helping me into the chair.

Sure enough, just a few feet from the top of the lift, our chairs soared right over the words "Marry Me Lori" written in the snow. I heard the woman in the chair ahead of me-Lori, I assumed—gasp as she read the words.

When we got off the lift, Lori stunned her would-be groom by punching him in the shoulder and skiing off. He stared after her, open-mouthed. Apparently she hadn't liked his proposal.

"Dude," I said, skiing up to him. "Maybe you shouldn't have written it in yellow."

WHAT ABOUT ME?

For some reason, people seem really surprised to hear that I have a steady girlfriend. Probably they picture me as one of those rakish bachelors who always has different women on his arm, which describes me pretty well except for the different women part.

Her name is Sarah, and she's a magazine editor. Everyone always tells me "Don't let her get away," to the point where I start wondering if maybe I should tie her leg to the piano.

No one has ever said to Sarah "Don't let Bruce get away."

Unlike my own situation, where I get along just fine with my ex-spouse and tolerate her husband the Fop, we don't communicate at all with Sarah's ex, whom I call the Gas Bag. I see him from time to time, because he is an author whose books have been very successful in feeding his ego. I went to a book signing of his once where his opening remark was "Let me answer the question you're all wondering." The Gas Bag gave every young woman in the room a smug look. "Boxers."

(I guess the question was "Who did that to your face?")

Sarah's conclusion from her divorce is that she married too young, too impulsively, and to a jerk. She says there's no sense rushing things between us, which works fine for me. I like being an independent single man, and really treasure the nights when we don't see each other—I'll make myself dinner, open a beer, and call Sarah on the phone and talk until bedtime.

Being afflicted with estrogen, Sarah was naturally hugely excited to hear about Sam's engagement, but she also asked about me, which proves to all you people who figured I was exaggerating her virtues that she's a good girlfriend.

"How do you feel about it?" she asked me.

"I guess I feel okay. I mean, they're just engaged, it's not like they're getting married. This really isn't any different than before except everyone keeps hugging each other."

"Okay, so you're going through denial, that's good, that's the first stage," Sarah told me.

"It's not a *stage*," I corrected her testily. "I don't have some sort of mental condition. It kind of pisses me off that you would say that."

"The second stage is anger," she said approvingly, nodding.

"How about if we agree that I get to handle this on my own without you doing a lot of analysis?"

"Bargaining," she noted. "The next one is depression, then acceptance."

I sighed. "Fine. Whatever. I don't feel like talking about it." I sat wearily in a chair.

"But can you at least admit that saying 'they're not getting married, they're just engaged' is denial?"

"Sure. All right. She's getting married. I get it. There, happy?"

"Yes, I'm happy. But are *you* happy?" she asked.

I looked at her pretty green eyes and read real caring there. "I honestly don't know. I get the sense that so much is going to happen between now and the wedding, I'm going to have a lot of different feelings. I'd rather not go through that."

"Because as a man, feelings make you uncomfortable," Sarah suggested.

"I'd say 'uncomfortable' qualifies as a feeling," I shot back.

"Because as a man, you want to be right," she interpreted.

"Because I *am* right," I responded. "Wait, right about what?"

"That you're going to have a lot of different feelings as this happens, and a lot of those feelings are going to make you very uncomfortable," Sarah said.

"Exactly," I agreed.

Boy, was I going to turn out to be right about that one!

HOW GEOFF DID IT

I had told Geoff I had an idea for how he should propose.

"Here's what you do," I advised him. "Swallow an aluminum tape with the message "will you marry me" stamped into it, wrapped around the engagement ring. Then go to the emergency room. When she sees your X-ray, she'll say yes, and then she can be in surgery when they remove the ring from your stomach and hand it to her."

I knew from Tom's experience with his proposal to Emily that the emergency room can actually be a very nice backdrop to a new engagement.

Geoff seemed to really appreciate my input, especially since I came up with this idea the first time I was introduced to him—back then, I had found bringing up the topic of marriage as soon as I met my daughters' dates an effective technique for weeding out boys. But when the time came for him to propose, he chose an entirely different method.

I know about this because I've seen the video. That's another new requirement in modern marriages: If at all possible the proposal should be videotaped, so that there's a permanent record of your boyfriend writing your name in the snow.

Another rule is that a prospective groom should tailor his proposal to match the bride, so if, for example, she enjoys going to the pistol range, you should write "will you marry me" on a paper target and then blast it with small-arms fire.

Surprisingly (given her personality) my daughter Sam isn't into weaponry, but she does love dogs. She fosters abandoned dogs, works with placement agencies to help lost dogs find homes, and has her own dog, a Labrador with the intelligence of shoe leather. Knowing this, Geoff worked to integrate her dog into his marriage proposal, though not by having the animal swallow a metal message that would show up on an X-ray or maybe later out in the yard. Instead, he somehow taught the dog to bring a wrapped box out of hiding and then sit, forelegs up in the air, while my daughter unwrapped the package and the screaming ensued.

I can't imagine how long it took for him to train the animal to accomplish this complicated trick—if he hadn't tried to involve her pet, Geoff and my daughter probably would be married and have two kids by now.

In the video, the dog appears pretty nervous, which is understandable—he had never proposed to anybody before. The dog, at the command "get it!" goes behind the couch, brings out a box, shakes it, jumps on it, and barks.

"Get it!" Geoff commands sternly. The dog puts his front feet on the box and pushes it around the room, tail wagging fiercely.

Sighing in disgust, Geoff gets up and retrieves the box, bringing it over to where my daughter sits puzzled on the couch. The dog lunges at the box, trying to grab it. Geoff gives it to the dog, who takes it in his mouth, shaking it.

"Now, sit up!" Geoff commands.

The dog stops wrestling with the box, cocking his head. The words sound familiar.

"Sit up!" Geoff commands again.

Miraculously, the dog sits, raising his paws, the soggy box in his mouth. "Take the box," Geoff suggests to my daughter. After a small struggle, she gets the box away from her dog. Smiling, unsure, she rips the soggy wrapping paper. Her eyes get big when she sees the small velvet container inside.

Geoff drops to his knees next to the dog, who begins licking him in the ear.

"Will you marry me?" Geoff asks, irritably pushing the dog's head away from his.

When my daughter screams, the dog starts to bark.

THE OTHER SHOE DROPS

I can tell something is wrong with my Valerie. The three straight days of the *Guess What, I'm Getting Married!* show have been wearying for all of us, but there is an odd tension in her eyes.

Of course, this is the same girl who wrote poetry in high school with titles like "Black Death, I Welcome Thee" and who once forcefully declared that it would be best for the planet "if everybody left." But I suspect she has misgivings about her sister's engagement, and when she shows up unannounced at my house without any dirty laundry to do or stuff for me to swallow to remove mercury from my blood, I know something is going on.

It's good timing: I was running out of reasons why I couldn't start work on a column that was due soon—by yesterday, in fact. I invite her in and let her find her own way to tell me what's bothering her. "So something's really bothering you about this engagement, probably because you think it's going to break up our family," I say vaguely.

She shakes her head. "No, that's not it."

"Your sister's engaged and getting all the focus, and you feel like you need more attention from your dad."

"No."

"You want to spend more quality time with me, just the two of us, without having to ask me to fold laundry."

"I promise, that's not it. Can I just tell it my own way?"

"Sure," I agree. "I want you to tell me in your own words. I know how difficult it can be, but I want you to know, someday you'll understand that a parent can have enough love for all of his children, and just because your sister is getting married doesn't mean I won't have time for you. We can clean my garage together this weekend, if you'd like."

"Dad."

"Okay, you tell it."

"The thing is . . ." She stares off for a moment. "Here's the thing."

"Yes?"

"The thing is . . . I'm engaged, too."

THREE

※

You Are In Charge of the Plan

The word "wed" probably grew out of the Germanic word *Wette*, meaning "bet" or "wager," as in, "I'll bet when Dad finds out I'm engaged, he'll wette his pants."

A father is to be forgiven if, upon learning that his daughter has agreed to marry some guy named Mulchy or Moldy, his expression is easily described by the cliché "deer in the headlights," though the sensation is more like "deer who has been *hit* by the headlights." There's a loud clanging sound as the brain jumps around inside the skull like a frightened cat, making it difficult for him to hear whatever it is his daughter is saying, especially with his long-dead relatives chanting for him to "move into the light."

The daughter will probably be kind enough to give him something to help him with the shock, like a beer, a stiff drink, or CPR. She'll answer his questions, which will usually be the following:

QUESTION NUMBER ONE: *What????*

ANSWER: *I said I'm engaged.*

QUESTION NUMBER TWO: *What????*

ANSWER: *I'm getting married, Dad.*

QUESTION NUMBER THREE: *What???*

After this, the sequence of questions usually repeats itself a few times.

I force myself to take in air and breathe it out, slowly and in control as if I'm having a baby. (In fact, I'm pretty sure I'm dilated to six.) Valerie's a sensitive person, and I can see real concern in her eyes, worry for the impact this is having on her father. I try to lift my hand to assure her I'm okay, but I'm still afflicted with what I assume is permanent paralysis and can only twitch. "Sam is going to kill me," she mutters.

"I'm okay," I finally gasp.

"I had no idea, Dad!"

"No, really, I'm fine. I just need a drink of water or Valium."

After a minute, I get up and get myself a glass of water. "Marty asked me a week ago, but we said we'd keep it secret until his father got back from his retreat."

"Who?"

"His father."

"No, who is Marty?"

Valerie glares at me. "My fiancé!"

I sit down. "Look, honey, I'm sorry. This is a bit of a shock for me, and I'm having trouble coming up with the right words to tell you there's no way you're getting married."

"Dad."

"Doesn't he know he's supposed to come and ask my permission first? This whole awkward situation could have been avoided."

"How am I going to tell Sam?"

"Valerie. Come on, you barely know this guy."

"I've known him since high school!"

"Well, I don't see how *that's* relevant."

"Dad, I'm getting married."

"Actually, no, you're not." I decide that I'm in what Sarah would psychologically call the "denial phase" and that I like it here. "Honey, you're too young to be married. *I'm* too young for you to be married." Something occurs to me. "Wait a minute. You're not . . . you're not . . ." I hold my hands out in front of my stomach in the universally recognized gesture for "having a really immense baby."

Valerie frowns at my sign language. "What, pregnant?"

The word makes me break out in projectile sweating. "Or anything *like* that," I say desperately.

"No, Dad. I'm not pregnant or anything *like* that."

I sigh, massaging my heart. "Then okay, good, you don't have to get married."

"I want to get married!" she snaps. "Dad, you're not helping. Sam is going to kill me. Like, in high school, when I tried out for volleyball, remember how mad she was and wanted me to pick another sport?"

"Which, if you think about it in retrospect, was pretty reasonable," I say. "So maybe this time you should pick something else. Don't get married, have a chastity pledge instead."

"Dad!"

"Valerie, you have so much growing up to do before you get married. You could travel to Europe without Marty. You could go back to school without Marty. You are so young, you will never again be so free to do anything in the world you want except get married to Marty!" I hold out my hands beseechingly.

I have nothing against Marty personally except that I don't like him. Well, even that's not true, I liked him fine until this marriage idea came up. He's a bit intense—I remember him lecturing me on how I should mulch my grass and build a compost heap for all my kitchen waste to mold in, and then I would have all this fertile soil with which to do whatever one does with fertile soil. The idea actually worked pretty well except my dog found the compost heap and ate it. No, it's not Mulchy the Compost King who's the problem, it's the idea that my younger daughter, the littlest girl, wants to get married.

"Dad," she said, calmly, firmly, and intransigently, "Marty and I are getting married. Deal with it."

I recognize the look in her eye. When she was little, Valerie used to delight shoppers at the grocery store by locking her limbs around our cart, tearing off a big hunk of air, and screaming "No!" when I told her it was time to leave. She wanted something—a chocolate cream pie, a makeup kit, a pet lobster—and wasn't going to let me pick her up until I gave it to her. Somehow she could make herself weigh more than a suitcase full of bricks, and as I struggled to get her in the air, her screams drew the attention of the store managers and the police department's Kidnap Response Unit.

What I learned then is still true now: Once she makes up her mind about something, there is no way it is going to change without a lot of screaming and crying, which I didn't feel like doing.

Maybe I could figure something out to alter the course of events, but for now, I have two daughters, and they are both engaged.

God help me.

A Wedding Is No Place for Emotions

Eventually, the father will recover from his initial shock, and then a miraculous thing happens: he adjusts to the new situation, he sees what has to be done, and he steps firmly into his position of Total and Complete Authority, of which, when it comes to situations like this, he has absolutely none.

Men were born to handle crises—that's why the world runs so well, with no wars or conflicts to speak of. And a wedding is no different from any other crisis, except for all the shopping. Once the father has accepted the idea that his daughter is getting married and that he is not allowed to shoot anybody, he'll take charge of the situation and see to it that everything goes according to plan. (Of course, *nothing* will go according to plan. If it did, it wouldn't be a wedding.)

Typically, the father's method of planning a wedding is to carefully identify each task that must be completed, along with the due date and some measure by which everyone will know that the task is completed.

TASK	*TASK DEADLINE*	MEASURE OF COMPLETION
Send wedding invitations.	*W-Day minus 160**	Everyone's tongue is all sticky.

Of course, he'll eventually realize that each major task is built from many other steps that precede it—"precedents," he may call them.

---

* W-Day is army-talk for "Wedding Day." Fathers should be allowed to inject the wedding plan with as many military terms as they want, like "search and destroy" and "total annihilation." This will make the whole affair more festive!

FATHER: *It has come to my attention that the sending of wedding invitations, which I have listed there in your Father's Plan for the Wedding Handbook as Step Five, has certain precedents.*

WEDDING TEAM: *Sir yes sir!*

BRIDE: *Dad, you are totally in complete authority with all your wonderful planning.*

FATHER: *This is no time for weepy sentiment, woman!*

BRIDE: *Sorry sir!*

FATHER: *Team, I will identify these precedents now, and then you will execute them and report back to me forthwith. Understood?*

WEDDING TEAM: *Sir yes sir!*

TASK	*TASK DEADLINE*	MEASURE OF COMPLETION
Decide who will be invited to wedding.	*W-Day minus 240*	The members of the family are no longer speaking to one another.
Determine the paper that will be used for the invitations. Linen is good, gold flake is better, and best is etched marble.	*W-Day minus 200*	The father's idea of a mass e-mail (what, you never heard of a "viral wedding?") has been overruled, and an order has been placed with the printer.
Pay 50% of the invoice for the invitations.	*W-Day minus 200*	We're out of money!

TASK	*TASK DEADLINE*	MEASURE OF COMPLETION
Pay the other 50% and pick up the wedding invitations.	*W-Day minus 175*	We're out of money!
Pay for and pick up the stamps.	*W-Day minus 170*	We're out of money!
Address the invitations.	*W-Day minus 165*	The bride is sobbing because no one is helping it is her wedding it is going all wrong she can't be expected to do this by herself she doesn't know half these people she's gaining weight it's the stress leave me alone.

See how organized it looks when the fathers take over? Of course, the actual process of making the guest list is a little more complex. Properly charted, it would look something like this:

Flow Chart of the Actual Process of Selecting the Wedding Guest List

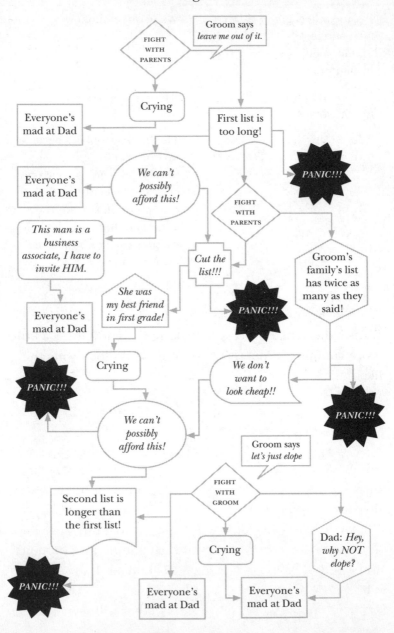

Marriages May Be Made in Heaven, But They're Paid for by Home Equity Loans

The father's method for handling such chaos is to assign everyone their tasks and, if they fail, follow up with a court martial and hanging. The very first item is to come up with a budget—it's good for everyone to agree on a spending limit that they can all ignore. The father will turn to the special wedding savings account he started when his daughters were born and take the money in there, which is none, add to it the savings left over from the college fund, which is negative, and throw in all of his extra money, of which he doesn't have any. This means that the wedding budget starts with whatever is in the couch cushions—you'll have to do your nuptials via fax machine.

Okay, ha ha, notice that when the father makes a joke like this, nobody laughs. Suggesting that the wedding will be anything less than a royal coronation is not funny to anyone.

Eventually, after a lot of calculating, calls to the credit card companies, and some tough decisions (*okay, I don't really need a new car, or a new lawn mower, or food*), the father will announce a number that represents what he thinks the budget should be.

This is not how wedding budgets are actually calculated, but it is sweet of him to try. Wedding budgets are built by the bride making a list of her requirements for bridesmaids, flowers, and ice sculptures of hearts (because nothing says "I'll love you forever" better than a heart that turns to a puddle of water in four hours), and then adding up how much everything will cost. There, that's the budget! Dad was doing it backward.

"This budget is unrealistic," the father will say, speaking

slowly and clearly to his daughter the way cops talk to someone on a window ledge.

"Of course!" the bride will snap. "I know it'll cost more than this!"

A CHALLENGE ONLY A FATHER CAN HANDLE

I spent a lot of time working on my Peace Plan—the formal, point-by-point set of stipulations and agreements that would bring about a cease-fire in what would undoubtedly be the biggest fight my daughters would have since they decided in grade school that they both wanted to marry Heath Leger. Valerie was right—Sam's reaction to the news that her engagement had been hit with a preemptive strike was likely to be volcanic.

Valerie asked Sam to come over to my house later that week to "talk about the wedding," as if anybody had been talking about anything else. As a father, I knew that I needed to come up with a really, really good way to avoid being present. But I also knew that it was my responsibility to be in the room to serve as protection for my dishes or anything else that might be thrown. That's where the Peace Plan came in. I figured that by the time I got to Peace Plan Point Number Twenty-Five—*Father shall be the final arbiter of all disputes and we agree we shall accept his judgment without complaint plus help him wash his windows*—they would have calmed down enough for me to get them to set aside any grudges or weapons.

I just needed to convince Sam that Valerie's engagement didn't steal her thunder—if anything, it *added* to her thunder! And then I needed to figure out what I was talking about. Thunder?

Sam arrived with a load of bridal magazines under her

arm. "I need everybody's help deciding the theme of the wedding," she declared.

"How about BYOB?" I suggested.

"Not funny, Dad," Sam said.

"Not funny, Dad," Valerie said.

"Excuse me for a minute," I said. I ran to my room to add another article to the Peace Plan. Point Number Seventy-Six: *No one gets to tell Dad that his jokes are not funny.* Then I printed it out and returned to the living room to find my daughters hugging each other and sobbing.

"What happened? Did Valerie and Moldy break up?"

"This is the happiest day of my life," Sam said.

"This is the happiest day of *my* life," Valerie countered.

"It certainly is a happy day," I agreed. "Um, but why?"

As it turned out, utilizing the "weddings trump everything" doctrine, Valerie and Sam had managed to dispel any rancor over the timing of their engagements without my intervention, which I found to be unacceptable. "There's bound to be a lot of bad feelings about all this," I observed. I pointedly handed them their copies of the Peace Plan.

"Can you believe it, Dad? Two weddings!" Sam glowed.

"I'm so happy you're not mad, Sam," Valerie said.

"Why would I be mad? You're my sister!" Sam declared, as if the two of them hadn't spent the majority of the past two decades fighting with each other. They hugged again.

"I'm so happy," they each said about ten times. "Aren't you happy, Dad?"

"Actually, I feel sort of like Poland after being invaded by both Germany and Russia," I said truthfully.

They gave me a blank look.

"Oh, Dad," my younger daughter said, "why would anybody invade *Poland*?"

"I think the best thing we can do now is read what I've

handed you, sign it, and then discuss how we're going to manage everything, with you writing down what I say," I told them.

They agreed that they would do this, but then got distracted by a discussion over whether Sam should have a "ring dog." When they left later that evening, neither one of them took their copies of the Peace Plan.

WE HOLD THESE TRUTHS TO BE SELF-EVIDENT

Once it sinks in that this is no joke, that your daughter is really getting married, you'll start working in earnest on the wedding plan. Immediately, several truths become self-evident:

Truth Number One: You are already behind schedule.
This truth can be particularly vexing if you don't even *have* a schedule yet, but the fact is that you should have been working on this thing since junior high school. There is so much to do: Trying to plan a wedding is a bit like trying to launch a rocket to the moon, except in a moon mission there are fewer details. You should probably quit your job so that you'll have enough time.

Truth Number Two: You, the father, are supremely qualified to make and execute the plan for the wedding. Nobody cares.
They don't want to hear that you've been in the military, or played on football teams, or are secretary of the interior. They don't want your advice, they want to plan every aspect of the wedding themselves and delegate lesser tasks to you, like paying for it. You have great ideas and they would appreciate it if you would keep them to yourself.

Truth Number Three: Your daughter's expectations are somewhere between unrealistic and insane.

Your daughter truly believes that everything will go perfectly, while you know that things probably won't even go well. You'll listen to endless conversations about flower arrangements ("The base of the centerpieces will be ringed with multicolored alstroemeria lilies and then peonies with two-inch blooms . . .") and shake your head. Flowers? They grow the way they want to grow, you can't make a flower behave like a toupee. Does she really think Uncle Bob won't drink too much, or that Cousin Ward can be persuaded to attend a wedding reception and not once mention life insurance? How are you going to prevent this whole affair from being a huge disappointment to your daughter?

Here's just a sample of what you're in for—the first conversation I had with my daughters about their wedding plans.

> ME: *Okay. First things first. I think we can all agree that it makes sense for you to get married at the same time—a double wedding, in other words, to save on expenses.*

> SAM: *No way.*

> VALERIE: *No way.*

> ME: *But won't the guest lists be more or less the same?*

> SAM: *Of course not.*

> VALERIE: *I'm not doing it.*

> ME: *Well . . . let's say the issue is not yet settled.*

> SAM: *I'd rather be set on fire than have a double wedding.*

> VALERIE: *I want to get married at dawn at someplace that is special to me, like the edge of the Grand Canyon.*

ME: *You what? You've never even been to the Grand Canyon!*

VALERIE: *That's not important.*

SAM: *That's not important, Dad.*

VALERIE: *The Grand Canyon dramatically illustrates what I believe, which is that the Earth is sacred.*

ME: *Well, I wasn't suggesting you not get married on* Earth.

SAM: *I want to get married in a church, with lots and lots of flowers. I already talked to the minister—it's only six hundred dollars to rent the space.*

ME: *Ask him how much to rent the Grand Canyon.*

SAM: *Since my wedding comes first, maybe Valerie could wear my wedding gown. That would save money.*

ME: *Not necessarily. I was thinking we could rent the wedding gown.*

SAM: What?

VALERIE: *You want us to wear wedding gowns from U-Haul?*

ME: *Well, why do you need to have a custom-made dress to wear for only five hours? It's not like you're planning to wear it again.*

SAM: *I want to own my dress so that I can pass it on to* my *daughter, for her to wear at her wedding.*

ME: *But you're not wearing* your *mother's wedding dress.*

SAM: *Oh, Dad, Mom's dress is like twenty-five years old, it's so old-fashioned.*

VALERIE: *I'm going to wear traditional Navajo garb.*

ME: *You're kidding, right? Is what's-his-name Navajo? I thought he was Jewish.*

VALERIE: *His name is Marty!*

SAM: *You're so insensitive, Dad. Why does it matter what religion he is?*

ME: *I didn't say that it matters, I just . . .*

VALERIE: *Why does it bother you so much that he's a Jew?*

SAM: *His religion shouldn't matter, Dad.*

ME: *I'm not bothered by his religion! I just asked about this Navajo thing.*

SAM: *Whether his religion is Jewish or Navajo shouldn't matter.*

VALERIE: *We're going to incorporate parts of the Jewish ceremony, plus some of our vows will be in Sanskrit.*

SAM: *That's so romantic!*

MY REASONABLE SUGGESTIONS

It's a good idea for the father to inject some sanity into the conversation by coming up with several reasonable ideas for how to save money on the wedding, all of which will be carefully ignored. It's not supposed to be reasonable, it's a wedding!

Here are the reasonable suggestions I made for saving money, and why they were rejected.

IDEA	REASON REJECTED
Buy our flowers from the grocery store instead of a florist.	Dad. A grocery store? You can't get flowers from a grocery store for a wedding!
We don't need a professional photographer. You can take digital photographs that are just as good as a pro can take, and fix them in Photoshop if you need to.	Dad. Photoshop? So the wedding pictures would be faked? You have to have a professional photographer, this is a wedding!
We could have a morning wedding and serve breakfast. Breakfast food is much less expensive, and no one will mind that we don't serve booze. This is a *great* idea!	Dad. What are you going to do, serve Frosted Flakes and French toast sticks? You can't have a breakfast reception, this is a wedding!
But Valerie's wedding is at sunrise.	Dad. The wedding is at sunrise. The reception will be a traditional tribal dance at night. Would you just let us worry about this part? Your ideas are crazy. This isn't some kind of joke, this is a wedding!
How about if we have edible flowers? That way, instead of serving dinner, people can just eat the centerpieces.	Dad. Stop.

How Moldy or Mulchy Proposed

Invariably, the first thing anyone asks the newly betrothed is "How did he propose?" even if the most appropriate question is "Are you out of your mind?" I had neglected to ask this of Valerie because I was afraid it would affect my carefully cultivated state of denial, but Sam wanted to know.

"It was kind of weird," Valerie began.

"Well, knock me over with a feather," I responded.

Sam gave me a look. She has this look she gives people right before she leaps up and smashes a volleyball so hard that it craters the floor, and that's the look I was getting now. Not wanting a crater in my floor or body, I decided to shut up.

"It didn't start out like a proposal at all," Valerie continued, while I reflected that I wished it hadn't finished like one, either. "I told you that Marty and I are going to adopt . . ."

"What???" I hyperventilated, no longer shutting up as much as I had been. "Adopt? You're going to adopt?"

"A highway, Dad. We went in to do the paperwork to adopt a highway, you know, that program where you keep the roads clean? Would you stop pretending you're having a stroke?"

"It's a heart attack, but sure, I'll stop. Wait, are you telling me you think you have to get married to adopt a *highway*? Like otherwise it would be illegitimate?"

"Dad," Sam snapped, "would you just let her tell the story?"

"Anyway," Valerie continued, "it is such a hassle. There's a waiting list, and they said they've had bad luck with couples because they break up and then fight over responsibility."

"So they have a custody battle over a stretch of highway," I translated. "Must be tough to decide who gets visitation rights."

"Dad," Sam said.

"Look," I said brightly, "I have an idea, why don't you call off the wedding and adopt my driveway?"

"The woman helping us said they really prefer to have married couples," Valerie said.

"And that's why you're engaged?" I responded, horri-fied.

"Dad," Sam said.

"No, of course not. But then later we drove out to the highway we wanted, you know, to look at all the litter, which is why we wanted to adopt it in the first place, and then Mar-ty's like, 'Maybe we should do what the woman said,' and I'm like, 'What do you mean,' and he's like, 'You know. The thing about couples,' and I'm like, 'What do you mean,' and he's like, 'You know, get married.' And I freaked out, and I'm like, 'Oh my God,' and he's like, 'Are you okay,' and I'm like, 'Oh my God,' and then finally I'm like, 'I have to think about this.' "

Piecing this together I realized that I was like, relieved. "So you're not engaged, then. You're in the I'm-thinking-about-it-and-it's-a-bad-idea stage."

"No, that was the next day."

"What? What was the next day?"

"Dad," Sam admonished, "would you just let her tell it?"

"So I didn't sleep at all that night," Valerie said. "But then I realized that Marty's been my best friend for most of my life."

"While I, on the other hand, have been your father for *all* of your life. You couldn't talk to me about it?"

"Dad," Sam said.

"So the next day we're on a hike. And I'm waiting for him to bring it up, but Marty doesn't say anything. And finally we're back at the trailhead, you know where I'm talking about? The parking lot?"

"Where the Porta-Johns are?" I asked.

"Dad," Sam said.

"And I'm like, 'So about what you said yesterday,' and he's like, he knows what I'm talking about, and he's like, all shy and doesn't say anything, and so I told him the answer's yes."

"And then you kissed!" Sam gushed.

"Yeah," Valerie agreed.

"That's so romantic, Valerie," Sam said, hugging her sister. I sorted through this statement in complete noncomprehension. What, exactly, was the romantic part? "Good old Marty," Sam praised.

"So when is good old Moldy going to come talk to me and explain himself?" I asked pleasantly.

"Dad," Sam said.

"We're going shopping for a ring together soon."

"That's so romantic!" Sam said again. Then she gazed proudly at her own ring, in which she invested none of her time selecting. From this I gathered that the most romantic thing for an engaged couple is to shop for a ring together and the other most romantic thing is for the groom to buy it on his own.

AN EVEN WORSE IDEA

There was, in my mind, a big difference between my older daughter's engagement to Geoff and Marty's pavement-oriented proposal to Valerie. As a father, I knew there were times when I saw dangers my children couldn't—such as when Sam took her ill-fated trip to Europe, where I'm sure a lot of bad things happened despite all the so-called happy photographs she brought back. I wasn't yet ready to forbid the marriage outright, which of course wouldn't make any difference anyway, but in my mind there were a lot of things that needed to get settled before I put a deposit down on the Grand Canyon.

Meanwhile, just making a list of things to consider for

the two weddings—What was the official theme? The official mood? The official odor?—was exhausting. Finally Sam came up with what would turn out to be the worst idea of the day.

"You know who can help us?" she mused. "My future sister-in-law. She's getting married the last weekend in April. She's been doing wedding plans for like a year and a half."

Though I had my reservations about a woman who needed more than a year to plan a wedding, I agreed that we could use some expert advice to help bring some of my daughters' expectations in line with reality.

"Her name is Alecia," Sam told me. "You'll really like her."

This turned out to be the most false statement uttered in the history of the world.

FOUR

~

Meet Bridezilla and the Devil Woman Who Spawned Her

The word "Bridezilla" is a combination of the words "Godzilla," which means "fire-breathing monster," and "bride," which means exactly the same thing.

Godzilla was created when atomic waste caused a placid dinosaur living at the bottom of the sea (picture Barney) to mutate into a frightening, ugly creature (picture Mick Jagger). Bridezilla was created when an engagement ring caused a lovely child (picture your daughter sitting in your lap while you read her a story about Barney) to mutate into a frightened, maniacal creature (picture your daughter clinging to a grocery cart, her face beet red, screaming *"No!"* until someone calls the cops on you). Godzilla swam in the ocean and fed on, well, Tokyo. Bridezilla does Pilates and feeds on, well, insomnia.

I suppose it is ironic that tremendous pressure is what created the diamond in the engagement ring, which is now causing tremendous pressure on your daughter. In the end, all that pressure resulted in a beautiful jewel, just as in the end, your daughter will be a beautiful bride. Between now and then, however, everyone will suffer.

It's easy to see what happens. A wedding seems pretty simple. People get dressed up, there's a ceremony, there's a party, everyone leaves, the father declares bankruptcy. But every step along the way is a minefield of potential disasters, of decisions that must be made, of competing advice and egos, of opinions from people on what simply *must* be done or the wedding will be *ruined*. (No one talks about the marriage, which is one of the key ingredients to forming a Bridezilla—the whole purpose of the wedding, which is to create a marriage, gets sort of lost in the discussion over which flowers best match the wedding's theme song.) So the very simple process of bringing a few people together for a celebration of love turns into something as complicated and unmanageable as trying to stage a Broadway production of *Cats* with real cats.

At the center of all this, the person who is the producer, director, choreographer, playwright, stage manager, and, above all, the *star* of this must-be-perfect show, is your daughter. The groom has already ducked out, saying "Whatever you think is fine," which is sort of like the airport tower telling a pilot "Land anywhere you want."

If your daughter has the strength of character to avoid becoming a Bridezilla, it is testament to willpower, to sterling moral fiber, to what an excellent, superior person you are. You did a great job raising her. But if she falls prey to the madness, you should blame other people. Relatives, friends, the wedding industry—it's a huge conspiracy, and you can't fault her for cracking under all that pressure.

To assist my daughters with their preparations, I had turned over one corner of my living room to the operation—Wedding Chaos Central, everyone called it, if by "everyone" you mean "me." I'd put up a giant whiteboard for ideas, suggestions, and tic-tac-toe. I'd carefully divided the whiteboard into sections, one for Sam's wedding, where she would get married in a church ceremony wearing a white wedding gown and then go to a reception that hopefully we could charge people to attend; and one for Valerie's wedding, where we would teeter on the edge of a cliff wearing Native American garb and then go lay siege to one of the white man's forts.

"The problem with all this stuff is that it makes no sense to me!" I complained to Sarah. "If this were a military mission, we wouldn't be dealing with outfits and music and what kind of vegetable matches the wedding colors."

"A military mission *would* be more joyful," Sarah agreed. "But don't armies have to decide what outfits to wear?"

"It's a uniform," I informed her archly.

"And don't invading armies have a band?"

"It's not a band, it's the drum and bugle corps."

"What about the flag, doesn't it have the official colors?"

"Sarah, would you please just accept that you don't know anything about military operations? I have to plan two weddings."

"I don't understand," Sarah responded. "Why do you have to plan? I thought their mother was involved."

"Oh, sure, Judy's involved, but they don't plan, they just talk about decisions. There's a big difference."

"Sure there is."

And actually, there *is*. One of the things that happens is that the bride will make a *decision*, as in, "the candles should have the scent of sandalwood" without a *plan*, like, "we will buy the candles at the Sandalwood R Us store on W-Day minus 20 and store them in Dad's broom closet and have them delivered to the church at W-Hour minus 16."

"Men are just better at identifying specific tasks and writing them down," I told Sarah.

"Whereas women are better at just doing them," Sarah said. She does that a lot, says things that initially sound like she's agreeing with me, only later to have me realize *hey, wait a minute!*

What I could see happening before my eyes, though, was that as each decision was being made, it influenced the other decisions, the way one person throwing up makes other people nauseated. (Sarah suggested I pick a more romantic analogy to use with my daughters.) Would the sandalwood candles match the wedding colors? Would the sandalwood scent be in conflict with the wedding flowers? What the heck was sandalwood? (I had a pair of old sandals in my closet, and though they weren't made from wood, they did have a pretty strong scent. Somehow I doubted this was what Sam wanted for her wedding.)

The dependency of one decision on another was making it more and more difficult to come up with a plan for the perfect wedding, and the pressure was building, threatening to turn them into Bridezillas if someone like me didn't intervene.

It's entirely possible, however, that some Bridezillas aren't made but rather are born that way. Which brings us to my daughter's future in-laws, Alecia, Geoff's sister, and Priscilla, the woman whose womb unleashed Alecia upon the world.

THE IN-LAWS—MAYBE THEY'RE CALLED THAT BECAUSE THEY SHOULD BE IN-JAIL

Like everyone else, I'd more or less forgotten about Geoff, who seemed far less relevant to the process than the guest list, which at that moment was stuck at a number more or less equal to the population of India. He'd faded into the abstract, as someone who existed only as an item on Father's To-Do List (Item 723: Pick out tux for Geoff).

No one but me had even read the To-Do List.

Geoff's sister Alecia was getting married, having gotten engaged some time around the sixth grade. This is how it seemed to me, anyway—in fact, Sam had taken to quoting Alecia so regularly on the necessity of giving various vendors time to make sure things were perfect ("Alecia says bridesmaids's dresses need to be ordered at least ten months in advance to make sure they match the wedding invitations") that I half-expected the woman to be the same age as Yoda.

I didn't really want to meet Alecia or her family, but I agreed to go to a lunch with Sam and Alecia to discuss wedding plans, because (as Sam explained) her mother couldn't fly in to town just for a lunch, and, as a writer, I "didn't do anything all day, anyway."

Valerie also came along, after first verifying that the restaurant served something besides meat because she is in what I refer to as her "permanent vegetative state." Sam reported that Alecia would be delighted to give all of us the benefits of her hard-won experience in the complex challenge of being engaged.

We arrived at the restaurant on time, but there was no sign of Alecia or her mother Priscilla. "So far this is not as bad as I thought it would be," I noted.

"Dad," Sam warned. "These people are our family now."

This didn't seem either accurate or fair, but I could tell that my daughter was feeling stressed, so I elected not to object.

"There they are!" A young woman called from across the room. An attractive blond woman in her late twenties, carrying herself with self-assurance, swept into view. Behind her plodded a solid-framed, expensively tailored woman in her mid-fifties who gave me a suspicious look as I stood up from the table.

"You're Bruce," Alecia informed me, enfolding me in a thick cloud of perfume. She hugged me and then Valerie while her mother Priscilla extended a formal hand in my direction. She had a grip like a can crusher.

"Well, now," Alecia sighed, settling down into her chair. "A bride is always forgiven for being late. Everyone knows she has a lot on her plate." She beamed at us, then nodded at my daughters. "Maybe you should write some of this down."

The waitress came to take our order, and Valerie asked if there were any vegetarian specials, which I, as a die- and artery-hard carnivore, felt was sort of a contradiction in terms. If vegetables were "special," we'd eat them for dessert.

"Vegetarians," Alecia mused after the waitress left. "They are such a problem. You'll find that people have all sorts of odd menu requests when you plan your reception, as if the whole world revolves around them and not the bride." Alecia gave Valerie a tight smile. "We've already come up with something for vegans, so you'll be fine at ours."

"Oh, I'm not a vegan," Valerie started to say.

"Whatever," Alecia responded with a wave of her hand. She turned and gave Sam her full attention. (I was to eventually conclude that Alecia had no interest in Valerie as a bride or a person because of the odd nature of Valerie's wedding plan.) "Now I'm sure you've been planning for this day your entire life."

"Since the day she was born," I agreed. My daughters gave me dark looks, and I shrugged. I glanced at Priscilla to see if she found this amusing, but her face was as dour as Churchill at Yalta.

"I remember when I was five years old, I was a flower girl in my aunt's wedding. It was the greatest day of my life. Everyone said I was prettier than the bride." Alecia looked to her mother, who nodded in confirmation. "That's why I won't have a flower child in my wedding. I don't want to be outshined by some kid." Alecia gestured for my daughters to write this down.

"You can't always control children," Priscilla growled. Now that I'd thought of the comparison, I couldn't shake off my mental conviction that this woman *was* Winston Churchill, or at least looked enough like him to be cast in a movie. "You can't control them on the beaches," I pictured her saying, "you can't control them on the landing grounds, you can't control them in the fields and in the streets . . ."

"I was actually thinking of having my dog be the ring bearer," Sam said.

"You are so funny," Alecia said humorlessly. She picked up a roll, looked at it disgustedly, then tossed it back in the basket. "Ugh. Carbs."

Valerie looked at her own half-chewed roll with a sad expression.

"Let me see your nails, both of you," Alecia commanded. Sam and Valerie offered their fingers for inspection, and Alecia gave them a pitying look. "Ladies, when I say I'm engaged, what do you suppose is the first thing people ask me?"

Is the guy an idiot? I wanted to reply, but I kept it to myself.

"My ring," she said impatiently, "they want to see my ring, it's what tells them you're not engaged to some loser. So your nails have to be *perfect*, or it looks like you're the loser." Alecia sighed, her burdens almost too much to bear. "Something I learned is that when you get engaged, everyone looks up to you, as their example on how to behave. So you have to make sure that when you go out in public, you are presenting the best possible look, not just for you, but for anyone who might ever want to get married someday.

That means manicures, pedicures . . ."—Alecia gave Sam's face an appraising glance—". . . waxing, photo facials, laser therapy—whatever it takes to make you look your best."

Valerie self-consciously dropped her hands into her lap.

"Oh my God, I totally forgot!" Alecia gushed. "We have the best news, Sam. You get to be in the wedding! You're a bridesmaid!"

Sam knew what was expected of her. "Oh my God, that's wonderful," she said back.

"You're wondering how this can possibly be true since my wedding is less than six months away. Well, here's the secret. Always make sure that the place where you get your bridesmaids's dresses has the ability to put in a rush order. That way, if you have to replace someone in your bridal party, like let's say your best friend gets pregnant which would ruin the lines of the dress, you can make a last-minute substitution." Alecia glowed at us. My daughters got the hint and wrote this down. "It costs more, but who cares."

I could name at least one person who cared, but held my tongue.

"It's an honor," Priscilla prompted.

"I'm honored," Sam answered promptly.

"And Valerie," Alecia said, "obviously you're invited, and we want you to bring Marty."

"Bruce," Priscilla said, speaking directly to me for the first time. I jumped, fighting down the urge to respond "Yes sir?" "I understand you have a son." She made it sound like an accusation, as in, "Why on God's green Earth would someone like you bring a child into the world, don't you care about the gene pool?"

"Yes, his name is Chris."

"Since we're adding Sam as a bridesmaid, obviously we need another groomsman," Alecia interjected excitedly.

"And one idea we had, well . . . wouldn't that be special, Chris and Sam, brother and sister? Geoff's already in the wedding, so he'll escort Sam, but that means we need someone to escort my friend Joyce."

"I am sure Chris would do it. It's an honor," I responded faintly. It felt to me that I was slowly becoming involved in yet another wedding, a sensation like being gripped by an undertow. An undertow with sharks.

"A handsome boy, I understand," Priscilla said gravely.

"Chris? Just like his father!" I joked.

Alecia and her mother exchanged worried glances. "Well, obviously we'd need to see him and all. I mean, it's just one idea. It's hard, though, to find groomsmen who are the right height," Alecia said.

"We've decided it isn't critical for the women, but we want the men to be a uniform height," Priscilla stated.

I decided I needed to think about that one.

"Chris doesn't actually look much like Dad," Valerie offered.

Alecia gave her a grateful smile.

"What about Sarah?" Sam asked. I knew she was just trying to be sensitive to my girlfriend's feelings, but I had sort of been hoping to leave Sarah out of it.

Alecia and Priscilla were exchanging the sort of glance that indicates they'd already talked this one over.

"We're having trouble with that," Priscilla admitted gravely. "Frankly—and I do hope we can speak candidly to each other, we are, after all, family—we'd prefer it if you were married."

"I'll see what I can do," I said. Both my daughters shot me a warning look.

"For the balance, I mean, everyone else who gets seated specially is married," Alecia explained hurriedly. "And since you're the father of Geoff's bride, we thought it would be nice if you could sit down in front, you know, with Judy and her husband."

"But it doesn't seem proper to seat you and your . . . friend," Priscilla pronounced delicately.

"I mean, who ever heard of the 'Girlfriend of the Father of the Bride?' Alecia said, moving her head in what I thought she meant as a humorous fashion.

"We just don't know how to explain it to everyone," Priscilla said.

"I mean, could we say she's maybe your assistant or something?" Alecia asked uncertainly. I could tell from her tone that this was the great idea that she and her mother had come up with, but seeing my expression caused her to falter a little bit.

I was feeling the stirrings of some real anger. "Tell you what," I said. Under the table, Sam nudged me, and Valerie was giving me the same "please don't embarrass me" face she'd been making at me since she was nine years old, so I bit off what I would like to have said. "Tell you what. Why don't we just do this. Let's not make any special effort to seat Sarah and me. Go ahead and put Sam's mother in the front, but Sarah and I will just be with everyone else in the back."

Everyone at the table thought this was a wonderful idea.

How Moldy or Mulchy Proposed

I sort of drifted off during the story of how Alecia's fiancé proposed, but I think I got the gist of it: a horse-drawn carriage brought a string quartet to serenade the couple, the guy dropped to one knee and recited some Shakespeare, specially trained geese flew in formation spelling out the words "I LOVE YOU" in the sky, and then the ring was hand-forged by Hephaestus, god of fire. Something like that, anyway.

Then Valerie was asked to recite her proposal story, which went like this: "Marty and I went on a hike, and when we came to the end, it was just such a perfect day, and he told me he loved me and asked me to be his wife. It was the happiest moment of my life."

I opened my mouth to ask what happened to my favorite part, where they drove along the highway looking for waste-paper, but Sam gave me one of her looks and I decided to let it pass.

"That's so romantic, Valerie," Sam said.

Valerie gave her a grateful smile. My heart went out to my brave younger daughter then, who felt so much empathy toward others she wouldn't even eat them unless they were plants, whose marriage proposal was so lacking in romance she had to fix it in postproduction, whose finger still lacked a ring, sitting here with Alecia and Priscilla, who had dismissed her as an inferior nut case because she didn't have the same values as they did.

"I'm proud of you, Valerie," I said. We smiled at each other.

"A hike," murmured Priscilla after a moment. She and Alecia exchanged dark, significant glances.

MORE ADVICE FROM PRINCESS ALECIA

I didn't write down any actual notes during Alecia's lecture on How to Have a Perfect Wedding, deciding that really what it all boiled down to was, Pick a Perfect Bride like Alecia. But here are a few tips that I recall.

TIP	EXPLANATION
Don't announce the engagement if it's not exactly the ring you want.	That way, your sweetheart will have time to save up more money. You're going to be wearing the ring for the rest of your life, so it's only fitting that the groom spend the same length of time paying for it. (This last part might not be exactly what Alecia said.)
Pick the dresses first, then the bridesmaids.	Think what a nightmare it would be if you picked a wedding party of all different body types and then tried to find a dress that would look perfect on all of them! What's important to remember is that while friends are temporary, your pictures last forever. In fact, why don't you just pay a bunch of professional models to be bridesmaids! (She probably didn't say this part, either.)
If you know that some kids are well behaved and attractive, go ahead and invite them, but if you are not sure about the children, put "adults only— no children please" on the invitation.	What's important on your day is that the guests, who are going to be in your wedding photographs, after all, add to your memories, not take away from them. How many times have you heard stories of supposedly cute kids getting all the attention, attention that should be focused on the bride? How many wedding pictures have you seen that are ruined because some scowling brat is standing in the middle? Only children who are both pleasant to look at and be around should be allowed to attend. So send "adults only" to the parents of homely or otherwise questionable children—you can always tell them later that a mistake was made with the invitations and you are sorry. No one will blame you, you're the bride! And if someone shows up with ugly kids, you can always stuff them in a sack full of rocks and throw them in the river! (Again, this final statement may not be precisely what she said out loud.)

TIP	EXPLANATION
Always remember, this is your special day. Everyone will be paying attention to you and no one else.	Hey, Alecia, how is this different from how you see it every other day? (I didn't say this, but I sure was thinking it.)

After our lunch, I looked up "brides" and "bridle" in the dictionary. It turns out that a "bridle" is a restraint designed to maximize control over something. I could think of no better word to describe Alecia's approach to her wedding, and sure hoped her future husband was comfortable with that metal bit in his mouth.

CONFRONTING MARTY

I wasn't ready to initiate the Running of the Groom for Good Old Moldy just yet, being of the opinion that through a combination of deft and subtle hints and suggestions, I was eventually going to talk Valerie out of getting married. (Example: "You're not really serious about this insane wedding thing, are you?") But I did want to have a warm, heart-to-heart, intimidating conversation with the young man, who despite having seduced my daughter with the whole drive-by litter proposal had still not spoken a word to me.

"It's the oldest trick in the book, you know," I told Valerie as we drove together to meet her so-called fiancé for coffee. "A man gets a woman to marry him not because she's in love with the man but because she's fallen in love with his children. Only in this case it's, you know, a highway."

Valerie didn't respond.

"So what did you think of Alecia?" I asked carefully. "Pretty nice, don't you think?"

"Oh my God!" Valerie blurted. "She is like so the opposite of what I want to be! Could you believe it when she said that all the bridesmaids have to have their teeth bleached so that they'll be the same color?"

"Sort of makes the whole getting married thing look like a really, really bad idea," I agreed.

"Dad."

"Well, look, Valerie, what about your mother, what does she say about this crazy idea of yours?"

"She says she loves me and that if I feel in my heart that I'm making the right decision, she'll stand by me because she only wants me to be happy."

"And that's supposed to be good parenting?" I sputtered.

Valerie looked pensively out the window. "I just don't want to become like Alecia," she muttered, more to herself than to anyone. Alecia's dark implications that there was a proper way to do things ("shouldn't you be writing this down?") and that if you didn't follow the rules exactly you would *ruin the wedding* had sobered up my younger daughter, who normally sat next to me in the car gaily complaining about my driving. And this was Valerie, who was honestly thinking of replacing the band at her reception with a showing of *An Inconvenient Truth*.

What I had to do, I decided, was help my children avoid Alecia's fate. I would not let anyone turn them into Bridezillas. That's the job of the Father of the Bride.

Valerie and I were both quiet as we swung into the coffee shop parking lot to meet her fiancé.

"He's not here yet," Valerie announced as we walked into the coffee place.

"Oh. Well, why don't you pick out a reasonable facsimile, then? That guy over there looks nice."

"Dad."

Moldy or Mulchy works in some supportive capacity at our local National Public Radio station. When he stepped into the café, I instantly recognized him as a kid who had been hanging around my house since middle school—who the heck thinks of marriage prevention at that age? I'd been satisfied with just making sure I kept the two of them out of dark rooms. Now he was planning to marry my daughter—it made me want to ask for a do-over, so I could be more intimidating this time.

Mulchy is my height, has dark hair and dark eyes, and had recently taken to growing a thick mustache in an apparent effort to appear unattractive.

"Who is he supposed to look like, Stalin?" I muttered out of the corner of my mouth.

"Dad."

"Sorry I'm late. It's really hectic. We're having a pledge drive over at the station," Moldy apologized.

"I love those!" I gushed.

Valerie gave me a warning look and we all sat down. A waitress came over. "I'll have a half-caf, sugar-free, fat-free, dulce de leche extra foam double macchiato," Valerie ordered.

"That's simple enough," I noted.

"Are you still serving the coffee where the profits go to support the mountain apes?" Mulchy wanted to know.

"Yes, but it's a lot more expensive," the waitress warned.

Moldy waved his hand in a cost-is-no-object gesture— after all, I was paying. "I'll have that in a triple shot latte. Is the milk organic?"

"Yes, of course," the waitress said.

"I'd like mine made with the gorilla coffee beans, too," Valerie interjected. The waitress nodded and then turned to me.

"I'll just have a coffee," I said. "No primates."

"Plain coffee?" the waitress demanded, astounded.

"Yeah, do you have that?"

"I'll have to see."

The waitress left.

"So, I'm glad we could do this," I said. "Now, let me understand—you two are thinking of getting engaged?"

"We are engaged, Dad," Valerie stated incorrectly.

"Engaged to be engaged," I compromised.

"Dad."

"Well, you're not wearing a ring. And Mold . . . Marty . . . has yet to ask me permission to marry you, which as you know in this state means you can't legally get married until a five-year cooling-off period," I bluffed.

Moldy and Valerie exchanged looks.

"We're just trying to find the right ring," Valerie explained.

"Do you know that the production of a single gold ring generates twenty tons of mine waste?" Mulchy said in an accusatory tone, as if I'd been digging up golden nuggets in my backyard and tossing mine waste over the fence.

"We also want a conflict-free diamond," Valerie added.

"Or maybe not a diamond at all," Moldy stated. Valerie gave him a look suggesting that if he stuck to this idea, the situation would be anything but conflict-free.

"You could go with recycled aluminum," I said.

Mulchy shook his head. "Impractical. Metal's too soft."

It made me happy that he had at least considered it.

"Well, look, Mulch . . . Marty, let me ask you something, man-to-man."

"Sure, Bruce," he responded.

I frowned. "I meant prospective-father-in-law-who-needs-to-be-treated-with-respect-and-fear-to-man," I corrected.

"Right."

"You and Valerie have known each other for as long, well, as long as an NPR pledge drive."

"Dad." Valerie gave me a stern look.

"Okay, but for a long time, right? So other than the need to give your highway parents with the same last name, why pick now?"

They looked at each other as if the question was completely unexpected. "Well, we've been sort of dating off and on since, like, sixth grade," he finally offered.

"And we're best friends," Valerie reminded him.

"And it's not like there's any other people we're interested in or anything," he plowed on practically.

It was on the tip of my tongue to restate Moldy's reasoning as, *"well, it's kind of become a habit, and besides, neither one of us currently has a better offer,"* but I elected to stay silent. It was as Valerie said—they were best friends. She knew all about his stern positions on how everyone else on the planet was bad, and his somewhat unromantic approach to their relationship didn't bother her, so why should it bother me?

But it did bother me. "Hey, did you two read about that couple, she was in kidney failure, so her boyfriend gave her an organ donation? And *then* they got engaged?"

"No, I didn't hear about that one."

"Well, it was in all the medical journals at the time," I said, meaning *People* magazine. "Anyway, now that guy, he deserved to be engaged to some father's daughter."

"Dad," Valerie said.

"He gave up a kidney? Whoa," Moldy said, contemplating.

"Exactly," I said smugly.

"Well, but if you were in organ failure," he went on with his studied practicality, "then I'd have to do it. I mean, I couldn't let you die, obviously."

Well, that one shut me up. Valerie gave him a look of such tender love that I felt as if I'd just conducted their wedding ceremony, right there.

Let this be a lesson to father's wanting to scare off unsuitable grooms: Don't bring up the organ donation thing, it's an easy lay-up.

"Okay, good," I said simply, and I felt Valerie relax in her seat next to me, the tension leaving her posture like an expressed sigh.

I could always catch Moldy alone and flay him alive later, if necessary.

Mulchy had to get back to the radio station to help them announce that there were only seven hours left in this current pledge block, and Valerie volunteered to walk him over, so I stayed and finished my very simple coffee while the staff of the café stood behind the counter and stared at me as if I were some kind of lunatic. The two lovebirds, still not officially engaged in my opinion, stood and chatted for a brief moment before turning away. They shared a kiss that was brief and a little awkward, like two people practicing a dance step they'd just learned.

Sam and Geoff were in the habit of saying good-bye to each other as if one of them were boarding a train to Russia. There are fish whose kisses are not as wet as theirs—I often turn away in disapproval, which doesn't seem to bother them in the slightest. (This isn't good—a father *should* bother his children at a moment like that. In fact, I've been considering ways to increase my bother factor, like clearing my throat, or shouting *"Incoming!"*)

Valerie's kiss with Moldy or Mulchy, on the other hand, was very much a dad-approved sort of kiss. You could get more germs just by walking by a water fountain than from such a dry, passionless kiss.

For some reason, though, this bothered me, too. Should two newly engaged kids really be kissing each other as if they were signing a nuclear arms treaty?

Valerie came back to the coffee shop, and she seemed happy as she drained the last of her half-caf, sugar-free, fat-free, dulce de leche extra foam double gorilla macchiato.

If Moldy or Mulchy made her happy, wasn't that all that mattered?

Unsolicited Phone Calls

Registering for gifts and visiting wedding Web sites can get you on the list for all sorts of unsolicited phone calls, like the one I received from my ex-wife's husband, the Fop.

I don't mind that, in person, the guy pretends to be all handsome and friendly, and I get that he makes a lot more money than I do. That's okay, there's no competition between us, and I'd like to see him try to write an entire book sometime. I'm dealing with a circumstance that is far from unique in this modern world—that of a "recombined" family, though I don't know of any rule that says I have to be combined with a fop if I don't want.

He doesn't call me very often, probably because he's intimidated by me, so I was surprised to hear his voice on the other end of the line when I picked up the phone one evening. After some pleasant fop-like conversation, he turned the topic toward the weddings.

"Two weddings, bet you never saw that one coming!" he exclaimed.

"Actually, I had sort of anticipated it," I said.

"Oh? Well, good. Look, Bruce, I know that being the father of two brides, well, that's got to take a pretty big bite out of the wallet."

Actually, the sensation was more like having my wallet swallowed whole, but I wasn't going to tell him that.

"We're managing just fine."

"I'd like to contribute."

"That won't be necessary, but I appreciate the offer."

"I thought you might say that. But look, don't you think that it's only fair to Judy to let her pick up some of the tab? They're her kids, too, right? Think how you'd feel if the situation were reversed, and I didn't want you to pay anything. How would you feel?"

I hated to admit that he had a good point, so I didn't. In the end, though, we decided he could send me a check and that I would do him the favor of depositing it. I would still bear the majority of the cost, but this way, he could feel like he was being some kind of big deal, when in reality all he was doing was preventing me from being homeless.

"And for the weddings, how are they going?"

"Oh, I've got both of them under control," I assured him. "Completely, absolutely, under control."

FIVE

❧

Industrial-Strength Pressure

A search of various Web sites reveals that weddings represent somewhere between a forty-five- and seventy-two-billion-dollar industry, depending on whether, during the year in question, Donald Trump gets married. To put it in perspective, that's about the same amount of money that the Department of Education spends in any given year, though to be fair, the Department of Education is only involved in the uncomplicated process of schooling all of the children in the United States of America and doesn't have to grapple with complexities like whether the bridesmaids should hold their flowers in front of their stomachs or slightly to the side.

In 1981, the total cost of weddings amounted to only seventeen billion dollars, so it's up 300 percent since then. This explosive growth in expenditures has been characterized by the wedding industry as "good." However, to fathers, these numbers raise the question "Why can't you get married in 1981?"

Your daughter may tell you, upon getting engaged, that

she wants a small, simple wedding, with just a few members of the family in attendance, followed by a sedate, modest dinner and an elegant Champagne toast. The wedding industry, however, wants her to have an event so hugely expensive it winds up being covered by *Vogue*.

The wedding industry has a larger advertising budget than your daughter, so guess who will win that one?

The first salvo in this battle to turn your daughter into Bridezilla comes in the form of bridal magazines, which each weighs as much as a phone book and will start appearing all over your home as if in a determined bid to cause it to sink on its foundations. (As a man, I'm here to tell you that there's nothing more disquieting than to find that *Weddings In Style* has come to replace *Sports Illustrated* in the bathroom magazine rack.)

The bridal magazines are filled with advertisements—in fact, it is sort of hard to tell the ads from the articles, since they both are full of pictures of what, as a man, I can only mentally register as "stuff." Many of the ads are for bridal gowns, and in them, the brides always look angry—maybe because they've had to starve themselves to fit into the things. Often they are doing their pouty look while sprawled out in exhaustion, as if the gown is not only as big as the Liberty Bell but weighs the same.

The people who ought to be angry are the bridesmaids, who are going to be asked to fork over a lot of money for a dress that will only be worn again if the woman gets arrested and decides to try to prove she's not guilty by reason of insanity. They're always smiling, though, because the bridesmaids are always happy for the bride, even when they're not.

The more helpful magazines often (logically) include the word "helpful" on the cover, as in, "Helpful Tips for Throwing Your Mother-in-Law Off a Freeway Overpass." And, though their frenzied focus on weddings can seem a little manic, it's a far, far healthier pursuit than the subjects covered in the video-gaming magazines my son used to read in high school. You can't really get married without them, though I'd say that by the time they start playing "Here Comes the Bride," you should put the magazine down.

When looking for a good bridal magazine, try to find one filled with stories told by brides who live in your price range, if you get my drift. The women who fly by private jet to a private island that was built just for the wedding have fascinating stories to tell, but I was far more interested in the ones who got married in Toledo.

One day I decided to skip working out and stack bridal magazines instead. (Usually I stick to a rigorous schedule of picking other reasons to skip working out.) When I was finished stacking, I had a tower that could fall over and kill anyone under five feet nine inches tall. Here's a sampling of some of the titles of the exciting articles my daughters had been reading:

- Fabulous Ideas to Make Your Wedding Absolutely Unique! (That's Right, If You and Every Other Bride Do What It Says in This Article, Your Weddings Will All Somehow Turn Out to Be Completely Different Than Everyone Else's. Don't Ask Us How This Can Possibly Be True.)
- Marriage Can Make You Rich! (But It Will Put Your Dad in the Poor House!)
- Bikini Waxing, Liposuction, Stomach Stapling: Three Things More Fun than Planning a Wedding!
- Saturday Weddings Are So Yesterday! (Unless It Is Monday—Then They Are So Day-Before-Yesterday!)
- Should Your Maid of Honor Take a Loyalty Oath? (Why Not, It Worked for the Nazis.)

- Meeting the Man of Your Dreams. (So Okay, You're Reading Bridal Magazines and You Don't Even Have a Boyfriend, Which Seems Crazy, But Who Are We to Complain? We Got Your Eight Bucks.)

MUST HAVES

Since your daughter has probably never planned a wedding before (not counting when she was age four and Baby Bear-Bear married Patty Coo in a ceremony attended by a stuffed dog and three Cabbage Patch Kids), it is only natural that she should seek to do some research into the subject of how to conduct a successful wedding, and you'll probably encourage her, completely unaware of the dangers lurking in such an activity.

PANDORA: *I think I'll open this box and see what's inside!*

FATHER: *Good idea!*

The trap for brides is baited with the words "Must Have." Everyone agrees that there are some things you simply Must Have, or the wedding will be ruined and your whole family will be run out of town by villagers throwing stones. For example, the bride Must Have a pair of very special shoes, beautifully handcrafted by Italian artisans out of leather from beautifully handcrafted Italian pigs. This despite the fact that the wedding dress is designed to reach from the bride's shoulders to a point about four feet below the floor. In other words, *no one will see the shoes.* She could stand up there in an old pair of basketball shoes. She could be barefoot. She could be *Bigfoot.* She does not need a pair of shoes that cost as much as my first automobile, no matter what her friends say. But a Pair of Very Special Shoes is just one item on the list of Must Haves.

7 MUST HAVES FOR A FABULOUS* WEDDING!

Engraved Matchbooks They should match the wedding colors, and they can't be ordinary matches, they must be special European matches, which look the same as American matches but are better because they are more expensive and more European. Every place setting should have the matchbooks, *even though no one is allowed to smoke*! (Emphasis added by father.)

Chocolate Fountains These are like water fountains in the mall, except no one throws coins in them (or so we hope). People dip things like strawberries, angel food cake, and fingers into the gooey flowing liquid, which looks an awful lot like the Missouri River in flood stage. Chocolate fountains are great for bringing people closer together because they will all share the same viruses. That's what a chocolate fountain is, a giant virus recycler. You simply must have one for your wedding so that your immune system can party, too.

And by the way, is this all new chocolate, or are we also sharing the germs from other weddings? (Question asked by father.)

Special Monogrammed Guestbook In fact, everything at the wedding needs to be monogrammed with the bride and groom's initials, from the wineglasses to the urinals in the men's room. The guestbook is important because

---

* The word "fabulous" is used constantly by bridal magazines, as if everyone getting married is gay.

without it, years from now, the bride and groom won't be able to remember who in their family has bad handwriting. Imagine all the wonderful hours the bride and groom will spend over the years, sitting together and leafing through the guestbook.

BRIDE: *Remember when Uncle Ron signed his name?*

GROOM *(sigh): Yes, I've never been happier.*

BRIDE: *And what about when Cousin Jeff signed his name.*

GROOM: *Those sure were fabulous times.*

BRIDE: *I'm sure glad we've got this specially monogrammed guestbook so we could spend hours and hours gazing at these fabulous signatures.*

GROOM: *Otherwise, the wedding would have been ruined.*

Since the guestbook will be lying open, so that no one will see its cover, why does it need to be monogrammed? (Logical question supplied by father.)

Flower Coffins You'll be relieved to know that advances in science have made it possible to create a special vacuum-sealed chamber to hold the wedding flowers in a pristine state forever, so the bride can display them on her mantle for years to come. It's sort of like decorating the living room with the body of Lenin.

But wait, didn't the flower bouquet get tossed over the bride's head into a feverish pack of single women who went after it like a loose football? No, you're forgetting about another Must Have—***Stunt Flowers***. This is a special bogus bouquet designed to look exactly like the wedding bouquet, but it steps in at the last second to take the abuse so that the wedding bouquet can be immortalized in the coffin. But wait, you cry, the person who catches the wedding bouquet is supposed to be the next person who gets married, even if it is Cousin Tina, who is having trouble meeting the right guy because just last month she was Cousin Ted, and hasn't finished her transition or even really started it unless you count her outfit. If the flowers being flung are not the real wedding bouquet, doesn't that break the curse? (Exasperated question from father.)

When I posed this question, I got this answer.

VALERIE: *Dad.*

SAM: *Dad. It's not a curse.*

ME: *So it's like what, a magic spell?*

VALERIE: *Dad.*

SAM: *Dad, it's not magic, it is just a tradition.*

ME: *But how does it make any sense?*

VALERIE: *Dad!*

SAM: *Dad, it is not supposed to make sense. It is a wedding.*

Wedding Favors A wedding favor is a special gift given to the guests as a thank-you for doing you the favor of coming to your daughter's wedding, eating all of the food, and, in the case of Uncle Bob at least, drinking free liquor until he winds up salsa dancing with Cousin Tina/Ted. Wedding favors remind guests (a) what a great time they had at your wedding, and (b) that they have something to throw away when they get home. There is a lot of pressure on the bride to come up with a wedding favor that is unique and fabulous—for example, how about a sterling silver bell, engraved with the bride and groom's initials? That way, when they are dashing for their getaway car (Valerie: Dad! It's not a getaway car. This isn't a bank robbery! Me: Right, a bank robbery involves less money), everyone can ring their silver bells. Then everyone who was at the wedding can have a reunion the next morning at the pawn shop.

> ME: *A bell made of silver? Wouldn't you rather have it be gold and diamond encrusted?*

> SAM: *Well, silver bells . . . get it, like the song? Because I'm getting married before Christmas. Soon it will be Christmas Day. Like that.*

> ME: *Why don't we just buy everyone a BMW and be done with it.*

> VALERIE: *Dad!*

> SAM: *Dad, stop. How would that fit on the table?*

Wedding favors must come in a Must Have **Wedding Favor Box**. These are fabulous gift boxes that are monogrammed with the bride and groom's fabulous initials.

> VALERIE: *Dad, we are really getting tired of your so-called jokes.*

How are we supposed to afford all the Must Haves? If we pay for all this stuff, we won't be able to afford the one thing we agreed we Must Absolutely Have—a wedding. (Financial observation cried out loud by father.)

A BRIDAL INTERVENTION

As the Must Haves pile up, the father may find it necessary to call for a Bridal Intervention.

An intervention is a process in which a family tries to talk, as a group, to one of its members about disturbing or addictive behavior. (In my family, we have interventions all the time, only we call them "holidays." Our approach is not to single out one person's behavior but basically to complain about everyone at the same time. In this way, no one feels ganged up on or gets any benefit from the process.)

Often during holiday dinners my mother will get very angry at my father, which otherwise rarely happens unless they speak to each other. When this occurs, she'll sometimes announce "I'm leaving" and walk out of the house and get in her car and then sit in the driveway because she forgot her keys. The rest of the family will go on eating and fighting as if nothing happened, though we won't forget about my mother because every once in a while she'll honk her horn to remind us she's still mad. One time my sister got so angry about something she went out to her car, too, and then because they were also furious with each other, my mother and my sister sat in their cars in the driveway and honked at each other.

Coming from such a loving family gives me the special ability to understand that someone can act completely crazy and yet, under the surface, be only somewhat crazy. So when I found my daughter Sam making her list of Must Haves and saw on it things like "Special box for the Champagne for the wedding toast (monogrammed?)" and "What else should be imprinted on the rose petals besides our initials?" I knew that an intervention was necessary.

Nearly every bride needs an intervention at some point, and nearly always it is the father who does it, because everyone else is *afraid*. At least, this is the only conclusion I can draw for why every single person in the family nods and smiles when the bride says things like, "Wouldn't it be wonderful if all the escort cards were silver ornaments hanging on a big Christmas tree, and that way people would keep them forever for their own holiday trees, except then I'd have to get a special box so their ornaments wouldn't break, and the box would have to match the special Champagne box, and it would have to be monogrammed and match the wedding colors!"

An escort card, by the way, is a card (or, apparently, an ornament) printed with everyone's seating assignments so that family members will know who has to sit next to Uncle Bob. The idea is that people come in, find their cards displayed in some attractive, theme-colored, monogrammed fashion, read their cards, and say "I'll trade you Uncle Bob for Cousin Tina."

A bridal intervention differs from a family intervention in that (a) most of the family shouldn't be invited, since they all thought the Christmas ornament idea was fabulous, and (b) no one winds up honking in the driveway. One can, however, enlist a neutral third party to help, someone good with conflict resolution, such as a minister, a priest, or Condoleezza Rice.

For my Bridal Intervention with my daughter Sam, I decided to invite Sarah, because everyone, even my own parents, likes her more than they like me; and my neighbor Tom, because he's a guy and agrees with me on everything and could bring sandwiches. I made an appointment (once your daughter gets engaged she won't be able to see you unless you give her at least a week's notice) and was somewhat surprised to see my daughter Valerie tagging along, standing on the doorstep next to her sister.

"You weren't supposed to bring reinforcements, Sam, this is sort of a gang-up-on-you thing," I explained in a kind, psychological-intervention sort of voice. "Valerie, maybe you should sit in your car and just honk occasionally."

"Dad," Valerie said.

We went into the living room and settled in for the big talk.

"Gosh, I know you're not allowed to eat meat, Valerie, because you have vegetarianism and everything," Tom said apologetically. "Would a . . . I have a BLT here, would that work?"

"Bacon *is* one of the more healthier vegetables," I remarked sarcastically.

"That's okay, I know you didn't expect me to come. I can just eat some lettuce and tomato on bread," Valerie assured him.

"I didn't expect you to come, either," I said in a friendly tone.

"But you're glad she's here, right?" Sarah said, as if feeding me a line I'd forgotten to say in a high school play.

"But I'm glad you're here," I echoed automatically. "Just surprised."

"I figured you're going to have some sort of 'father' talk about how the wedding is getting out of control, so I decided I should get mine over with, too," Valerie replied.

"It *is* out of control," Sam blurted. "There's so much to do, I can't get started. Everything depends on everything else! Like, if we have a destination wedding, that means when we come back the reception should have a theme of, like, where we went to get married, Hawaii or Cancun or whatever."

"Hawaii? Cancun?" I sputtered.

"But it's close to Christmas, so I thought a Christmas theme would be wonderful, but I don't want to get married with green and red bridesmaids! And the invitations, they can't be sandals at Christmas, and then I have to pick out a dress, and the wedding favors . . ."

"Hold on, *Hawaii*?" I demanded.

"I remember when I started journalism school, there was so much I had to decide at once," Sarah mused thoughtfully. "I had to find a place to live, I had all my studies, I had student loans, my car broke down . . . It was awful."

Tom and I exchanged a glance, wondering how to get her off this irrelevant tangent.

"Yes, that's what it's like *exactly*," Sam cried.

"But this is a wedding. I think the Apollo program provides a better model," I said. Tom nodded agreement.

"A better paradigm," Tom said. "We say that word at work a lot, and it probably applies here."

"What I eventually decided is to make myself sort of a logic tree. Like, what decisions need to be made first?" Sarah continued. Both Sam and Valerie nodded vigorously.

"What flavor cake will you have, do you think?" Tom asked.

"So there's no sense worrying about themes and invitations until you know if it is a destination wedding, right? That's the most important. *Then* you can worry about the next decision," Sarah continued.

I felt that this Bridal Intervention was going very poorly

because I was not doing most of the talking, but I couldn't think of how to get it back on track.

"You're exactly right," Sam said. "I've been focused on the details, but I need to make the big decisions first!"

"Some people like sprinkles on their cake. Now, I'm not much of a sprinkle man, myself. Wrong sort of paradigm," Tom observed.

"We've been talking about the Grand Canyon at sunrise, but there's an *enormous* canyon on the Hawaiian island of Kauai," Valerie said speculatively. "I bet that would be acceptable."

All the women beamed, happy that my daughter might consider Hawaii somehow acceptable.

"I had a chocolate fudge wedding cake in 1988 that I still dream about," Tom noted.

As a result of a fatherly Bridal Intervention like the one above, a wedding can go from completely out of control to sort of out of control. What I said was exactly right: The wedding plan needed to be viewed as a big decision tree. I felt good because my daughter had been in danger of turning into a full-blown Bridezilla, but I saved her with a well-constructed intervention, plus there were sandwiches.

A SAMPLE DECISION TREE

The decision tree concept that I explained to my daughters has a basic father-approved structure: The most important decisions drive the less important decisions, the way tree limbs branch off from the trunk.

Here's how the decision tree was working for my daughter before the Bridal Intervention:

Figure A:

Typical Wedding Decision Tree

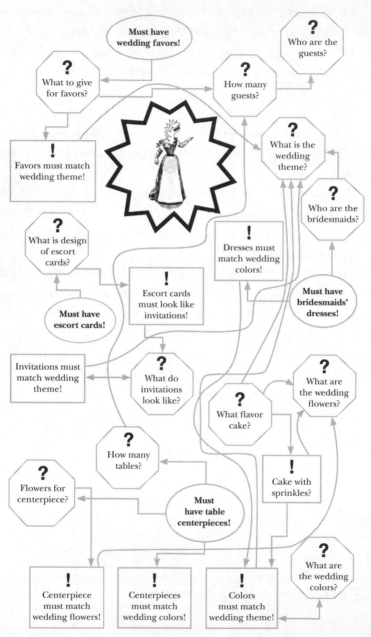

Here's the decision-making tree (designed by the father of the bride) once the Bridal Intervention has been held. See how much simpler it is?

Figure B:

Father-Designed Decision Tree

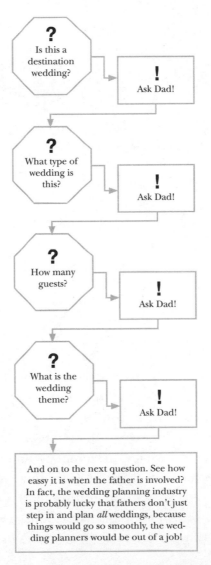

And on to the next question. See how eassy it is when the father is involved? In fact, the wedding planning industry is probably lucky that fathers don't just step in and plan *all* weddings, because things would go so smoothly, the wedding planners would be out of a job!

Everyone's decision tree will be different. For example, here's how the groom sees the decision tree:

Figure C:

Groom Decision Tree

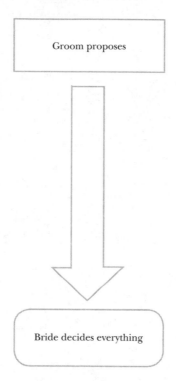

Most of the time, though, the decision tree will look like the one in Figure A. Here's what to consider.

1. Is This a Destination Wedding?

A destination wedding means that some number of people will travel to someplace for the ceremony and/or reception. Due to the high cost of flying, the wedding party and guest list is usually very small, though it should be noted that to be successful, you should make sure you have at least two people there (the bride and groom). Places like Hawaii and

Tahiti are more popular than places like, say, Cleveland and Duluth.

Often people who go off to a destination wedding will come back and have a reception, but the whole pomp and circumstance of formal vows, with the men wearing tuxedos and the bridesmaids dressed like sight gags, is avoided.

2. What Type of Wedding Is This? (Besides Expensive)

Is this a traditional, or nontraditional, wedding? (Both have a lot of traditions.) Is this a get-married-in-a-church and then everyone-gets-lost-going-to-the-reception wedding (the "religious ceremony") type? Is this a cash bar ("cheap") or open bar ("Uncle Bob will for sure be there") type? Is this a sit-down dinner ("formal") or everyone-can-eat-snacks-from-the-vending-machines ("profitable") type?

3. How Many Guests Will Be Coming?

Deciding on this will determine the exact measure by which you can't afford to get married.

Of course, if you are going with the (father-suggested) vending machine idea, you can theoretically open the event to the public. Otherwise, though, your previous decisions are driving some of the considerations here. Let's say, for example, that your younger daughter is thinking about going to the Grand Canyon (or the still-acceptable alternative, the Waimea Canyon on the island of Kauai, Hawaii). That's a destination wedding, though how we are going to get there without using any internal combustion engines that harm the Earth, I have no idea. Clearly, though, there's no guest list for the ceremony, which will be conducted by a holy man of some religion that no one belongs to except him. It's also going to be a nontraditional wedding, which means that instead of doing nonsensical things because they are traditional, you will do them because they are nontraditional.

If it is a formal sit-down dinner your daughter craves, the guest list is limited by the size of the room, since it turns out the Superdome is already booked. The price per plate is also a factor, though no one seems to be bothered by this particular detail except maybe you.

4. What Is the Theme of the Wedding?

Judging by the way everyone acts during the planning stages, the theme of most weddings should be "Everyone Is in a Bad Mood."

Most fathers are surprised to hear that there even is a theme. If you quizzed them after a wedding as to what they thought the theme was, they'd probably answer, "I'm Missing the Ohio State Game." But themes are very much on the mind of most brides, because bridal experts state emphatically that you Must Have a theme or the marriage will be doomed. Sometimes the theme is driven by the location or the time of year, though care must be given to the exact wording. So "It's Beginning to Look a Lot Like Christmas" is better than "It's Snowing in Cleveland." Or themes can be a single word: "Joy" or "Love" is probably better than "Bloating" or "Smallpox."

When it came to my older daughter's decision tree, the answers were simple, so we only had to listen to her talk about it for maybe thirty hours straight. In the end, she decided that she would rather have the wedding be local and the honeymoon be destination, so that she wouldn't have to bring her father along on the trip, even though I am very good at organizing such things and when she was growing up she really appreciated how I always was telling her what to do to have fun on vacation, like go fishing with me. She wanted a sit-down dinner, and she wanted to limit the guest list to only those people from her life who were breathing. The theme, surprisingly, would have nothing to do with

Christmas—in fact, her decision that the theme would be "Hot August Nights" completely changed the schedule, bumping everything up by a couple of months. Gone were silver bells, wreaths, and Tom's idea that they should be married by a minister dressed up like Santa Claus. Now the colors would be warm and they would be married by a minister dressed up as Neil Diamond. (Again, Tom's idea.)

"Who?" Valerie asked, bewildered.

"His album, *Hot August Nights*," Tom explained. "That's what Sam's theme is based on."

Sam and Valerie looked at each other and shrugged the way I used to look at my sisters and shrug when my parents asked me how there could be a Talking Heads song without talking in it.

Valerie's decision tree was a little more complex. She wanted a destination wedding because where we lived was apparently not close enough to the Earth. However, good old Moldy now objected to the Grand Canyon because he had read somewhere that it was full of tourists, and tourists are loathsome creatures because they go to places for fun, as opposed to the reason why Moldy would go there. What he wanted, apparently, was an enormous geological feature (like a mountain, a 200-mile-long gorge, or a polar ice cap) that no one had ever noticed before. He wanted a nontraditional wedding that made, in his words, "the right political statement." The number of guests wasn't an issue, though I was privately betting that he didn't have any friends except my daughter. As a wedding favor, each guest would receive a personally tailored computer-generated report on their "carbon footprint."

"It doesn't look to me like Valerie's wedding is ever going to happen," I remarked to Tom. "Somebody better figure out a way to break it to their highway."

Sarah disagreed with me. "Why would you say Valerie's wedding isn't happening?" she asked me. We were in my kitchen—it was my turn to cook, so I'd gotten Chinese takeout.

"If you'd watched *Apollo 13* as many times as I have, you'd just have a sense of these things," I responded.

"You like Marty, though," she said.

I had to think about that one. "When Valerie was a teenager, she was so dark," I finally said. "I used to call her slumber parties 'coven meetings.' She didn't smile for two straight years. Then she came out of it and started showing she had a sense of humor again."

"She laughed at your jokes," Sarah translated.

"Exactly. But around Moldy, I don't know, for some reason I get a whiff of the old darkness, you know? It's like there's some part of her that she put away but Mulchy brings out in her whenever he's around. So yeah, I'd really, really like it if they didn't get married. Also, I'm worried about falling into the canyon."

"But you know you can't stop it, right?" Sarah asked softly. "If she's determined, she's going to get married. With or without your approval."

I nodded. "Yeah, I agree, it's a really stupid system."

Ironically, I was talking about this very problem with Tom, how odd it was that a father couldn't just veto a fiancé and be done with it ("a sensible paradigm," Tom called it), when Valerie burst into my home, her face flushed with excitement.

"I got a ring!" she announced, throwing her hand out in front of us.

Tom and I stared in amazement.

"The diamond's from Canada. Conflict-free," she continued happily.

It looked like a completely normal diamond ring, a gold band with a pretty jewel in the center. "A simple but elegant design," I said out loud, quoting from a bridal magazine (See? I told you that a good one can be helpful.) She gave me a pleased look.

"It's made from recycled gold."

"Recycled?" Tom said in disbelief. I could tell by the look on his face that he was picturing the plastic sack of beer cans in his garage.

"I'll explain it later," I told him.

"Marty said the Grand Canyon is fine, it's not like the tourists will all be up at sunrise. Oh Dad, I'm getting married, I'm really going to be a bride!" She actually hugged herself with excitement, and I felt my resistance to Marty melting like an ice cap exposed to global warming. If he made her this happy, who was I to judge?

"Okay, I have to go. I'm going to work on my decision tree!" Valerie kissed me on the cheek and virtually skipped out the door.

THE #1 MUST HAVE: A FATHER

Picture the wedding industry as a horde of invading marauders who have launched a blizzard of arrows at your daughter. The father is the only thing that stands between her and this incoming salvo—he must raise his shield and protect her. (There's not a father in the world who wouldn't like this analogy.)

Sure, if it is really important, there can be wedding favors (which could, I still insist, be dispensed from vending machines), but if a bride starts making lists of all the decisions she needs to make, she'll quickly become buried in the details. Helping her prioritize her list, making and keeping the choices that are most important to her even if it means the wedding invitations might not precisely match the wedding flowers, is a sure way to help prevent her from evolving into a Bridezilla.

This isn't to say that the Bridezilla Alert was over and that we could all come out of our bridal bomb shelters. The pressure was still on my daughters—in fact, it was about to get much, much worse.

SIX

≈

You Need Professional Help

I was late to Sam's Emergency Wedding Meeting because I was driving around the block, desperately trying to think of a good excuse for not attending. My reluctance had nothing to do with my daughter, for whom "emergency" pretty much described everything about her wedding, but with her future in-laws, Alecia (Bridezilla and Geoff's sister) and Priscilla (British prime minister/Geoff's mother). (I'd started calling Priscilla "Priszilla," but Sam begged me to stop for fear I'd say it to her face, as if I ever would do such a thing unless it was by accident.)

This meeting was called because it was *their* emergency—the two 'zillas—which I could only assume had something to do with the major networks refusing to preempt their evening broadcasts in order to be able to cover Alecia's nuptials.

When I finally, reluctantly, went up to Sam's door and was admitted into her apartment, I was surprised to see that Geoff was there as well. "Well hi, Geoff," I greeted cheerfully, glad there would be some testosterone in the meeting besides mine. "I'd forgotten all about you."

99

I turned to Sam. "Hey, Sam, look, it's Geoff! Remember him?"

Nobody was amused. Priscilla gave me a blood-tears-toil-and-sweat look, and Alecia gazed into the distance, as if awaiting the dissipation of some unpleasant flatulence. Sam's expression indicated that she felt as if I'd just testified against her at her murder trial.

Somehow, though the room was well lit, where Priscilla sat the corner was deep in shadow—a gathering storm, if you will.

After about five minutes of obligatory chitchat,* Alecia identified the crisis that had her and her mother in a state of nuptial DefCon 2: Sam's decision to have her wedding at the end of August meant that Alecia's wedding was totally ruined.

Apparently the theme of Alecia's wedding was "Celebrating the Wonder of Alecia in Springtime," or some such, which put Sam's theme in competition.

"Why would a springtime theme be in competition with, with . . ." I groped for the right Neil Diamond song. " 'Sweet Caroline?' "

"Dad, it's Hot August Nights," Sam hissed at me. "Stop trying to be funny."

I was pleased to hear that I had been funny, though I wasn't sure what I'd said that qualified. "Well, okay, but what's the big deal?" I still wanted to know.

"It's the colors," Priscilla rumbled from her dark corner, her voice like a room full of alligators coming awake. I

---

* Sample of chitchat: I found the most *adorable* clasps for the *necklaces* that match the *colors* of the *flowers* of the *air* of the *theme* of the *joy* of the dance . . . (I may have dozed off, but my brain kept registering sounds.)

glanced at her cold face and then looked hastily away—the woman truly frightened me.

"Exactly," Alecia breathed, as if we all understood. Which, of course, we all didn't, since I was truly baffled. "The colors."

Priscilla made a sound in agreement, it sounded like "kack!"

For the uninitiated, weddings don't just come in themes, they also come in colors you never heard of, like "atmosphere," "persimmon," and "vengeance." The colors must match the theme—if they don't, the couple will not be allowed to get married—that's the law.

"But I don't even know my colors yet," Sam said falteringly.

Alecia gave her a smile that somehow didn't look smiley. From my angle, it appeared her canine teeth were a half inch longer than her incisors. "Yes, but Sam, summer colors and spring colors are all very much alike. Pastels. Pinks. See?"

I could see that Sam was struggling not to say, "Yes, Alecia, and you're an idiot," so I interrupted. "Okay, but what are you saying, that you're worried that you and Sam will have some of the same colors?"

"No," Alecia said, turning her chilling smile on me, "I'm saying it's not happening."

"Sorry?"

"It's not happening. I have been planning my wedding for *too long* for something like this to go wrong."

"Sam, your wedding is less than seven months away. That's not enough time to plan something to be proud of. The Christmas theme was better," Priscilla growled.

Alecia nodded. "I was okay with that one, too. But not this."

I realized I was out of my depth, here. On television shows, when someone starts talking this crazy, the cops always hit them with Tasers. So was Alecia actually implying that if her wedding, more than four months earlier than my daughter's, shared a few of the same colors, it would somehow be a disaster? Wouldn't walking out of a church legally married to Alecia be the trump disaster?

"So you're saying that if my daughter wears white, and you wear white . . ." I said slowly.

"*No,*" Alecia snapped.

"Bruce," Priscilla said. "Many of the people attending Sam's wedding will have been at Alecia's wedding. So you see?"

I nodded. "Yes. Well, no."

"You understand, right, Sam?" Alecia demanded, deciding I was too dense to participate in the conversation.

I turned to look to my daughter—if she understood, maybe she could explain this whole thing to me in terms that didn't cause my brain to implode. But what I saw on her face made my heart seize: She looked both trapped and wounded. These were her future in-laws, and she felt powerless to do anything in the face of their implacable audacity.

"Powerless" is not my daughter's natural state. When she glanced at me, I didn't see the volleyball champion who hit the ball like cannon shots over the net, I saw a little girl being told by her friends that she wasn't welcome to play horse with them on the sidewalk.

My heart started to pound. My first instinct—which was to stand up and punch Alecia in the nose—I dismissed out of the sure sense that her mother would come out of the shadows and sink her teeth into me like a badger. But I knew I was going to do something—they were ganging up on my little girl.

I was opening my mouth, sort of wondering what would come out of it, when Geoff surprised me.

"So what?" he asked flatly. Everyone peered at him—they had apparently forgotten he was there. He looked completely relaxed and confident, though his eyes held a coldness I had never seen before. "This is our wedding. We're going to have the colors Sam wants," he continued factually. "I don't care if they're like yours, Alecia. In fact, I don't care if they are exactly the same."

"Oh, this is so not happening. *Mother*," Alecia implored.

"Geoff," his mother warned.

Geoff shrugged. "Wait, I have the perfect idea. Let's tell everyone in our family they have a choice, they can go to *your* wedding, or *my* wedding, but not both. That way, they won't be offended by seeing the same colors!" Geoff beamed at the two stricken women, and I had a sudden sense of which of the two weddings would attract the most family members. "Sam and I won't have to go to your wedding either, Alecia," he continued. "So that way, no one can possibly think that Sam stole any of your fabulous ideas."

In the silence that followed you could have heard Alecia's talons growing.

"Or maybe," Geoff continued reasonably, "Sam picks the colors she wants, and nobody says another word about the subject. Ever. Not to me, not to Sam, not even to your maid of honor." He sized up his sister. "Your choice, Alecia. You want a competition between weddings, let's make it a real competition. The winner gets all the guests."

I found myself, for the first time, regarding my future son-in-law with real admiration for the decision I'd made to let him marry Sam. He was willing to stand up to his own mother to protect his soon-to-be-wife, something most men have trouble doing. Heck, I wouldn't go after Priscilla with anything less than an elephant gun.

Alecia declared through a brittle smile that she never intended for her comments to be anything but advice, seeing as Sam was new to the dark science of wedding planning and Alecia had been doing it for two decades.

Geoff cocked his head. "Sounds like we're still talking about it. Is that what we're doing? Because that means the wedding smack-down is on." He stared Alecia right in the eyes. "Bring it."

Another silence, both more charged and more enjoyable than the first, followed this comment, and then Priscilla cleared her reptilian throat. "So tell me, Sam," she asked carefully, "have you given much thought to floral arrangements?"

A FESTIVAL OF MUST HAVES

A hundred years ago, frontier towns were visited by wandering carnivals that would put on elaborate cabarets while pickpockets infiltrated the crowds and took people's money. Today, those carnivals have been replaced by wedding shows.

I have to confess, how something so lacking in entertainment could be called a "show" is beyond my understanding. A wedding show is to "shows" what a funeral party is to "parties."

"Dad," Valerie said when I made this apt observation.

A wedding show is where purveyors of the Must Haves gather together under one roof and lure huge crowds of future brides inside and subject them to powerful drugs, like chocolate, until every woman is a mindless zombie numbly signing up to receive free information about everything from eyelash braids to parachute weddings.

"Dad!" Valerie warned.

"Well, as much as I agree that some members of the family should be shoved out of an airplane, I am not going to learn sky dying just so you can get married," I replied.

Wedding shows need to be held in large venues, such as football stadiums, county fairgrounds, or Nevada. Sometimes there are other events going concurrently with a similar theme—the day we went to the wedding show, the fairgrounds was also hosting a body art symposium and a gun and knife festival. I felt it was very appropriate.

Our stated purpose in attending this event was to get "ideas," even though in my opinion we had too many ideas already.

You Are Cordially and Elaborately Invited

In this age of faxes and e-mails, it is no longer necessary to send out formal wedding invitations, though nobody but the father seems to understand this. Instead, brides want a wedding invitation in their colors, reflecting their theme, and printed on special card stock made from trees that were raised listening to Beethoven and given daily foot rubs. The imprinted letters should be so thick and raised they might well be written in toothpaste; people will be able to read the invitations just by running their hands over them.

Inside, the wedding invitations should be little decorations—miniature Champagne bottles, colorful silk flowers, studded snow tires. The purpose of these decorations is to introduce everyone you are inviting to the joy of extra postage. Also in the invitation should be a separate invitation for the reception, a separate card announcing where the couple is registered, a separate card requesting an RSVP, a separate envelope for the separate card requesting an RSVP, a ribbon for no good reason, tiny sheets of tissue paper that separates the separate stuff, and then something "extra."

"Extra," I repeated when I heard this. "The invitation is already going to look like an envelope from Publisher's Sweepstakes, what do you mean, 'extra'?"

Apparently, it is fashionable these days for the bride to insert something unique inside the invitation. A photo of the happy couple on a date, perhaps, or maybe a poem, or one of the bride's baby teeth. This extra thing adds extra weight—you'd spend less on stamps if you were the Unabomber.

"The extra item is up to you," the professional wedding-invitation guy will say. Apparently, you don't have any choice for any of the other stuff, but when it comes to the extras, the bride is afforded some choice. In this way, the wedding-invitation industry is generous and wonderful.

CASH REGISTERS

Like dogs, all weddings need to be registered. Unlike dogs, however, there is no special discount if the people getting married are neutered, though I think we can all agree that there are some people—Alecia, as an example—who could make this a better world by not ever reproducing. Or talking.

The very first thing brides are urged to do after getting married is to register for her gifts, which is sort of like fantasy football, only involving shopping. The bride can spend several days building her ideal "team" of dishes, appliances, furniture, and private airplanes, and at the end of it she doesn't have to pay a thing. In this way, the wedding industry is certain it is protecting itself against the bride backing out of the engagement—if she goes through with the wedding, she gets all these fabulous gifts!

One of the top questions asked by brides is how to get

their guests to give cash instead of gifts without sounding ungrateful and tacky—which I think we can all agree is an ungrateful and tacky question. The philosophy seems to be "Hey, if I'm marrying this guy, I expect to be paid in cash, not in waffle irons." Though I guess there are circumstances where I would agree with this: If I were marrying Alecia, I would want someone to pay me ten billion dollars.

At the wedding show, several vendors have set up kiosks so that brides can register right there on the spot. Their friends and sisters can register, too, even if they are not engaged, an activity known as "collective hysteria."

My favorite booth at the wedding show displayed "necessities" the brides needed to remember to put on their registry. The list of necessities included a heart-shaped pancake griddle, a panini grill, and a stone kitchen toad that reacted to beeps from the microwave by announcing "Something's cooking in the kitchen!" in three languages.

Carbo-Bombing

The next stop in the wedding show is the aisle where all the cake designers provide samples of their wares. By the end of the aisle, everyone will have consumed the equivalent of one whole wedding cake, which is made of sugar, flour, saturated fat, and sugar.

The wedding cake isn't chronologically the next step in the wedding process, but the people putting on the show want everyone stoned on glucose before the next aisle, which is where the jewelers are hawking their wares. *Why not spend ten grand on the wedding rings?* the groom is supposed to think. *Might as well, I've had so much sugar I'm losing my pancreas.*

If the couple has already purchased their rings, the

jewelers are unappeased: what about the bridal gift? (In some weddings, the bride and groom privately exchange gifts. He gives her something she really wants, like jewelry, and she gives him something he really wants, like nudity. Or more typically, she gives him cuff links or some other item in a demonstration of the fact that she doesn't understand testosterone.) The jewelers show necklaces, earrings, and other items to the few grooms at the show, who stare numbly at the display, realizing that their jewelry buying didn't end with the engagement ring, but rather has just begun.

I phoned my son from my cell phone so that I could ignore my daughters as they held up diamond earrings and claimed that Sarah wanted a pair.

"Hey, we're actually not too far from your school, you should come over," I told him. "We're at the gun and knife show."

"No, you're not, you're at the wedding thing."

"The wedding thing that's part of the gun and knife show," I corrected. "Anyway, you should come over just because of all the single women."

"Single *engaged* women," he corrected.

"Plus free cake," I said desperately. "Look, I need someone to talk to, both of your sisters have gone lunatic."

"They're not laughing at your jokes," he translated.

"Right."

"Well, I'm not coming. If I go, Terri will go—Terri my girlfriend," he said, answering a question I didn't ask.

"I know who Terri is," I groused.

"Sure. And if Terri goes to a wedding show, she's going to drag me over to look at engagement rings. I do *not* want to have that conversation with her again."

"Okay," I said bitterly, "but don't ever ask me to buy you a howitzer. You had your chance and you blew it."

A PERFECT DAY

Over and over at the wedding show, vendors would say brightly, "It's your wedding and you want it to be perfect." I decided that "perfect" was a term that belonged right up there with "Must Have" as a key phrase in warping a perfectly normal daughter into a Bridezilla.

Chic Chair Couture. To achieve perfection, even the chairs need special outfits for the wedding, so that they wind up draped in sheets as if heading off to a Klan rally.

"Dad!" Valerie said.

Picking out a chair outfit and shopping for these outfits can, to a man, be just as tedious as shopping for any other kind of clothing. The difference, I suppose, is that while at a clothing store the man sits on a chair outside the dressing room and waits for the person he's with to come out and model the outfit; when it comes to this type of shopping, the man sits on the actual model.

I questioned whether it would be considered rude if a chair wore white to a wedding and was given looks that I interpreted to mean that everyone had gone temporarily insane.

It's a Vision Thing. One of the vendors at the wedding show was an eye clinic touting LASIK surgery so the brides could actually see who they were marrying. He also sold different-colored lenses, so that the bride could have eyes in whatever color she wanted. There was even an odd, Satanic-red lens he sold (that I dubbed "Eye of Priscilla"). He admitted that he hadn't sold any of these to future brides but he did move a couple to some people who wandered in from guns and knives.

Lights, Camera, Action. There's more to a perfect wedding than having a wedding photographer—you also need for every table to have a digital camera so that you can remember your wedding while it is happening. A videographer needs to record the reception, capturing your relatives dancing, for blackmail purposes. Video streaming allows people from all over the world to log onto your Web site and watch in real time as bottles and bottles of Champagne are consumed by Uncle Bob.

So not only is your daughter supposed to put on a perfect show, but the show itself will be subject to Nielsen ratings. No wonder she's stressed!

It's Not Enough Just to Feed Them. The perfect wedding has something unusual at it besides Cousin Ted/Tina. Why not rent a vintage juke box, a photo booth, or an MRI machine? Or hire a professional choreographer to teach everyone to dance, music-video style, to a song by Snoop Dogg. Maybe Alecia could entertain the guests by hanging upside down from the rafters with her wings folded over her face.

You may think I'm making a so-called joke about the synchronized dancing, but this is actually a fairly popular option. On the Web I even found a wedding party mimicking the choreography of Michael Jackson's "Thriller," in which the people dance like zombies (which, come to think of it, is sort of how Uncle Bob moves by the time the bar closes).

Deck the Halls. A wedding simply wouldn't be perfect if every square inch of the church and reception hall wasn't decorated in the official colors, right? Imagine the trauma if one of the guests were to accidentally catch sight of some unadorned walls. For outdoor weddings, aisle liners are a must—fake leaves, fake pine cones, fake Astroturf.

Get There in Excess. The limo should be large enough to hold the entire wedding party plus the guests. Besides stereo systems, full bars, and sky lights, modern limos can contain foot massagers, hot tubs, and theme parks.

One trend is to rent a vintage automobile, like a 1938 Rolls Royce, to take the bride and groom from the church to the reception, in order to experience high insurance rates. My observation, which was that Uncle Bob had a 1966 Dodge Dart he would let us borrow, fell on deaf ears.

No wonder the organizers of the wedding/tattoo/gun and knife show put up a large tent for fathers to go and buy things to use to stab themselves. A wedding show is filled with things you never thought existed or cared about in the slightest, though the women in your life will mysteriously know all about them, as if they watched a video about it when they were still in the womb.

If your daughter is dragging you off to a wedding show, stop at the entrance, give her all of your money (at least, all the money you haven't given her yet) and then go off and buy yourself something that uses gunpowder. By the time she emerges, hyperenergized by what she has just seen, you'll be so pumped full of testosterone you won't even be able to hear her.

THE PROFESSIONAL WEDDING PLANNER'S PLAN

As it turned out, we all had preconceived notions of what a professional wedding planner would be like. I wanted someone who would make everything easier, facilitating a lot of the grunt work and maybe changing the oil in my car. Sam wanted someone who "got the whole vision" and was a member of the Association of Bridal Coordinators. Valerie wanted someone who "shared the same values" and was a member of the Environmental Protection Agency.

After reading about each coordinator in the booklet from what I was calling "the bag of worthless crap," Sam decided the

person we should speak to was Lindy Love-Lloyd, who promised in her literature to "literally obliterate any obstacles to *your*
perfect wedding, no matter what or who they might be."

I reflected that the word "obliterate" would appeal to
anyone facing the prospect of a mother-in-law like Priscilla.

Lindy Love-Lloyd looked to be in her fifties, a wiry woman
with a voice husky from smoking or perhaps yelling at Marine
recruits. "Two weddings! My goodness. That's wonderful,"
she said when she heard what was going on.

I frowned over this blatant misuse of the word "wonderful."

"Would either of you like some chocolate-covered peanuts?" Lindy offered.

Both of my daughters shook their heads. "Oh, no," Valerie said. "We've had too much cake already."

"Good," Lindy approved.

"I'll take a couple," I interjected. They were pretty tasty.

Lindy took notes as Sam described what she wanted at
her wedding, which was considerably more detailed and
alarming than I had heard previously. I leaned in to remind
everyone who was in charge. "It sounds like the theme of this
wedding should be 'A Return to Eden' and not 'Song Sung
Blue.' "

"Hot August Nights," Sam corrected.

"Dad!" Valerie hissed.

Lindy looked at me over the tops of her glasses. "Mr.
Cameron, you know what a purse is?"

Was this a trick question? I couldn't see the trap, so I nodded. "A purse," I lectured, steepling my fingers, "is an over-
sized wallet with straps that contains things a woman needs,
like lip goo, face stuff, nail remover . . ."

"A purse," Lindy rasped, "is an accessory. A woman carries it at her side. Understand?"

"Sure," I agreed. "Though there's a kind of purse called a 'cluck' purse that a woman carries in front . . ."

"That's what you are, Mr. Cameron," Lindy interrupted.

"Sorry?"

"You're gonna be by her side at the wedding. You're a purse, get it? You're an accessory that holds money. It's my job to look at the plan and see if there are problems, and then obliterate those problems. Your job is to not be one of those problems. Got it? You're a purse."

Valerie and Sam beamed at this for some reason, apparently forgetting how much help I had already been.

"Well . . ." I said, intending to correct her without saying the words "look here, you stupid idiot."

She held up a hand. "Not a talking purse. Just a purse."

Sam and Valerie were both giving me the "stop it, you're embarrassing me in front of other people" look that I'd seen on their faces pretty much continually since they were four years old. I decided for the sake of peace in the family to be quiet for a bit and let Lindy Love-Lloyd the Obliterator continue her interrogation, which she carried on in a style that she must have learned when she was running the gestapo. She wrote down answers from each daughter, nodding thoughtfully as she contemplated obliteration.

"Okay." She whipped off her glasses, put them on the table, and pinched her nose. "You," she said, pointing to Sam, "you're in good shape. You don't need help with planning, you need help with execution. You've decided on most of the important details. My opinion, you've got enough time, you could save money at this stage and just keep going the way you're going. A wedding planner can help, but why don't you see how far you can go without getting stuck. When it gets closer to the date, we'll talk. But you got a good head on your shoulders."

"Thank you," I said, knowing what she really meant was that I had done a good job raising my older daughter.

"Just keep your dad out of it, and you'll be fine."

I cocked my head, not sure I'd heard right.

"But you, Valerie, you're a mess."

"I know," she agreed sadly.

"You can't have a wedding theme around, what was it again?" Lindy wanted to know.

"Toxic waste," I volunteered.

"The purse is talking. The purse needs to shut up," Lindy said without even looking at me.

"The theme is, you know, Earth-Friendly. Or, We All Need to Get Along, like that," Valerie said falteringly.

"You need help *now*," Lindy said. "You don't have a plan. You don't have a date. You don't have a budget."

"Actually . . ." I began, fully prepared to discuss the budget.

Lindy went right on talking, obliterating my interruption. "You should talk to a few other planners, see who you like. You want, I'm happy to help you. I've dealt with challenges like yours before." She gave me a meaningful look, for some reason. "Important thing, you need to get your plan into shape. At the rate you're going, you're never going to have a wedding."

Both of my daughters were somber as we left, not even cracking a smile when I suggested we visit the gun and knife show to see if we could pick up some silver bullets for Alecia. Lindy Loves-Lunch or whatever her name was had really splashed cold water on their moods.

"Well, that Lindy was certainly quite a piece of work," I remarked as we sat on the bus that would take us back to our car as soon as we could agree where I'd parked it.

"Wasn't she wonderful?" Sam said.

"My god, she made so much sense!" Valerie blurted.

"What? You want to hire the Obliterator? Your father can come up with a wedding plan as easily as she can."

"Oh, Dad," they said together.

A FATHER'S WEDDING PLAN

Wedding planners would have you believe that the act of standing up in a church and saying a few words and then going to dinner is so complicated that it would defeat the Army Corps of Engineers. I, on the other hand, felt perfectly comfortable saying we could get along without Lindy Love-Lost's assistance, by initiating a wedding plan that Tom and I would draw up on the whiteboard in Wedding Central.

FATHER'S WEDDING PLAN	
INDUSTRY SUGGESTION	FATHER'S REASONABLE ALTERNATIVE
A wedding cake "topper," which is sort of a tiara for pastry. These can be a (sterling silver) representation of the monograms on everything else, or a (jewel-encrusted) replication of the wedding flowers, or (ridiculously overpriced) miniature statues of the bride and groom.	Go to the toy store, buy a bride and groom doll set, and you're good to go. Also, why do you even need a cake? What's wrong with, say, toast? (For a breakfast wedding, I mean, which I still insist is a really good idea.) A wedding cake costs as much as a compact car and tastes just as bad. (For the record, Tom thinks the wedding cake is necessary even if the wedding is for breakfast, arguing that there's not much difference between wedding cake and a frosted doughnut, which is what he has for breakfast all the time, anyway.)

INDUSTRY SUGGESTION	FATHER'S REASONABLE ALTERNATIVE
Professionally crafted wedding bouquets and other flowers.	Get married outside and let nature provide the flowers and other decorations. (If it rains, look at it as nature providing the bridal shower.) I spent a lot of money last fall putting in some flowering shrubs that look great except for where the dog dug them up, and Tom will come over and cut the grass with the new riding lawn mower his wife didn't want him to buy, but if it was for a wedding she couldn't possibly still object, right? During the reception, Tom could give rides to the kids on the thing, charge them a buck, help offset the cost of the wedding.
Engage a professional band. Pick either a local band with lots of experience in weddings or go upscale a bit and hire the Rolling Stones.	Two words: wedding karaoke. That way you don't need to pay for a wedding singer—the crowd supplies its own!

My daughter Sam read the whiteboard in disbelief. "This isn't a plan at all, it's just a bunch of random dumb ideas," she pronounced. "It's not even funny."

"I thought the lawn mower ride was pretty amusing," I responded.

"That's right, it's all a big joke to you."

I was shocked to see tears in her eyes. "Hey, hey. Sam. Look. I'm sorry that Tom made all these stupid jokes, we were just having fun. I know it's serious."

In the end it was decided that Lindy Love-Less would consult on an as-needed basis with Sam (though I still insisted that the title and authority of Wedding Planner logically belonged to me), and that Valerie would employ her services as a full-on wedding planner and problem obliterator. I couldn't argue, as their mother offered to pay for it.

My personal philosophy is usually that we don't need any so-called experts, because I am pretty much an expert in most subjects, being a man and therefore someone who is good at making stuff up. But I saw that Lindy was an antidote to the MBPS—Must Be Perfect Syndrome. With a professional running around doing her obliteration, my daughters were temporarily convinced that the wedding would, in fact, be perfect—so the stress on them to accomplish the impossible was, at least for now, abated.

That's what I thought, anyway.

SEVEN

❧

You Can Feed All of the People Some of the Time, or Some of the People All of the Time, But You Can't Feed a Wedding Party

I suppose there is a time in every major endeavor when the plan moves from the abstract (hey, wouldn't it be fun to put some people on the moon, maybe take some videos?) to the concrete (it's t minus 10 and counting, did anyone remember to pack oxygen?).

And so it is with weddings. After what seems like months and months of unspecific anxiety over all the details that need to be decided, the anxiety will suddenly become very specific. We're really going to launch this sucker!

(Note to fathers: Daughters do not appreciate it when you speak of their upcoming wedding as a "sucker.")

For me, the "this is really happening" moment occurred when we went shopping for her wedding dress.

The tradition of impossibly large and impractical wedding dresses comes to us from medieval times. The woman wore a heavy veil and, thus disguised, made it through the entire wedding ceremony without the groom having a good look at what he was getting into. Only when his fate was sealed was he allowed to raise the veil and gaze upon his new wife's face, an act that gave birth to the phrase "buyer's remorse."

If the groom were truly unhappy, he would reach out and tip over the large candles illuminating the church, causing an immediate fire. Everyone would rush from the building except the hapless bride, who, caught in folds of cloth, would expire from smoke inhalation.*

Like most heterosexual men, I think wedding gowns look ridiculous and are about as sexy as an army parachute. Take the gown that Donald Trump's most recent wife, Melania, wore to her wedding: It looked to me like what would happen if you fed a white 1998 Volvo station wagon to the car crusher. Take a look at a picture of Melanoma at her wedding if you don't believe me, there is serious damage to both the front and rear crumple zones. The dress is rumored to have cost more than a hundred thousand dollars and weigh fifty pounds—almost 30 percent of the weight of an Apollo space suit. And which would you rather have? You must admit, it would be a lot more fun to have a space suit in your closet than a wedding dress.

But, like most heterosexual men, my opinion on the matter doesn't matter to anyone. Even the groom's opinion doesn't matter—he's not even allowed to see the thing until it's coming down the aisle at him like a giant white bowling ball.

So I was shocked and bored when Sam informed me that in top secret negotiations, she and her mother Judy decided that while the final decision on the dress would naturally fall to the two of them, the initial foray into the world of wedding dresses would involve me. Once we had winnowed the

---

* Yes, I am making some of this up. Well, all of it.

selection down to a just a few, her mom would come to town and seal the deal.

"I don't think that's a good idea, honey," I told my daughter. "I don't think you want your father helping you pick out the wedding gown. I'm not sure it's even *legal*."

My daughter always knows how to appeal to my soft side, though, getting me to agree just by sweetly saying "but without you there I'm afraid I'll go over budget."

The first step in picking out a wedding dress is to attend a wedding fashion show. As special events go, this one is about as exciting as watching a tree grow in your yard. You sit on uncomfortable chairs while women charge down a long wooden stage, holding their gowns so they don't fall over. Each one of the models is thin to the point of organ failure—backstage they're probably hooking themselves up to a dialysis machine.

Listening to the reactions of the crowd, I concluded that wedding gowns come in three types: beautiful, gorgeous, and fabulous. I was willing to bet that none of these labels would describe the price tags.

"Dad, would you quit scowling?" Valerie hissed at me. "You're ruining this for Sam."

"Isn't that why you invited me?" I asked.

It took me a while to figure out why they *did* invite me. My normal response to all that cloth draped across the female frames was to give them a "tent" rating ("pup," "army surplus," and "Barnum and Bailey"), but other times I didn't think the gowns were funny at all: They were sexy. As a father, I had trouble appreciating the idea that my daughter would show cleavage, or even *had* cleavage. So when a model came out in a clingy gown, I would grow very quiet.

Whenever I grew quiet, Sam and her sister put the gown on the rack of dresses to show their mother.

A few weeks before this, when I asked my ex-wife what she had done wrong to raise her daughters to be so obsessed with weddings, she sent me a videotape. It turned out to be one that I shot when my girls were age nine and six, respectively, and they had both received bride outfits for Christmas. I had forgotten all about it, but I could clearly be heard behind the camera saying, "Who's the pretty bride? Who's the pretty bride?" while my daughters primped.

Sarah seemed to think the tapes made some kind of point.

"How could you say that?" I fumed at her.

"I'm just trying to be objective," she told me.

"I don't want objective, I want you to be on my side," I complained. "You know what this is like? This is like when Sam played football in elementary school."

"I didn't know about this," Sarah responded. "Football? Are you sure you didn't just imagine it?"

"What? No. She played football, full tackle, and let me tell you, she was good. It was her favorite sport, and she told me that she was going to try out for the middle-school team. And that's when I had to break it to her that this wasn't the sport for her. She loved tackling people, and she was fast and strong, but football is a game for people with a lot of muscle mass. Like me."

"Like you," Sarah repeated, nodding.

"Right. So I told her she would have to pick another sport, because the boys were going to be much heavier than she was, and it wasn't fair, but that's just how it was going to be."

"And this relates to going shopping for wedding gowns how?" Sarah asked.

"I don't know!" I answered. "I'd just like it if somebody, just once, would tell me I'm right about something!"

Anyway, after the Running of the Brides, the fashion show switched gears to bridesmaids' outfits. The same anorexics who had been brides were now demoted, and came out in the latest styles and fashions for the women whose job it is to stand next to the bride and look ridiculous.

"Dad, would you quit laughing?" Valerie hissed at me.

After the show you are treated to the personal dress consultation, in which the people from the wedding shop flutter around making cooing noises as your daughter comes out of a back room wearing one gown after another.

Fighter pilots often describe flying as "hours of boredom interspersed with moments of sheer terror." That's what it's like to go with your daughter to look at wedding gowns. You wait for her to come out, you nod that yes, the gown is beautiful/gorgeous/fabulous, then you look at the price tag, clutch your chest, fall to the floor, and turn blue.

I promise you, get a room full of fathers and show them the prices on some of these gowns and there won't be a dry pair of pants in the place.

It takes longer to change into a wedding gown than to overhaul the engine on Uncle Bob's 1966 Dodge Dart. The wedding shop, knowing that men can't sit through the ordeal without going comatose, thoughtfully provides reading materials—*bridal magazines.* Or if you want, you can stroll the halls, which is a bit like going to the Museum of Wedding Must Haves—there are displays everywhere of stuff you never imagined even existed. (The Wedding Cake must be beautiful! It must be cut with a beautiful Wedding Cake Knife! The Wedding Cake Knife needs to be displayed in a beautiful Wedding Cake Knife Stand! The Wedding Cake Knife Stand must sit in a special Wedding Cake Knife Stand Tray! Everything must be monogrammed!)

You can also look at wedding veils, which represent a tidy profit to the wedding industry the way Windows represents a tidy profit to Bill Gates. Veils are made from tulle, a cloth that sells at any fabric store in rolls of twenty-five square yards for seven bucks. A really extravagant veil, then, one that could not only hide the bride's face but also her mother's, would have about fifty cents worth of tulle in it. Of course, by the time you add ribbons, some rhinestones, lace, and whatever else goes on them, you might have a couple of bucks worth of materials invested in an item that then sells for several *hundred* dollars.

That's okay, though. After the wedding, you can always eBay the thing for twelve bucks.

"Dad, can I talk to you?" Valerie said in a voice so sweet and gentle I automatically was suspicious. She pulled me down the block to a coffee shop and bought a half-caf, sugar-free, fat-free, extra foam double latte because she wasn't in the mood to order something complicated. I ordered coffee, nonspecial, nonfancy, no la-la or extra hoity-toity.

"Okay, look," Valerie said with a sigh. "I'm not sure how to say this, but you're ruining Sam's wedding."

"What do you mean, I'm 'ruining' the wedding. The wedding can't be ruined until the day we have it."

"Dad. All of your so-called jokes about how much stuff costs is really getting old. I mean, don't you think Sam is under enough strain already?"

"Okay," I argued, "but I'm helping to pay for most of it, don't you think I should have a say in how my money is spent?"

Valerie stirred her fancy-pants coffee. "Okay, but . . . you know Sam, right?"

"Yes, I've met my daughter."

"Dad. I mean, you know she's not going to want, like, a twenty-thousand-dollar wedding gown. She wouldn't do that. You saw her looking at price tags. The really expensive ones, she's not even trying on."

"Apparently we have different definitions of the term 'really expensive.' And did you see those veils?"

"Dad, this is a wedding! What are you doing?" My daughter shouted, her voice so loud the chemists at the coffee bar stopped injecting foam and stared at us.

I blinked. The last time my daughter Valerie yelled at me this loudly was at an airport security check, when I told her she had to put her My Little Pony through the X-ray machine. She was a few years older now, and mostly spoke to me in the soft tones people reserve for mental patients.

"You know what this is about?" she stormed. "This is about you wanting to be in charge. It has nothing to do with the budget. You just complain about costs because that's the area where you have the veto."

"No, you're wrong," I informed her, a little angry at her thoughtless accuracy. She waited for me to explain, but when I went to my brain for an intelligently crafted argument, all I got back was *We got nothin'. You're on your own.*

I realized I had fallen prey to the danger that all fathers run into when they get involved in the wedding plan. We're men, so we like to be the boss. Worse, we're the fathers, so we always feel we know what is best for our daughters. But questions about whether the invitations should be "pastel" or "muted" make no sense to us, so we feel like we're losing control. The only way we can reassert our authority is to wield the ultimate club of the purse strings. It all comes from male insecurity.

Not that I carry a purse.

"So okay," I admitted grudgingly. "I can see how some of what I've been doing might have been misinterpreted."

"So even though you're wrong, I'm still not right," Valerie translated.

"I'm comfortable with that statement," I admitted.

"So would you just give Sam a break?"

"Okay. I'll try not to make as many jokes about how much the wedding is overcosting me."

"Dad!"

"Okay!"

Since I had Valerie alone, I asked her how her wedding plan was coming with Lindy Love-Lorn. "The woman hasn't called me for advice, so I imagine she hasn't really gotten started obliterating," I said smugly.

Valerie told me that Lindy had researched several spots along the rim of the Grand Canyon to show Marty as possible places for the ceremony. The wedding party would be just immediate family who would ride in on horseback, and Lindy had found the place to rent the horses. Lindy had located a Navajo elder willing to conduct the ceremony, though Marty now wanted Al Gore. Valerie's dress would be made of hemp, and Lindy had located several shops that sold such a thing.

"Good, then when we're done, we can sit around a camp fire and smoke your dress," I noted.

Lindy had found a place that used recycled, nontoxic, biodegradable ink and paper for the invitations. Valerie thought it would be nice to give donations to an animal shelter as wedding favors; Marty wanted to give out starter packets for compost heaps. Lindy had located and priced the starter packets, and had determined that yes, they could be monogrammed. Lindy had found lodging deals, caterers, and other vendors for the ceremony and was now drawing up plans for a reception when we all returned.

"So really, Lindy hasn't even gotten started," I summarized. "I'm much further along with Sam's plan."

"That's great!" Valerie gushed. "So you settled on a church?"

"Well, no."

"A place for the reception?"

"Um, not yet," I allowed.

"Is the guest list finalized?"

"Almost. Well, not really."

"But you've figured out who is in the wedding party?"

"Do you mind if I take some notes?"

"Dad, what have you figured out?"

"Tom wants chocolate cake," I said triumphantly. "He says that's the best, and I agree."

"Tom? Who cares what kind of cake Tom wants? What does Sam want? What does Geoff want?"

"Geoff?"

"Her fiancé! Remember him?"

"Geoff," I mused, writing it down.

By the time I returned to the bridal shop, Sam was wearing yet another wedding gown. This one laced up the back and gripped her around the chest like an iron maiden.

"Can't . . . breathe," Sam said faintly.

"Sam! Do you know how much stuff we have to decide? Where's the church? What flavor cake? How many horses?"

"Dad!" Valerie said.

"We don't have time to pick out a dress!" I stormed. "We need to get some critical things decided immediately! This sucker is really happening!"

My daughter looked like she had swallowed a wedding veil. Valerie moved to her back and began furiously unlacing, and the blue faded from Sam's face. "This one is a little tight," she said calmly.

THE WEDDING NEEDS TO BE AS UNIQUE AS EVERYONE ELSE'S

As the bride sets out to plan her perfect day, she's under a lot of pressure to come up with something that will surprise and delight her guests, a unique treat, like having Warren Beatty do birdcalls. A good place to start is the location—why have the reception in a reception hall, of all places? There are so many other, unexpected locations, like, say, a prison riot.

Unique Locations for the Reception

Location: Aboard a Yacht

Pros: During the ceremony, the father of the bride can troll for salmon. And, due to the law of the sea, the happy couple can be married by the captain of the boat, saving money because instead of hiring a minister, you can just have your neighbor Tom do it.

Cons: Instead of crying, some people will probably be barfing. Also this is sort of difficult to pull off in, say, Iowa, though you could always just put the yacht on a trailer and park the thing in the parking lot at Wal-Mart.

Location: Prison Riot

Pros: No one will expect it! It will feel very spontaneous and exciting, and even the most hard-bitten guest will cry (once the guards have fired the tear gas).

Cons: The cons.

Location: At the Zoo

Pros: The wedding party can be made up of orangutans, and the bride and groom can ride in on a yak. You'll save money on dinner because the guests can just have snow cones and cotton candy.

Cons: You probably aren't allowed to fish during the ceremony.

Location: The Floor of the U.S. Senate
Pros: Be the first time something gets accomplished there in a long time.

Cons: The ceremony might be interrupted by senators snoring.

Location: Online (My idea!)
Pros: Save money by preparing a fabulous dinner and e-mailing digital images of it to everyone (don't forget to have a vegetarian alternative for people who don't read meat e-mails). The vows can be sent via text message so that people can enjoy your ceremony while stuck in traffic or sitting in boring meetings. This is a great idea and I wish everyone would stop laughing.

Cons: Apparently some people think this idea is evidence of mental illness. They need to learn to think outside the wedding box.

When the Wedding Gets in Your Eyes

As the above exercise illustrates, even when the father resolves to stop making jokes that are hilarious (as opposed to "so-called") about the cost of everything, his input is still considered unnecessary to the actual planning of the wedding.

Much of this has to do with your daughter's "vision" of the wedding, as if angels came to her in the middle of the night and give her a PowerPoint presentation. Since you can't possibly see her vision, your ideas are worthless.

Sensible You: *Instead of a sit-down dinner, how about a buffet line? That way people can pick what they want*

to eat, and you don't wind up with a bunch of rubber
chicken.

BRIDE: *That's not my vision!*

SURPRISED YOU: *Your vision is rubber chickens?*

BRIDE: *No!*

PATIENT YOU: *Then what is your vision?*

BRIDE: *Not a buffet line!*

EXASPERATED YOU: *Okay, so what do you want to have for*
dinner, then?

BRIDE: *Everybody's pressuring me! Nobody's helping!*

A wedding vision is therefore similar to what Supreme Court
Justice Potter Steward said about pornography, "I shall not
further define it, but I know it when I see it." Only in this
case, no one can see it.

Your daughter will not appreciate having her wedding
compared to pornography, so you might as well say "this
sucker is like pornography."

So there you are: cut off from the vision, your great suggestions (like the online wedding that is clearly not mentally ill) scorned, prohibited by law of Valerie from using
the budget as a conversation starter, no longer in charge,
your (Las Vegas–comedian level) jokes dismissed without so
much as a smile—and still, through it all, you're expected to
somehow help your daughter.

People keep saying to her that it is all so exciting, and I
suppose it is, the way being chased through the woods by a
guy with a knife is exciting.

That's always been the father's job though: to stand by his

daughter and help her through difficult times, even when his presence is expressly not requested.

How Moldy or Mulchy Proposed

I agreed to meet with Lindy Lug-Nut and Valerie to help the wedding planner with all of her issues, and arrived at the lunch place slightly after the two of them did.

"Sorry, I got held up by, you know," I said, waving my hand so they would assume that it was something important and not just that I'd spent all morning trying to find my television remote. I grabbed a menu.

"Valerie was just tellin' me how Marty proposed," Lindy rasped at me, her voice like a guitar played with a nail file.

"I'll just have a roast beef sandwich," I told the waitress when she came over.

"Oh, well . . . we don't have roast beef," she responded.

"Dad. It's a vegetarian restaurant," Valerie informed me.

"What? Then what are we supposed to eat?"

"I don't know . . . vegetables?"

"So nothing, not even turkey?" I demanded. "What about fish?"

The waitress shook her head. "Oh wait, you might like the veggie burger."

"Veggie burger? What the heck is a veggie burger?"

"It's a burger made with . . . veggies?" the waitress guessed.

"Dad." Valerie turned to the waitress. "He'll have the veggie burger. Carrots. Potatoes. Iced green tea. Okay, Dad?"

"Sure." I put a smile on my face. "Sounds deliciously fibrous." After the waitress left, I asked Valerie very reasonably why she would pick a restaurant like this when she knows I like to eat food that eats food.

"They sell my eco-friendly, cruelty-free cosmetic line here," she answered.

"For what, to dip the french fries in?"

"So then what happened?" Lindy asked, mistakenly feeling that there was a more important topic than lunch.

"So then . . ." Valerie got a dreamy look on her face. "We hiked to the very top of the hill, and the sun was just coming up. He got down on one knee and said that he had always loved me and couldn't imagine life without me. Then he gave me the ring and asked me to marry him."

"Wait," I interjected. "Who are we talking about here?"

"That's really romantic," Lindy buzzed.

"*Very* romantic," Valerie affirmed, looking like she could pass a polygraph.

I opened my mouth to inject accuracy, then thought better of it. I felt sad, and not just because they didn't have roast beef. The fact that Valerie needed to embellish her proposal to make it palatable made me want to put my arms around her for some reason.

The food arrived, and I took a bite of veggie burger. I could tell by the way it felt when I swallowed that my stomach had no idea what it was looking at. I nodded at Lindy Loch-Ness. "So, Lindy, Valerie says you have some questions for me."

"Yes. We need to know the budget figure, she doesn't have that."

"Okay," I agreed reasonably. "So let's go through it, starting with the guest list. Since you're planning to hold the ceremony on the edge of a cliff, I take it we're not inviting Cousin Ward, who's afraid of heights."

"No, let's not go through it."

"I . . . what?"

Lindy leaned forward. "The guest list is under control. The location is under control. I have it all under control, got it?" She reached into her briefcase, pushing aside whatever illegal weapons she carried in there, and pulled out a sheet of paper. "I got three figures on here. You pick the number. I'll take care of the rest."

If she thought I was going to be intimidated, she had another think coming. I looked her dead in the eye so she would know who she was dealing with. "I don't have a pen," I said icily.

Lindy produced one. After some hesitation, I circled the number in the middle. Both Lindy and Valerie smiled.

"Perfect," Lindy said, sticking the paper back in her briefcase.

"Well, it would help to know what the lower figure would get me and also what sort of extras we'd be getting for the higher number," I groused.

Lindy shrugged. "Don't got a clue. The fathers always pick the middle number."

DISASTER STRIKES

Valerie walked me to the car. "Thanks so much for coming, Dad. You've been so great through all of this."

"What father wouldn't be willing to have lunch with his daughter, even if it causes a bowel obstruction?"

"You know, it wouldn't hurt you to eat a lower fat diet."

"Valerie, you may find this difficult to understand, but my goal with food is slightly higher than just to have it 'not hurt.'"

"How is Sam's wedding plan coming?"

"Fine. We're way ahead of where you are with Lindy Lunk-Head."

"That's great! So you have the reception hall booked?"

"Yes. Well, no. Look, my real concern is your wedding. Are you sure Lindy knows what she's doing? She seems disorganized—that whole three-number monte she pulled in the restaurant, I think she was just faking her way through it."

"Oh Dad, yes, I think she really does. I finally believe it, Marty and I are really getting married."

She gave me a big hug, and despite my misgivings, my heart melted like soy cheese on a veggie burger.

BRIDAL 911

My daughter Sam and I have an understanding: She is to knock on my door before she comes in and removes my appliances. So I was surprised when I heard my front door bang open and then her steps as she virtually ran into the living room.

"Oh my God Dad you will not believe it this is the worst thing that could possibly happen!"

"The wedding invitations don't come in ecru?" I guessed.

"Alecia fired her MOH!"

"Her M . . ."

"Her maid of honor!"

"This is horrible!" I agreed. "Even if we have no idea why it matters!"

"Dad, she wants *me* to be the maid of honor! Me!"

"Really? I had no idea you two were that close."

"We're not. We despise each other!"

"Then what happened, everyone else turn her down?" I joked.

"Yes!"

I asked her to explain, and it came out in a rush. Alecia fired her best friend as maid of honor for "being such a bitch." But all the rest of the women who had been conscripted to stand next to Alecia on the basis of being attractive, but certainly not more attractive than the bride, didn't want the job, especially since this was the second MOH Alecia had downsized.

"Well, okay, but look, is it really so bad? So you stand in a different spot during the wedding, so what?"

Her eyes bulged. "Do you have the slightest idea what the maid of honor does?" she demanded.

"Of course," I huffed. "But why don't you tell me your interpretation, and I'll say whether you're right or wrong."

It turns out there is not a heck of a lot of difference between "maid of honor" and "personal servant," except that maybe the personal servant doesn't have to wear a huge bow on her butt.

WHAT A MAID OF HONOR IS MADE TO DO

The origin of the wedding party can be traced back to the time when an unwanted suitor would invade a family and remove a young female against the family's will—back, in other words, to a time known as "Moldy's proposal." To successfully conduct the kidnapping, the groom would assemble a raiding party that would fend off the armed response by the father. (I'd be willing to go back to this arrangement right now.)

The wedding party began wearing stupid outfits to ward off evil spirits: Supposedly, the uniform look achieved by having the groomsmen dress like headwaiters and the bridesmaids dress like prom rejects would confuse the evil spirits, who would not be able to identify which couple was the bride and groom and would return empty-handed to their home in Alecia's body.

The two most important positions in the wedding party are the maid of honor, whose job it is to assist the bride, and the best man, whose job it is to stand next to the maid of honor in pictures. Here are just a few of the maid of honor's duties:

1. Location Scout

The first duty of the MOH is to help the bride decide on the best location for the perfect event. In this way, two women drive around town doing research and lunch, completely unconstrained by budgetary considerations. In Alecia's case, however, the location of both the ceremony and the reception were set. Her first choice for the wedding—a Catholic cathedral—was turned down by the priest because neither Alecia nor her fiancé were Catholic. (Alecia might have had a shot anyway had she not gotten angry and said something to the effect of "Well, how much do I have to contribute to be made Catholic for a day?")

2. Help the Bride Go Postal

As every father knows, it is pretty easy to use the computer to print up a bunch of labels and slap them on envelopes, but daughters want invitations with painstakingly fancy handwriting on them. The MOH is usually roped into helping with this process, which takes a lot of lunches to get through.

Alecia's invitations had already gone out, so all Sam was asked to do in this regard was follow up with those people who had been mailed invitations but had not yet sent a gift. Seeing that the prospect of doing this made Sam physically ill, Alecia (over lunch) suggested some of the following phrases to help the conversation get started.

- Will you be bringing your gift to the wedding?
- Do you need help selecting the perfect gift?
- Most people have gifts in already, is there a problem?

Sam said having this script in front of her made her feel like a bridal bill collector.

3. Tell People to Sit On It

As far as most people are concerned, it doesn't matter where they sit at a wedding reception, as long as it isn't so close to Cousin Ward that he can initiate an insurance interrogation. But for others the seating arrangement is interpreted as a statement about their status at the wedding, and they will be hurt and outraged if they aren't seated at an important table. It's like high school, where the popular kids sat at one lunch table, the less popular kids at a lesser lunch table, and so on all the way down the line until the last table, where I sat. (It sounds silly, even petty, but it can be deadly serious. I know of one woman whose best friend from grade school broke off their relationship forever because she felt that she was assigned a lower status seat at a wedding.)

For Alecia there was another consideration: Her wedding party's table would (of course) be the center of attention, and therefore the subject of most photographs. She knew people nearby would inadvertently be caught in the frame, so the tables nearest hers needed to have only attractive people sitting at them, even if they didn't know one another.

4. Land a Burning Airplane

Everyone who sees a bride dissolving into a puddle of tears or breathing radioactive fire will say something like, "You're getting too stressed, you need to delegate!" The beleaguered bride will gratefully grasp this advice, but unless she has a father who is as on top of things as I am, the only person to whom she can delegate things is the MOH.

That's okay, though, as the MOH is being well compensated, if by "well" you mean "not." She will, however, at least receive a nice gift. (In Sam's case, this turned out to be a photograph of Alecia.)

5. Create a Cult of Personality

The MOH should plan every detail of the bridal shower and

bachelorette party and should mercilessly hound people until they agree to show up. These are events where the bride is the center of attention and everybody gives her gifts and maybe donates a kidney. Alecia wanted three (showers, not kidneys).

"Three bridal showers!" Sam fumed. "Do you know how hard it is to get people to go to even one?

"Well, shouldn't you invite different people to each one?" I asked.

"Different people! How many friends do you think someone like Alecia has?"

"Including you?"

"I hate her!"

"Then none."

"Exactly. And Alecia thinks it would be 'cute' if we handmake all the guests little gifts instead of buying them gifts. What can I possibly make that will convince people to sit in a room and listen to Alecia talk about herself for an hour?"

"Earplugs?"

"I'm not the maid of honor. I'm the maid of doom," Sam said, burying her face in her hands.

TIME TO OBLITERATE SOME PEOPLE

After tallying up the second amended guest list, I concluded the only way we could afford to feed everyone at the reception a sit-down dinner was if we fed them something pretty inexpensive, like peanut butter and ice.

"Too many people," I told Sam. "Can you reduce it to a more reasonable number, like three?"

Here's the problem with the wedding guest list: It grows all by itself, adding names in the middle of the night when you're not looking.

Let's say you want to add your neighbor Tom. This makes

sense, because he's a good friend of the family and has a new bass boat. Plus, Tom has done a lot of consulting on the wedding plan, even if his entire contribution thus far can be boiled down to saying "chocolate cake."

But if you invite Tom, what about your other neighbors? You don't want them angry at you, especially since your dog keeps pooping in their yards. One of your neighbors works at the same place as you, so now you have to invite your other colleagues at the job or they won't cover for you when you're late. And since everyone at work knows about the wedding, don't you have to invite key clients?

By the time you're finished with the process, you've got a hundred people coming, and only nine of them have ever even met the bride. And that's just your list—turns out, the bride wants to invite some people, too. And so does the groom! His whole college fraternity is planning to come, not because they like weddings, but because they like open bars.

It's easy to see how spending grows out of control. You can either (a) decide on a budget and then spend more than that, or (b) decide what you want to do, calculate the cost per person, multiply it by the number of guests, and then spend more than that.

Therefore, as you finalize your plans, you should keep in mind the one truism of all weddings: This will never work.

EIGHT

❧

Three Weddings and a Father

Not only did I have my own daughter's weddings to deal with, but, just as I'd feared, I was getting swept up in Alecia's plans as well, unable to resist her gravitational pull because she was, after all, the center of the universe. This really irritated me—men don't usually even care much about their *own* weddings, why should I care about hers? It was too much to expect from a male of my gender.

From a man's point of view, a wedding plan proceeds much like a pregnancy—after the initial flurry of, well, excitement, not much seems to happen for a long time, and he can't understand why the woman is throwing up. Gradually, though, he starts to notice changes, and after awhile he becomes convinced that not only is a big event coming that will change his life forever, but that he's a big part of it.

Sam's fiancé, Geoff, seemed to sort of come to attention when we were out checking on the wedding chapel. I saw his expression as he glanced around the room, picturing that one day in August, he would walk into this place a single man, and then walk out a few minutes later a husband. He looked a little overwhelmed, and I wondered if he was thinking of bolting for the door. But then Sam called him down to the front of the chapel to stand with her, and he relaxed, smiling into her eyes.

Marty, on the other hand, seemed somewhat detached from his own wedding plan, though to be fair he was very busy at his radio station because they were having another, or the maybe same, pledge fund drive. Lindy Loose-Lips the Obliterator was pretty much in charge anyway, advising me that the details of my own daughter's wedding were on a need-to-know basis, and I didn't need to know.

The Fop, however, did need to know, or so he thought. He phoned me one night to complain. "Lindy isn't telling me anything, she just says it's under control," he said.

"You're not getting intelligence from the front lines, so the battle plan is getting lost in the fog of war," I translated for him.

"Huh?"

"Lindy doesn't talk to me much, either."

"I'm used to running things. I run my own company, for God's sake."

"I run my own company, too," I objected.

"Right, well, sure, but there's a big difference in the size of our operations," the Fop replied.

I found myself getting a little irritated. Men don't appreciate it when other guys brag about their size of anything. "Exactly," I said. "You have all kinds of people helping you, while I have to do everything myself."

"Okay. Okay. I'm just saying, I'm paying for Lindy's services."

"I said I'd pay. You don't have to pay," I replied.

"No, it's fine, it's not that! It's just that she told me I'm a houseplant, you know? I'm supposed to sit there and not say anything."

"Ha! I'm a purse."

"What?"

Though it pained me to say it, I told the Fop that I didn't have any power over Lindy the Obliterator, either—she was like a rogue agent, behind enemy lines, operating (as we say in such circumstances) "off the reservation."

"I have no idea what you're saying to me," the Fop confessed.

He has a long way to go before he gets promoted to purse.

KEY DECISIONS

Sam's wedding plan was coming along nicely, though—it turns out I have a real flair for this, and could probably turn it into a career except that the whole process nauseated me. We had already made several key decisions based on a consensual approach that involved a lot of immature eye rolling and foot stomping—but then, I've never been very good at handling arguments.

Decision #1: Venue

Bride's Idea: A lovely chapel on a small lake. The couple would depart from the chapel in a horse-drawn carriage, which would wind its way through the woods to a gazebo, where the rest of the wedding party would meet for photographs. Meanwhile, the guests would take their own transportation to the grounds of a country club on the other side of the lake, where they would enjoy an open bar until the couple arrived for a sit-down dinner.

Dad's Idea: I put a lot of time and effort into locating an aluminum building off of I-70 that could serve as a place for both the wedding and the reception. People could sit at

folding tables and watch the wedding and maybe eat peanuts and popcorn out of bowls.

Bride's Response: As lovely as the abandoned tool and
die factory sounds, we want to be married in a place that will
pass the health code.

Dad's Response: The best wedding I've ever been to was
Cousin Ted's. He got married in an aluminum-pole barn
with folding tables, peanuts on the table, a keg of beer, and
a buffet of cold meats. He and his bride were dirt poor, but
we danced until dawn in that place.

Bride's Response: And didn't he get divorced?

Dad's Response: Because he became Cousin Tina! He and
his—her—ex are best friends; they even go shopping together.
Don't you and Geoff always want to be best friends?

Bride's Response: Like, after the divorce? Or maybe the
sex change?

Dad's Response: Um . . .

Bride's Response: I'm really touched that you'd like to
try to recapture the joy of Ted's wedding, but wouldn't you
agree that no two people are alike? Especially when Ted is
those two people? I want to get married in a chapel and have
the reception in an elegant place.

Dad's Response: Okay, but what's with all these horses? I
haven't ridden a horse since sixth-grade summer camp, and
now between you and your sister it's like we live on a Pon-
derosa. It would be far more romantic to use Tom's boat to
ferry you across the lake, and imagine how sweet and wonderful it would be if we caught a special wedding fish!

Compromise Decision: The chapel, the horse, and no
trolling, even if the trout are biting.

Decision #2: Guest List

Bride's Idea: Each family may invite a total of one hundred
guests, even though Priscilla says she has that many friends

in her Ladies Lunch League alone. Of these, we would expect that fully 10 percent would not be able to make it. Geoff's fraternity brothers will not be invited, which is good because otherwise several people would probably wind up being tossed in the lake at some point.

Father's Idea: Send out invitations that say "instead of inviting you to our wedding, a donation in your name has been made to the local public radio station pledge drive." Good Old Moldy really likes this idea, by the way.

Bride's Response: Valerie's fiancé is named Marty, Dad, and we've cut this list down as much as possible. Everybody keeps telling me people I *have* to invite, even you.

Dad's Response: When did I ever do that? Name one.

Bride's Response: What about Tom and Emily?

Dad's Response: Well, you can't very well ask Tom and not his wife, honey.

Bride's Response: But why do we have to invite Tom at all?

Dad's Response: You have to invite Tom, for heaven's sake!

Bride's Response: See? You just told me I *have* to invite someone.

Dad's Response: What's your point?

Compromise Decision: We'd invite 150* people and hope that half of them came down with the flu. Plus, Cousin Tina can come as her own date.

Decision #3: The Theme

Bride's Idea: I want Hot August Nights, so we'll have lots of bright colors and summer flowers.

Dad's Idea: Is *that* what the theme is? I've been telling people it's Cracklin' Rosie. Well, look, I have no problem

---

* The average number of guests at a U.S. wedding is 167. There is some debate in my family whether inviting 150 people meant we were "better" or "worse" than the average.

with this idea at all, probably because I can't see how it costs anything. I didn't know you liked Neil Diamond that much.

Bride's Response: I don't like Neil Diamond. I just want the theme to be Hot August Nights. I can't help it if he did an album by that name.

Dad's Response: You know who looks a little like Neil Diamond, only bald? Cousin Ward. Maybe he could get up and sing a medley of songs about life insurance.

Bride's Response: I want a band.

Compromise Decision: The theme is Hot August Nights and we'll have a band and nobody will be allowed to sing unless the band plays the Neil Diamond song "Cherry Cherry," which I performed in the eighth-grade talent show and still can belt out really, really well.

Decision #4: Meals

Bride's Idea: I want a sit-down dinner offering a choice of either chicken or a vegetarian meal.

Dad's Idea: Fried eggs.

Bride's Response: We're not doing a breakfast wedding, that's already been decided. I want a sit-down dinner offering a choice of either chicken or a vegetarian meal.

Dad's Response: Okay, how about this? We could hand out poles and let people fish off the dock and fry up what they catch. This would be a really unique way to have a wedding, and I feel very strongly we should do it this way.

Bride's Response: I want a sit-down dinner offering a choice of either chicken or a vegetarian meal.

Dad's Response: Well, how about a buffet? We could set out cold meats, everyone could build their own sandwich. Valerie can eat a lettuce and tomato sandwich, I know because I saw her do it once. I feel very strongly we should do it this way.

Bride's Response: I want a sit-down dinner offering a choice of either chicken or a vegetarian meal.

Compromise Decision: We would have a sit-down dinner offering a choice of either chicken or a vegetarian meal.

Decision #5: Wedding Favors

Bride's Idea: I would like each guest to receive a little bamboo fan. They don't cost much, they are very pretty, and when people step outside, they can use it to fan themselves.

Father's Idea: I am really, really strongly against the idea of wedding favors. We're already feeding them and giving them drinks and entertaining them with a band plus my singing. I don't see what a fan has to do with anything anyway.

Bride's Response: The theme is Hot August Nights. A fan only costs a dollar, and then the little sleeve they come in only costs another dollar or two dollars with the monogram.

Dad's Response: But a couple of dollars a person adds up to real money when you multiply it by the fifty people who don't have the flu. Tell you what, we could give out free tickets for a ride in Tom's boat, and he could whip them around the lake once or twice, that'll cool them off. Wait, what is the theme again?

Bride's Response: I really like the fan idea, and Tom is not bringing his boat.

Compromise Decision: We'd have fans in little monogrammed sleeves and buy 150 of them, and Tom's boat will remain in the garage, just as Emily predicted.

SNAKES ON A BRAIN

Though a father can be very reasonable and compromising, offering helpful suggestions and being very supporting, wedding stress can still strike like a snake, injecting poisonous fear and anxiety into a bride's nervous system until she becomes paralyzed. Tom nodded thoughtfully when I told him this.

"Or like an alligator," he said shrewdly.

"What's like an alligator?" I asked, puzzled.

"I was just thinking of, you know, cool animal attacks. Like snakes, alligators, sharks."

"Tom, this is my daughter we're talking about here," I said sternly. "Can you see how an alligator attack might be a little upsetting to me?"

As if responding to a summons, the front door crashed open and my daughter Sam stormed in. "You know, even the SWAT team knocks first," I informed her.

"We waited too long to book the hotel! There's no way to get a block of rooms now. Everyone coming from out of town will have to stay all over the place. This is a disaster!" she announced, falling onto the couch as if bitten by a snake but not an alligator.

"That doesn't sound so bad," I ventured.

"Are you kidding me? Everyone will be scattered. Do you know how difficult it will be to organize that?"

"Why not let them just find their own places. The ones who aren't up to the task, well, that will be sort of like natural selection."

"Dad!"

"Well, look," Tom said, trying to help, "my brother owns this aluminum building off I-70, we could set up some cots or something . . ." He frowned at my warning look. "What?"

"Oh sure, cots in an abandoned factory, and I could change the theme of my wedding to Hurricane Katrina," she responded. "I don't *even* have time for this. Alecia's having her third and final bridal shower in less than four hours. I have to pick up the drinks, the food, decorate her living room—they've been different decorations every time!—

make sure the right music is on her iPod, set everything out, call everyone to make sure they're coming, and then be there when everyone arrives and somehow make sure they have a good time, or at least pretend to."

"What's Alecia doing during all of this?"

"Her nails!"

"Well, I know it is taking a lot of effort, but at the end of all this, you'll have a really close relationship with your sister-in-law."

"I hope I never see her again as long as I live. Do you know what she came up with today? Love letters from the bridal party." She nodded at my blank expression. "Uh-huh, I didn't get it, either, so naturally Alecia acted like I'm stupid for not understanding it instantly. We're going to set out her stationery at the shower tonight along with special pens that have to be in her colors that I spent all day shopping for yesterday. And everyone in the bridal party is supposed to write down wonderful thoughts about Alecia and give them to me, and then throughout the year I am going to mail them to her at special, random moments so she'll get these love letters all during the first year of her marriage."

I tried to imagine what a wonderful thought about Alecia would look like but was unable to do so without including some of Tom's alligators.

"So it's like I'm not off the hook, I'm her maid of honor for the year! Oh, and what do you bet that when she thinks of it, she'll want everyone at the reception to do the same thing. Instead of dancing, everyone will be at their tables writing, like we're all taking our SATs."

"Are we going to have to sign the letters, or can they be anonymous?" I asked innocently.

She grinned wickedly, then frowned at me. "Don't even think of it, Dad."

"But you were thinking of it," I pointed out. For a moment we were back to being just father and daughter, her upcoming wedding the furthest from our minds.

"Thinking of what?" Tom wanted to know.

"Thinking that there simply aren't words to describe how much we love Alecia," I told him.

Tom shrugged. "I think she's sort of a creep."

"Oh, get this. I get an emergency call from Alecia today at work. I was in a meeting and Brenda sticks her head in and says I have an urgent call and I'm assuming something horrible happened to Geoff and I rush out and it's Alecia. Want to know what the problem is?"

"She didn't make it back to her casket full of dirt by sunset?" I guessed.

"No. Her look-alike wedding doll is *ugly*."

I glanced at Tom's face—I've seen more comprehension from my Labrador. I'm sure I didn't look any more clued in, either.

"She paid a fortune for this custom-made doll—in her dress—that's supposed to be her exact duplicate," Sam explained. "And she says it doesn't look anything like her and it's ugly and she wants me to somehow get her money back."

"Does it look like her?" I asked, curious.

"Yes! I mean, as much as a doll can look like a person. I don't know what she was expecting."

"Well, can we stick pins in it?"

Sam laughed, then reached into her backpack and pulled out some papers. "Okay, decision time. These are the designs for the cake."

I sifted through them thoughtfully, pretending that they didn't all look exactly the same to me. A wedding cake is just a pile of regular cakes, really, with something fancy on top of it like the Imperial Crown of India or maybe just a live monkey playing a harp. The bakers sometimes added decorative objects, like what appeared to be pearls, flowers, or gold coins, none of which were edible. Maybe for wedding favors we'd give out the Heimlich maneuver.

"I like the butterflies," I murmured, picking one at random.

"I will not have my wedding cake decorated with *bugs*," Sam shot back. "God, Dad, do you have to make a joke about everything? This is really hard to do and you're not helping."

I have to admit, this hurt me a little—I wasn't joking, there really was a cake with butterflies or maybe moths on it.

Tom cleared his throat. "You know, Sam, sometimes getting married is like being bitten by a poisonous snake."

She stared at him in disbelief.

"I mean, it can take over, infecting your whole system, you know? Until even the sweetest person gets full of poison."

"Tom, thanks for sharing," I said. "That may be the dumbest thing you've ever come up with."

Sam's eyes were full of tears. "Oh my God, you are so right, Tom. This really is getting to me. I'm sorry, Dad, I didn't mean to yell at you. I'm just . . . this has been really, really hard."

"It was actually my idea. The snake, I mean. Tom wanted alligators."

Tom nodded shamefully.

"I just want a simple cake, you know? One that tastes good. One that is, is . . ."

"Chocolate," Tom prompted.

She smiled, wiping her eyes. "Yes, Tom, Geoff wants

chocolate, too. So I don't care what Alecia says, we're going to have a simple chocolate cake, with white frosting. I like this one here, but . . ." she said while she gave me a trembling smile as she held out a photograph, "it's also the most expensive."

I looked at the picture. It was simple, not at all encrusted with jewelry or other potential lawsuits, but the price was more than double what we'd decided. Tom reached out and took it from me.

"Tell you what," he said. "Let this be our treat. Me and Emily."

Sam drew in her breath in surprise.

"I figure, I'll wind up eating most of it anyway." Tom grinned.

My daughter gave him a hug that nearly knocked him over, kissed his cheek, and then, with a quick glance at her wristwatch, announced she had to go. We watched her head out the door, her steps much lighter than when she came in.

"That's really nice of you, Tom," I told him, meaning it.

He shrugged. "Oh. I got a question, though."

"Yeah?"

"Who's Geoff?"

ROLL OUT THE CHICKENS

Not everything about planning a wedding has to be stressful, though it will be. The closest you can come to relaxed enjoyment is the food tasting, though brides can even turn that festive occasion into a personal meltdown.

Naturally, my son showed up for the meal selection portion of the ordeal. "I've been eating dorm food," he said, shrugging.

The chef popped open a few bottles of wine and started rolling out the dishes: Roasted Chicken, Ginger Chicken, Chicken-Fried Chicken—there were so many varieties I was nearly overcome with emotion.

"If only," I choked, "we could get up from this table and have you be married without going through the trouble of the wedding, that would make this day perfect."

My daughter, however, became nothing but gloomy somewhere around the Chicken-Stuffed Chicken, and by the time we got to the Chicken with Chicken Sauce, she was downright depressed. I thought it would perk her up when we all agreed that the Chicken Chicken à la Chicken was the best (another decision made; as soon as I found where I put my list I would check it off), but she remained solidly down in the doldrums.

You know why brides get depressed at the tasting? Because they're *eating*.

Bridal magazines scream at their readers, "Lose Those Pounds You Fat Pig!" and "If You Can't Drop 35 Pounds You Shouldn't Get Married!" (These may not be the actual headlines, but you get the idea.) A bride is supposed to weigh less on her wedding day than at any other point in her life, including birth. She can personally lay waste to a thousand chickens at her reception, but prior to that she should not eat anything except oxygen. The goal is that by the time she stands up to take her vows, she should look like Lara Flynn Boyle after six weeks of fasting.

The fact that your daughter looks absolutely beautiful doesn't matter because it is only your opinion. She stares into the mirror and sees the reflection of Meatloaf staring back. She even says it to you:

"I'm fat."

What Not to Say When Your Daughter Tells You She's Too Fat to Get Married

1. You're not fat!
Wrong. This means you don't care about her, you're not listening to her, you're not looking at her. Of course she's fat—she's getting married!

2. You have plenty of time to lose weight if you want to.
Wrong. Oh, you thought this was clever, didn't you? What did you do, practice in the mirror? She doesn't have plenty of time, even if she's not getting married for five years. And you carefully avoided expressing any sort of opinion about her statement, which is the same as holding her by the shoulders, shaking her, and spitting "You're fat!" into her eyes.

3. I think someone is breaking into your car.
Wrong. Nice try, though. You thought you could avert disaster by changing the subject, but what you don't realize is that for a bride, there is simply no topic more important than this one. By changing the subject, you're saying you don't care about her.

4. You look beautiful in your wedding gown!
Brilliant! But wrong. You thought you could convince her that it doesn't matter what she thinks she looks like naked; she'll be wearing enough cloth for Christo to cover Miami. Instead, you just reminded her that when she gets married, everyone will be looking at her globules of fat. Take three steps back.

5. Okay, yes, you're fat.
Are you crazy?

6. Oh honey. Here's some money.
This one will work. She'll hire a personal trainer, and he'll make her suffer, and she'll lose the pounds that she sees as unnecessary and you see as unnecessary to lose, and when she finally stands up there on her wedding day, thinner, fitter, and more svelte, she'll think she's too fat.

8 Simple Things Go Wrong on Alecia's Wedding Day

In trying to figure out why anyone would want to tie the knot with Sam's future sister-in-law, Alecia, the only thing I could come up with is that if you were married to Alecia you wouldn't have to buy a pit bull. Yet the countdown to her wedding day proceeded in an orderly fashion, if by "orderly" you mean that she would call my daughter in the middle of the night and scream instructions.

As is true with military incursions, natural disasters, and other unpleasant experiences, not everything was perfect as the day of Alecia's wedding arrived. As of 8:00 a.m. on the big day, here are the things that Alecia was complaining about.

1. The flowers aren't fragrant enough.
The wedding flowers had been delivered by truck caravan and unfortunately they smelled like flowers. It wasn't clear exactly what else they were supposed to smell like, but Alecia was reportedly furious. What she wanted was a "fragrance of spring," so that every year after that, when winter receded and flowers began to bloom, people would be reminded of

Alecia's wedding and maybe call her and thank her or buy her presents. Now, I don't know where on planet Earth the spring season smells like the fifty thousand lilacs, tulips, and gerbera daisies Alecia had assembled—inside a hothouse, I suppose—but I felt pretty confident that even though the fragrance wasn't strong enough to suit Alecia, a lot of people were going to have allergy problems after her wedding. Alecia, however, was angry—and wanted Sam to "do something about it."

2. It's cloudy outside.

Alecia apparently thought that for her wedding, the people in charge of the weather for April would deliver a sunny day. Worse, it was too humid. Sam knew what humidity did to Alecia's hair, it made it totally frizzy! If it got all frizzy, it would be impossible to have it perfectly sculpted! Alecia's hair was supposed to be so lovely that when people saw it they would fall to their knees and weep. Now, people would not leave the wedding saying that Alecia was the most beautiful bride in the history of *Homo sapiens*, which was the goal here, in case Sam was forgetting. The wedding would be completely ruined and that certainly wasn't Alecia's fault.

Sam added the weather to the list of things to do something about.

3. Grandpa looks old.

The family to which Alecia belonged had been unwisely reproducing for generations, and Grandpa—Priscilla's father—was still alive (and probably feeling guilty for what he had helped unleash upon the world). Apparently his nose hairs were visible, his skin was blotched and white, and he'd had the audacity to get outfitted with dentures without checking with Alecia to see if it would be okay. Everyone could tell he's got false teeth! (Which was apparently worse than if he hadn't gotten them, in which case everyone could tell he *needed* false teeth.) Alecia seemed to imply that Sam should somehow take Grandpa aside and young him up.

4. Alecia's ex-boss had RSVP'd and apparently planned to attend.

Alecia had been shocked to find out that her company had no policy for allowing people who were getting married to take time off—she had assumed that if you got six weeks for having a baby, surely they'd offer at least that for people who were engaged! Alecia had been forced to quit her job so she could concentrate full-time on having her nails done. She sent a wedding invitation to her former employer because the man was rich and could afford a nice gift, but she never for a moment thought that he'd be so rude as to show up at the wedding. Now, when people met him, he would explain that Alecia had worked for him answering phones and not as a fashion model. The whole thing was embarrassing and Sam needed to figure out a solution!

Sam added to her list the task of getting Alecia a retroactive promotion.

5. One of the bridesmaids' kids was sick!

At the last minute, one of the bridesmaids had called to say she wasn't sure she could make it because her three-year-old son had a fever and a bad cough. Alecia was so furious she hung up on the woman, unable to say what she was thinking, which was probably that she didn't care if the woman drowned her son in the bathtub, it was Alecia's *wedding day* and her bridesmaids had to be there! Sam needed to call the woman, apologize for all the expletives, and try to figure out a solution to the whole mess.

6. There was an emerging pimple on Alecia's face!

This was the biggest problem of them all! What would happen if Alecia's face, upon which we would all be gazing with adoration and worship, was somehow marred by a hideous zit? Everyone would hate Sam, that's what would happen, because they would know that the pimple was caused by stress and that Sam's job was to reduce the stress on the bride! So Sam had better find an emergency dermatologist and somehow schedule an appointment and get a police escort and get the thing lanced or whatever, because Alecia did not have this much plastic surgery to have her day ruined because Sam was incompetent!

7. *Alecia was swelling up.*

As a way of giving extra burdens to Sam, Alecia invented a new tradition wherein she and her soon-to-be-husband would share a very special candlelight dinner, just the two of them, served at a cozy table at a very expensive restaurant, before the two of them went their separate ways and got trashed at their bachelor/bachelorette parties. The menu for the special dinner was to be a complete surprise that Sam was to plan without input from Alecia except that Alecia really liked shellfish in drawn butter and liked asparagus but not broccoli and was not eating potatoes because of the carbs and steamed mussels are nice and instead of Champagne they should have a nice white wine like a Rodney Strong Chalk Hill Chardonnay and dessert should be crème brûlée with raspberries and whipped cream. Sam gamely arranged for a lobster dinner, the wine, the asparagus, and the dessert in a restaurant with curtained tables and even paid for it as a gift to Alecia, which turned out not to be all that exciting because apparently Alecia had expected Sam to pay for it all along. But Alecia felt that the special dinner wasn't really very special; for some reason the lobster wasn't very delicious, and Sam had forgotten the steamed mussels.

Worse, Sam must have not given very specific instructions to the chef, who must therefore in his ignorance put too much salt on the food, because when she woke up on her wedding day, Alecia was all puffy! She looked like she had gained two pounds! It was all Sam's fault! Alecia was so angry she wasn't even speaking to my daughter except to issue instructions.

8. Where's the joy?

Everyone should be bubbling over with excitement and pouring compliments and attention on Alecia. Instead, everyone seemed cranky and tense. Sam, as the maid of honor, was like the head cheerleader. It was her job to get everyone excited for this special day, and instead Sam was moping around looking burdened. It made Alecia furious to see Sam acting like that, Sam needed to shape up! "Act happy!" Alecia screamed at Sam. "This is my wedding day!"
In response to this last demand, Alecia's mother Priscilla gamely attempted a smile, but her facial muscles were unused to the maneuver and the best they could furnish was a spastic twitch in the corners of her mouth before the mirth vanished like the British evacuating Dunkirk.

I assumed there had been a time in her life when Alecia wasn't a horrible creature—like, when she was first conceived. But I refused to believe that the pressures of a wedding could turn a normal person into an Alecia—you had to start out a twisted soul.

Through it all, my daughter persevered. She bit off every retort, never once saying to Alecia what I wanted to say, which was something like "Die, you miserable dog." Sam bent but never broke, and I was proud of the effort she was making.

If she could take this amount of pressure and not crack, I knew my daughter could handle her own wedding without losing her composure.

I was, of course, wrong.

Meanwhile, though, the clock was ticking on the big

event. Soon Alecia would be walking down the aisle. We'd eat, drink, dance, and then she'd leave. We'd all throw rice because we were not allowed to toss rocks. She had a two-week honeymoon coming up—two full weeks without Alecia. It sounded like heaven.

All we had to do was get through the next twelve hours.

NINE

≈

Bride of Frankenwedding

Most monster movies follow a basic formula. First, the monster is either made, discovered, or both. Maybe it was lying dormant for millions of years, but wasn't dead because it ate a lot of antioxidants. Or maybe it was a normal animal that was irradiated by energy from outer space or too much talking on a cell phone. Second, the monster starts making its presence known by doing subtle things like lurking in the shadows or eating the neighbors. Third, there is a final, climatic scene where a bunch of people are assembled and the monster rampages, destroying everything and killing almost everybody before it dies.

A wedding is like the third stage of a monster movie, except instead of killing the bride, everyone shoves her in a limo for the groom to deal with. For this reason, I prefer a monster movie over a wedding any day.

Alecia's big day started with a noon meeting of just the ladies in the wedding party, who got together for a light lunch and a last shot at having Alecia to themselves to worship before they had to share their worshipping with everyone else at the wedding. I wasn't present at this particular event, for which I am eternally grateful, but my daughter advised me how it went—since it was the last time any of them would have to endure the agony of Alecia as bride-to-be; Sam called it "The Last Suffer."

Meeting Minutes of The Last Suffer

1. Opening Remarks—Alecia

Alecia opened the meeting by noting that it would be a glorious day for all of them, due mainly to the fact that the bride is Alecia. She then generously acknowledged that her wedding party was made up of women to whom she will always owe gratitude for being her bridesmaids, just as she is sure that they were grateful to Alecia for inviting them to be in the wedding, so the gratitude sort of canceled itself out.

2. Reflections on Perfection: What Does it Mean to Be Perfect?—Alecia

Alecia provided random musings on how the wedding will be absolutely perfect. The colors are perfect, the clothing is perfect, and it goes without saying that the bride is perfect (though Alecia did, in fact, go ahead and say it). Someday she hopes that the women in the room can be the brides in their own perfect weddings, modeled after Alecia's. (No reference was made to the two bridesmaids who are married already. Perhaps now that they have seen this wedding they will rethink their own situations, get divorced, and start over.)

3. Oh, the Tacky Gifts I've Received! Humorous Observations—Alecia

Comedy-style ruminations were then delivered about some of the stupid, cheap, and ridiculous wedding gifts Alecia has received and will return for cash.

As a bonus, Alecia detailed the personality flaws of the tacky people who sent the substandard gifts.

An example was made of a sterling silver samovar that Alecia's great-aunt Rebecca (or, "not-so-great-aunt Rebecca," as Alecia called her in a continued demonstration of her comedy-style wit) said was supposedly hand-carried by their great-great-great-grandmother on the boat from Russia and is both ugly and real old. Not only is it tacky that this not-so-great family member didn't spend a dime on the gift, but Alecia can't even return it so it will probably wind up in the closet for Alecia's husband to toss his spare change in, and then when it is full of change they can buy something Alecia really wants with the money.

4. Unscheduled Interruption: The Sick Child Phones—Bridesmaid

The babysitter of the bridesmaid whose little boy has inconsiderately become ill phoned his mother, who was forced to leave the lunch to attend to her child. Alecia graciously covered any awkwardness by addressing the remaining bridesmaids and offering shrewd criticisms of the woman and the woman's bratty kid. Clearly, Alecia felt her "one mistake" was selecting this particular person as a bridesmaid.

No mention was made of the other bridesmaids who had been fired.

5. Question and Answer: The Bridesmaids Ask Alecia About Her Wonderful Wedding—Alecia

Alecia solicited questions from the bridesmaids and gave them advice about marriage, love, and life, all subjects in which Alecia is now an expert by virtue of having been engaged for what seems like most of her adult life. Though no actual questions were asked, Alecia spoke for twenty minutes.

6. Compliments from the Bridesmaids—Bridesmaids

At her urging, one by one the bridesmaids stood and addressed Alecia on the subject of the wedding and their gratitude for (a) Alecia inviting them to be in the wedding party, (b) Alecia having such a wonderful wedding, and (c) Alecia. Alecia responded to each compliment by reminding the individual bridesmaids of additional reasons why they should be grateful to Alecia for all of the above.

7. Concerning the Schedule of the Day: Every Moment Is Tightly Choreographed—Maid of Honor

Sam took the floor to advise all the bridesmaids on what will happen over the next several hours, a plan as complicated as an assault on Ice Station Zebra.

Aside from Alecia: "And nobody else better have a sick kid ha ha."

8. Everyone Pays for Her Own Lunch Except Obviously the Bride: Surprise—Alecia

Though they were not forewarned, the bridesmaids had to divvy up the bill, covering Alecia's meal because as the bride she shouldn't be expected to pay for anything.

9. Adjourn: Final Remarks—Alecia

Alecia explained that she has said everything she can think of and anything more would just be repeating herself, and then demonstrated the truth of this remark by repeating herself.

Spray-on tan immediately followed.

I didn't have to ask Sam what the spray-on tan was all about because I saw it: Alecia, worried that some of her bridesmaids might not have uniform complexions, directed that all of them would be spray-painted with tanning stuff.

"You look fine," I assured Sam, who was fuming over the outcome.

"I look like George Hamilton," she shot back. "I have to go, we're having our armpits waxed. Which we're all paying for, twenty-five dollars."

"Twenty-five dollars! I could have my whole car waxed for that," I said.

"Dad," Valerie warned. She pulled me aside and explained. In waxing, warm wax is painted over the body part and then, when it has dried, two KGB interrogators come in and rip it off, removing all hair and joy from the area.

There seems to be some controversy over which is more painful: body waxing or giving birth. To a flaming lava baby. With horns.

At least after labor a woman winds up with a baby—all she gets after armpit waxing is the tendency to wake up screaming in the middle of the night and, in the case of Alecia, a vicious rash.

I didn't know it at the time, but shortly after Alecia endured her armpit ripping, her skin started to itch and turn red. Sam came back from running an errand to find the bride dancing around the hotel room, scratching under her arms like a monkey.

Apparently Alecia was somewhat irritated that Sam laughed so hard she had to lie down.

We were five hours away from the wedding.

BRIDAL EMERGENCY KIT

One of the duties of the maid of honor is to prepare for everything that could possibly go wrong, so that the wedding will go off without a hitch even during an attack by locusts. Key to this process is the assembly of the Bridal Emergency Kit, which contains items to cover, well, bridal emergencies. Here are the things that belong in such a kit:

1. Needle and thread, so that if the wedding gown falls apart, they can quickly sew a new one.

2. Breath mints, so that if anyone wants to talk to Alecia, they'll have perfect breath with which to do so.

3. Panty hose, so the bridesmaids will have nylon stockings to wear if they decide to rob a 7-Eleven.

4. Tissues, for people so overcome with Alecia's beauty they cry, or at least can use the tissues to pretend to be crying.

5. Money, for tips and also to bribe people to pretend to cry.

6. Duct tape, in case someone has ignored the admonition included in the invitation and has brought a small child who might make noise during the ceremony and thus needs his lips sealed.

7. Glue gun, in case the duct tape doesn't work.

8. Spare groom, in case this one comes to his senses and bolts from the church.

9. A copy of the bridal vows, which Alecia has written herself and memorized but in her nervousness might forget, depriving everyone of joy.

10. Painkillers, to help us all get through Alecia's bridal vows.

11. Several credit cards, which the groom will ceremoniously hand over to the bride to remind her why she is getting married to him.

12. Groom's prescription medication, which might explain why *he* is getting married to *her*.

13. Wristwatch, so you can keep checking to see how much longer you'll have to endure this whole thing.

14. Money, to give to Alecia because that makes her happy.

AS LOVELY AS A SWAN

My daughter Sam, in her role as Alecia's *Gruppenführer*, assigned me the role of driving my son to Alecia's wedding chapel, because apparently groomsmen can't drive themselves. This meant I was en route to the church several hours early and that I wasn't happy.

"A groomsman is, by very definition, a guy who has his own transportation," I griped to my son.

"I do, Dad. I have *you*." Chris grinned at me.

"Now who's making so-called jokes?"

"You have to do it because Sam says. If you don't do what Sam says, she puts you on the phone to talk to Alecia. That's what happened when I said I couldn't make it for the tux fitting and needed to reschedule. Believe me, you don't want that."

"Okay, you're right," I agreed. "But why does Sam have to be the wedding obliterator? Why didn't they hire someone like Lindy Lynch-Mob?"

"You didn't hear? Alecia has had three wedding planners. They all quit, like those bridesmaids."

"The bridesmaids quit? I thought they were court-martialed for failing to obey orders on the battlefield."

"Alecia told a couple of them they had to lose fifteen pounds." He regarded me with twenty-year-old wisdom. "Women get all tense and freak out over weddings. It makes them happy."

I told him that if, at his age, he had managed to figure out what made women happy he could quit college and grow rich on the lecture circuit.

Actually, he wanted my advice. He was worried because his girlfriend was spending far too much time reading Sam's bridal magazines and talking about the wedding for his comfort. "She keeps saying things like, 'for my wedding, I want the groomsmen wearing gray tuxes.' And then she, you know, *looks* at me. What am I supposed to say to that?"

"Tell her the dollar is down against the Euro, give her something else to worry about."

"I mean, I'm still in college, and then I'm going to go to medical school so that you're always poor." (He probably didn't say the "poor" part, but that's always what I hear whenever he discusses his plans for converting my future income into tuition payments.) "What does she think, that we're going to get married now?"

I shrugged. "It's like UFOs. Somebody spots a flying saucer over Mexico City, the next thing you know, people are seeing one every day," I explained romantically. "So once one woman gets married, they all want a wedding. It eventually burns itself out or turns into a trip to Roswell, New Mexico."

"Is Sarah like that?"

I thought about it. "Well, no, she already had a wedding like Alecia's, only it was worse because she married her ex-husband the Gas Bag. You don't do the huge wedding thing twice—it's like catching mono, one bout and you're inoculated for life."

"Weddings are like UFOs and mononucleosis. Got it. Thanks, Dad, these talks really help when it comes to dealing with the ladies," he deadpanned.

"I'm just glad I can give you my wisdom, or really give you anything that doesn't involve me writing a check."

"So are you and Sarah ever going to get married?"

I don't know why, but with a son it is sometimes possible to forget you're a father and just talk like buddies. I've never been able to drop my protective shield with my daughters the way I now did with Chris.

"The thought doesn't terrify me," I admitted. "But look, I've got two weddings, and you in college for the next several decades . . . I'm not sure now would be the time."

"So she'll wait?" Chris asked.

"I don't know," I replied honestly. I drove for awhile in silence, thinking about it. "Women see marriage as a sequential step on the relationship continuum," I finally said. "Men see it as a step in their lives. So for men, the questions are, 'Am I ready? Do I have enough money? Is my job secure?' For women it's, 'How long have we been together?' "

We pulled into the church parking lot. He regarded me for a moment with that startled look children his age get when it suddenly occurs to them that their parents are not complete idiots. "Yeah, that's it," he said. Then he grabbed his tux out of the backseat. "Okay, I'm going in."

He closed the door, then bent down and rapped on the window. I lowered the glass. His eyes regarded me steadily. "I hope you don't wait so long that she winds up dumping you. I like her."

"Me too."

"Besides, I doubt you could find another girlfriend now, or even get a *date*," he observed.

"You know, I so could have done without that last comment."

He grinned at me and trotted away. He headed to the side of the building, following signs that my daughter Sam had carefully placed to guide the groomsmen to their dressing room, while I wandered in the front door to see what was going on.

Alecia was up at the altar, spitting at the minister. Disaster had already struck: The minister was vetoing part of the ceremony. Sam stood by while Alecia's anger boiled over.

"This can't be the final word. Not on this day. No, I won't. You can't. No!" Alecia shouted, madly scratching her armpits. She whirled on her heel and stomped off.

"Looks like things are going pretty much as expected," I remarked to my daughter, who rolled her eyes at me.

"I'm sorry, she's just a little tense," Sam apologized to the minister.

The minister nodded. "That's okay, I've done a lot of these before."

"Are they always this wonderful?" I asked him innocently.

He regarded me with wry humor. "Let's just say I far prefer doing funerals."

Sam moved her head close to mine so she could whisper. "Alecia decided a few days ago that she wants the bridesmaids to enter carrying candles. So I got these glass candleholders from the craft store and painted them with the right colors, but the church won't allow it because they're afraid people will catch on fire," she explained.

"And burning humans is against church rules or something? Because there used to be a time when they were really into stuff like that."

"I guess. I thought it was dumb anyway," Sam said, "I mean, they're already carrying flowers."

"But it would be sort of festive if the bridesmaids ignited."

"Stop, drop, and roll," Sam replied, grinning at me. Then she checked her watch and sighed. "Okay, I've got to go help with the dress, and then Alecia wants to spend half an hour alone in private contemplation with just the photographer there to take pictures of it. I wonder what else will go wrong?"

We found out an hour or so later, when the guests began to arrive. Alecia's love-theme (as opposed to all the other themes) was something like, "I Am Like a Swan, I Am Beautiful and I Mate for Life, So Don't Even Think You Can Get Out of It." To punctuate the point, live swans were supposed to stand at the church door and greet people as they arrived by maybe shaking hands or something. The groomsmen were to assist the swan wrangler and ensure that the birds didn't get bored and wander off, though no measures had been taken to see that the groomsmen didn't get bored and wander off.

My son summed up the swan problem succinctly. "Those suckers are *mean*," he told me with feeling. Apparently the swans, far from wandering off, had established the top steps of the church as their territory, and were attacking anybody trying to get in.

"Well, what does the swan wrangler say?" I asked.

"He says swans are *mean*. He says he told Alecia this but she said she didn't care because the swans were part of her vision."

Sarah came in and sat beside me, lovely in a dark blue dress. "I've just been bitten by a bird," she informed me.

"You'll be okay as long as you've had your shots."

"Shots? For what, bird flu?"

When a couple of bridesmaids showed up in their lurid pink and yellow puffy dresses, the swans panicked, thinking they were giant attack flamingos. They took off, soaring over a fence and taking shelter in a backyard swimming pool. The swan wrangler couldn't get over the fence and looked frustrated.

People swarmed in. Valerie and good old Moldy arrived, and my daughter and Sarah talked about their shoes for five minutes.

I shrugged at Moldy, who seemed to be in a really bad mood. "The swan get a piece of you?" I asked him.

"There shouldn't be swans, they don't belong here, this isn't their natural habitat."

"They don't normally nest on the top steps of a church?"

"Of course not."

I remembered that Mulchy had majored in biology, so he probably knew what he was talking about.

"It was just hard to find birds that had the same personality as the bride," I explained.

"Dad," Valerie said.

Moldy had more complaints. "Did you see how many SUVs there were in the parking lot?" he asked me. "People don't think, they just get in their gas guzzlers and drive."

"If they'd given it some thought, they probably wouldn't have come," I agreed.

"Shhh," Valerie admonished both of us, though there was nothing to see or hear, or interrupt.

From up in the balcony a cellist began playing—probably Yo-Yo Ma. The crowd hushed. Geoff, all tuxed up, came down the aisle with his mother on his arm. Priscilla walked with Churchilian dignity: a riddle, wrapped in a mystery, covered in taffeta. As she walked, she nodded at people she recognized in the crowd, but not me. Standing at the back of the church was the man I assumed was her husband, and, to my astonishment, he bore a passing resemblance to Franklin Delano Roosevelt. They were perfect for each other!

"We could reenact the entire Second World War right here," I murmured to Valerie.

"Dad!"

Marty frowned a little because he was against war. Sarah's lips twitched in a smile. Geoff dumped his mom off and stood at the front of the church.

Then a woman wearing a ballet outfit came down the aisle, twirling *en pointe* and tossing black and red rose petals in the air, which landed on women's pastel spring dresses in puffs of dark pigment. The minister paled at what the flowers were doing to the carpet.

"They're monogrammed," I said to Valerie, showing her a rose petal. Mulchy snorted in derision. I decided I was starting to like the guy.

"We're not ripping the petals off of a bunch of flowers at our wedding," he said to Valerie. She nodded in a way that said, "Shut up now."

When the ballet woman had stained her way to the front, she turned and sang Elton John's "Candle in the Wind," the Princess Diana version, to remind everyone that Alecia reminded everyone of Princess Diana.

When the wedding party came down the aisle, grinding the rose petals into the carpet under their feet, I gazed with pride at my beautiful daughter in her stupid dress. "Wow, look at the bow on Sam's butt," I said. "You could tie an aircraft carrier to the dock with a bow that big."

"Dad!"

Finally the groom passed up his last chance to flee and was standing expectantly at the altar—for how stupid he must be, he was entirely unremarkable, just a young, sort of fleshy man with dark hair: Fop Jr., I decided to call him. The minister smiled, and the crowd turned to look toward the back of the church.

Alecia's dress was full of rippling folds in the front, sort of like a car hood after a teenager's first driving lesson. Everyone stood to get a better look at the thing. "It cost ten thousand dollars," Valerie said in quiet awe. I stared—give me a couple dozen yards of fabric and a staple gun, and I was pretty sure I could come up with the same design. Her father strolled with her, batting the flowing veil out of his eyes, while Alecia radiantly absorbed everyone's worshipful adoration.

The minister had a lot to say for a guy whose only real question had to be "Who is going to clean my carpet?" During his sermon I sat and studied my son, who looked so handsome, mature, and distracted, and my daughter, whose skin matched all the other bridesmaids in Stepford uniformity, and it occurred to me that this was all really happening, my children were really growing up and were launching their own independent lives with my financial assistance.

While the minister spoke, the lone child in the room, the bridesmaid's sick son, coughed and then said, "I sorry." People laughed, and Alecia looked into the crowd like a swan guarding a church, her eyes sizzling. Thus distracted by the child criminal, she forgot herself and scratched viciously at one of her armpits.

Next, Alecia turned to her groom—Alecia had written a poem.

ALECIA'S POEM

My love is like
The gaze of God
My kisses sweet as candy
And while my beauty
You may laud
You too
Do come in handy.

I have waited
All my life
For this
My wedding day
And now I'll be
A perfect wife
At least
That's what you'll say

Anyone
Would love me

But it's for you
That my heart lifts
Because of how you treat me
The way
You bring me gifts

You may not be
The richest guy
But honest I'm not mad
If there are things
That we can't buy
The worst I'll be
is sad

Like the swans
Who never part
Neither one can leave
You now are
Deep in my heart
And when you die
I'll grieve

So take me love
And know this true
You are now all aware of
I'm really glad that I have you
And me that you'll
Take care of

Alecia beamed at the people in the church. "It's okay to applaud," she said, so people did.

"Call Hallmark, see if they are interested in doing a 'Narcissistic' line of cards," I murmured to Valerie. She dug an elbow into my side, grinning.

Then came something I had never seen before: my son brought over a chair and Alecia sat, extending her leg. Her groom carefully removed her right shoe. Sam stepped forward and handed him what was unmistakably a glass slipper, which the groom then placed on the bare foot.

"The charming prince puts the glass slipper on his love, just like in *Cinderella*," the minister intoned, looking mildly disgusted.

"*Cinderella*, it's Alecia's favorite part of the Bible," I said out of the side of my mouth to Sarah. She elbowed me, too—I was going to wind up with more bruises than if I'd spent the day in the Roller Derby.

As if he heard me, my son Chris started to laugh, biting his lips to keep it silent. Instantly the giggles swept through the bridal party, the women telegraphing their helpless laughter with the shaking of their bouquets. Alecia glared at them in fury, which just made it more difficult for them to maintain control.

There were more Alecia rituals—she and her groom poured Champagne into the slipper and drank from it, Alecia kissed the rings before they put them on, Alecia scratched her armpits—but my focus was on my children, who were practically purple with the effort of restraining their laughter.

I've never been more proud.

Finally the groom broke, bursting into a guffaw that let everyone else off the hook. A deep cleansing laugh swept through the church, while Alecia stood and made her enemies list.

Then it was over. The string quartet in the balcony, which

I had started to think of as "the band," played the theme song from the movie *Titanic* (a slightly less expensive disaster), and eventually everyone streamed out of the church and stood to watch the fire department in the neighbor's backyard, trying to help the wrangler catch the swans.

At the reception, my daughters, who had just been through an excruciatingly lengthy wedding, wanted to talk, at excruciating length, about weddings. I realized as I listened to their chatter that I had become something of an expert in wedding-speak, and could easily translate what they were saying.

A FATHER'S TRANSLATION OF WEDDING TERMS	
WHEN THE BRIDE SAYS	IT MEANS
It will be a storybook wedding!	The story where the monster destroys Tokyo.
I have the perfect vision for my wedding colors!	Somehow people are supposed to match the paint chips in my head.
My bridesmaids' dresses are the type that could be worn again to a formal party or event.	They will never be worn again.
I just want my new husband to be happy.	What makes me happy makes him happy.
My wedding cake will be so romantic!	It's going to be expensive and taste bad.
We just couldn't stand not being married and completely on impulse decided to elope!	The baby's due in August.

WHEN THE BRIDE SAYS	IT MEANS
I'm going for just the basics, I don't need a lot of expensive extras at my wedding.	Just the basics will be expensive.
My fiancé is so relaxed, I really envy how calm he is with all that is going on.	If he doesn't start helping I'm going to kill him.
Swans mate for life. I want everyone to be greeted by a pair of beautiful, life-mated swans.	By "greeted" I mean "bitten."

Alecia's reception got off to a slow start because the bar didn't open in the reception hall until the wedding party arrived. Sam informed me later that Alecia stated that she didn't want people having fun until she got there, so the bartender stood firm, even when people started offering him money.

Finally the doors blew open and the band leader announced the arrival of the bride and groom, Sam applauding so everyone would know that the proper response was to clap and not follow their instincts and throw dinner rolls.

The tables were ornately set, each napkin folded precisely into the shape of a swan (a professional origamist had been hired for the purpose). The wedding favors were boxed in swan-shaped containers and were little sterling silver hearts with the wedding date etched into it. On impulse, I gave mine to the bartender without giving thought to how much it would infuriate Alecia to see the hearts piling up in the guy's tip jar.

Okay, maybe I gave a *little* thought to it.

The wedding table was set up front as if it were on a stage, and not ten minutes into the evening somebody started to clink his spoon against his wineglass. This set off a chorus of clinking, and Alecia, her lips tight, briefly smooched her new husband, and then said something to the wedding singer.

"The bride requests no clinking tonight, this isn't that kind of wedding," the guy said into his microphone. Meaning, I guess, the kissing kind.

Everyone clinked in understanding, and kept clinking until Alecia gave her husband another dry, emotionless peck on the lips.

I grinned, finally having some fun.

Prior to dinner, Franklin Roosevelt stood, took the microphone, and serenaded his daughter, singing a song I'd never heard before but had lyrics that went something like

You're so beautiful
No one is as beautiful as you
Everyone wants to be you
But nature could only make one of you
You're so beautiful
Those swans were really stupid

These may not have been the exact words, but you get the drift. I was impressed by the quality of the old guy's voice, and told Valerie, who shrugged.

"Sam said it's prerecorded by a professional. He's lip-synching."

After the song there was more glass clinking, and Alecia lip-synched a kiss with her husband. His expression seemed to indicate he was starting to wonder what had happened to the girl who once made out with him in the backseat of his car.

Next we were treated to a PowerPoint presentation of

pictures of Alecia, smoothly narrated by the wedding singer, who described the high points in Alecia's life, which seemed to be:

1. Alecia is born. Everyone rejoices.
2. Alecia discovers mirrors. Life will never be the same.
3. Alecia is the most popular girl in her school. It takes three schools before this is so.
4. Every single photo of Alecia, including those in third grade, is a glamour shot. It also is apparent that Alecia is photographed more often than Britney Spears.
5. Alecia has several parties at her house, proving how popular she was, in case you had any doubts.
6. Sometime in high school, her parents began paying for Alecia to be professionally photographed doing things like sitting in their garden looking at leaves, sitting on a beach looking at the ocean, or sitting in their den reading a book (in the picture she's holding the book upside down).
7. Alecia gets engaged, and the world rejoices, though her new husband looks more unenthusiastic with each passing moment.

After that, though, the guests seemed to wake up to the fact that it didn't matter what Alecia wanted anymore—she had lost all her power when she said "I do," and now this was just a party where everyone could drink free alcohol and invent new ways of dancing (perhaps I was the only person to do this). The whole evening threatened to break out in fun, though twice Sam had to stop whatever she was doing and track down Alecia, who was barricaded in the ladies room.

"Everyone's ignoring her," Sam told me when she had finally coaxed the bride back out into the open. Alecia sat glumly at her seat at the table, watching her new husband dance with one of the bridesmaids.

"Well, she's just sitting there," I pointed out.

"Her wedding dress is too long for her to dance in without running the risk of falling, and that would ruin everything."

I pictured it in my mind, Alecia falling on her face. "I'm not sure I agree with that," I said slowly.

There were a few more things to go through, such as the cake cutting, or, as I liked to call it, the ceremonial food fight. Everyone got a big laugh when Alecia's groom shoved a big piece of cake into her mouth, smearing her cheeks with frosting, though it was slightly less amusing when Alecia grabbed a handful of frosting and socked him in the jaw with it.

The wedding cake was a delicious concoction, if you like sugar-flavored lard. "Put some of this under your pillow tonight," I advised Valerie. "You'll dream of your dentist."

The stunt bouquet was trotted out and Alecia flung it high over her shoulder, and the ladies went after it like it was a jump ball in the NCAA Finals. Several of them seemed to get a piece of it.

Then it was time for the big send-off. Instead of rice, the crowd threw confetti, each paper shred imprinted with the sentiments like "We love you, Alecia" and "The most perfect couple on earth." The happy couple got into their car, which was Chitty Chitty Bang Bang.

I'm serious, it was Chitty Chitty Bang Bang. Alecia had somehow tracked down the current owners of the original car used in the movie that was based on the book by Ian Fleming, who was also the creator of the James Bond books. I decided that when it came to Ian Fleming's creations, Alecia's husband would probably have been happier if he'd had the car from *Goldfinger*, the one with the passenger ejector seat.

"Thank you all, I love you all, thank you for the fabulous gifts, or if you forgot to bring yours, you can send them to my mother's house!" Alecia called as they lurched off down the street in Chitty Chitty Bang Bang.

My son slid up next to me. "I'm going to guess that their marriage is going to have a lot more 'Chitty Chitty' than 'Bang Bang,'" he observed.

With Alecia gone everyone could finally relax and have fun. I watched Sam and Geoff dance, smiling and chatting with each other, and saw Valerie trying to drag her fiancé on the dance floor, though Moldy refused, probably because he felt dancing was against the environment.

I showed Sarah some of the new steps I'd invented, and she seemed really impressed. Then a slow number came on and we moved closer.

"You look really beautiful tonight," I told her, going from memory because at that moment all I could really see was her ear. "Are you having fun?"

"I've never danced like this before," she responded simply. I decided to take it as a compliment.

"You know, my son asked me when you and I are going to tie the knot."

She pulled back to look into my eyes. "My, how much have *you* had to drink tonight?"

"I'm just . . . you've probably been wondering . . ."

"Am I waiting breathlessly for you to get tipsy and raise this subject at the wedding of someone you can't stand? Is that what you're asking?"

Put that way it didn't sound as romantic as I'd intended. Sarah was grinning mischievously at me. "I never said you were breathless," I pointed out.

"Honey." She snuggled close and put her head on my shoulder. "You've got a lot on your mind right now, let's not add to it. There's plenty of time."

I decided that Sarah and I needed to be alone. I went to say good-bye to my daughter. "You did a really good job, Sam. You got her married, and nobody beat her to death," I told her. "My favorite part was when Alecia left."

"It was a very special moment for me, too," she agreed.

"So did being the maid of honor give you a lot of good ideas on what to do for your wedding?"

"Mostly what not to do."

"Ah."

She regarded me with the competitive gleam in her eye that I recognized from countless championship volleyball games. "I'll tell you one thing, though. My wedding is going to be a *lot* better than this one!"

TEN

~

Though Bridal Showers May Come Your Way, They Bring the Flowers for Which You Pay

Legend has it that the first bridal shower was held in Holland, where a poor Dutch boy (have you never noticed there were never any *rich* Dutch boys?) wanted to marry a girl, but the girl's father forbade it.

You can tell this was a long time ago because the father got a vote.

Normally, the father's decision would have been the end of it because this was a most excellent time in history, but the Dutch boy felt that the girl's father was being unreasonable, which is a father's right, and so everyone should have just shut up. The Dutch boy appealed to the people in the town, who liked the Dutch boy because a few years earlier he had saved Holland by sticking his finger in a leaky dike.* They "showered" upon the bride-to-be all of the things she would need to start her own household, like, I don't know, Dutch Boy paint.

---

* Let's just say I'm combining two stories for the sake of efficiency.

The father became angry at being overruled and sacked the village.* Therefore the lesson in all of this is the father is always right.

In modern times, the bridal shower has become less about ignoring the father and more about having the event at my house. At least, that's the conclusion I reached when I was told that my daughter Valerie wanted to have a shower for Sam in my living room.

"What for?" I asked. "She already has everything she needs because she took them from my kitchen. And didn't she already have one at your mother's house?"

"Dad. Stop it. She does not have everything she needs. And that one was out of town, we need to have one here."

"Well, wait, I thought the maid of honor planned the showers and evicted *her* father."

"You're not evicted, you can come. And I *am* Sam's maid of honor, and she's mine."

"You're kidding." I stared at her. "Well, don't you think that's something you should have consulted me on?"

"Why?"

Okay, she had me there. But I pictured when Valerie was first born, how after a week at home Sam announced that we should send the baby back because "it wasn't working out." As far as I knew, that opinion hadn't changed much. "Don't you remember how you would fight every single morning over who got to use the bathroom to put on makeup?" I asked her.

"Dad, that was high school. We are so much more mature now. We know how to share things. Like last week Marty and I had a Margarita party and Sam let me use her blender without me even asking."

---

* This is what should have happened, anyway.

"That's *my* blender. Sounds like you know how to share *my* things."

"So who's being immature now?" she wanted to know.

"Okay, so tell me about this surprise bridal shower that I'm having at my place."

"It's not a surprise, Sam knows about it."

"But I didn't," I pointed out.

Valerie proceeded to explain to me about bridal showers, which I should have paid attention to but found I was unable to due to the subject. So everything I know about bridal showers I learned firsthand, which is this:

BRIDAL SHOWERS: WHAT EVERY FATHER SHOULD KNOW

Here's all a father needs to know about bridal showers:

1. Don't go.

BRIDAL SHOWERS: WHY FATHERS SHOULDN'T GO

To understand why a father doesn't belong at a bridal shower, one must first understand the nature of the two most powerful chemicals in the universe: testosterone and estrogen.

Testosterone is a hormone that, in small amounts, produces healthy reactions like a resistance to disease, authority, and common sense. In large amounts, it causes NASCAR.

Estrogen is a hormone that causes Hugh Grant movies.

When women get together in the same room, they start to excrete estrogen in the form of rapid conversations and compulsive chocolate consumption. Men, on the other hand, pretty much keep their testosterone to themselves, unless they want to have a hockey game or a war.

Now, all men have a little estrogen in them, called their "feminine side." Women like it when men get in touch with their "feminine side," so men will pretend to do so, believing it will allow them to get in touch with the women's "feminine parts." However, for the most part, men are afraid of estrogen and will do anything to avoid being exposed to it for too long for fear of becoming what I suppose we could call a "Wimp-zilla."

At a bridal shower, the estrogen is thicker than frosting on a wedding cake. If a man is exposed to such an event for more than half an hour, he will have to watch all four *Die Hard* movies just to reset.

Of course, I didn't know any of this. I just thought I should attend the thing since it was being held in my house and there would be cookies. Besides, as my daughter's official self-proclaimed wedding obliterator, I wanted to make sure that no decisions were made about Sam's upcoming nuptials without my input, advice, and veto.

Bridal showers come in themes, but not the same theme as the wedding because that would mean saving on the decorations. Valerie considered and rejected several themes before hitting on the perfect one for Sam's party, though again, I wasn't really paying attention, but here are some of the examples.

Viva Las Vegas Shower!	The house is decorated to look like a casino. Everyone gambles using fake money. A professional dealer can be hired if you're concerned you're not generating enough expense. During the middle of the party, some Mafia goons come in and beat everybody up.

History Shower!	Everyone dresses as and behaves as a famous person from history, such as Marie Antoinette, Joan of Arc, or Caligula. People guess who each guest is supposed to be based on their comments (Marie Antoinette: "Let me eat cake!").
Death Valley Shower!	The heater is turned up really high and no one is allowed to drink water.
Parents Are Out of Town Shower!	The hostess pretends she is a teenager and her parents are out of town for the weekend. Her friends all come over and throw up on the carpet. The party ends when the neighbors call the police—the guests exit by running out the back door and scaling the fence.
Presidential Debate Shower!	The hostess poses insipid questions to the guests, who do their best to answer by completely evading the topic.
Arriving at the Los Angeles Airport Shower!	Every guest brings a suitcase. The suitcases are all placed in another room, and then the guests spend the rest of the evening waiting for them to come out.
Divorcée Shower!	At some point in the evening, all the talk about weddings leads one or more of the divorced women in the room to speak bitterly and at great length about what a jerk her ex-husband is. (Can be combined with other themes.)
Iron Curtain Shower!	Priscilla and her husband explain to the guests the decisions they made at Yalta.

BRIDEZILLA, THE SEQUEL

Something really unfortunate happened on Alecia's honeymoon: She came back. Infused with postbridal happiness, she had apparently been calling Sam almost daily with helpful suggestions and complaints about her wedding gifts. Naturally, Valerie felt she had to invite the woman to my house, which made me unhappy because if you recall vampire lore, once you invite the monster into your home she can destroy you with impunity.

The theme for Sam's shower was "A Gathering of Goddesses." Every woman was to come dressed as a goddess of some kind, which meant they could wear tiaras, which are like wedding-cake toppers for people. The guests were all supposed to guess which goddess you were. So if you suddenly turned to the person next to you and hit her over the head with a broadsword, you might be Athena, goddess of warfare. (Or you might just be trying to get to the last cookie.)

When I have a few of my friends over, I usually decorate the place by setting the remotes on the coffee table. Valerie wanted something more elaborate, so she rented some fake columns from, I don't know, columnists, decorated them with fake ivy, set out fake grapes, and had a cake made to look like Mount Olympus, which is the place in Greece where the gods ate dessert.

The guests were to arrive at seven, so at about six fifty-five I started to wonder what I should do for a costume. Valerie wasn't available to consult—she was on the phone with Moldy discussing globalization. But I figured I could come up with something. Maybe I could carry a hammer and be Thor, god of thunder. Or I could tip Tom's boat upside down in my front yard and be Poseidon, god of bad movies. Or I could just stay the way I was and be Dad, god of my family.

When the ladies arrived I decided I was glad I had stuck with Dad, because their costumes were so elaborate and well planned that I doubt I could have pulled anything off, even if I did the hammer thing. Most of them wore tiaras, except

Sam, who wore a helmet with horns sticking out of either side of it.

"Let me guess . . . you're Sam, goddess of motorcycle gangs."

"No," she told me, "I'm Brynhild, one of the Valkyries. Where do you want me to put my blender?"

"*Your* blender. Ah yes, Brynhild, goddess of extreme irony."

Sarah came in dressed as Eirene, "Goddess of peace, because I figured that's something you could use," she told me.

"You must have heard Alecia is coming," I responded. I regarded her costume with admiration. "Somehow you make a toga look beautiful. You could really do a lot better than a guy like me," I informed her.

She cocked her head. "You really don't approve of men dating the women you care about, even if the man in question is you, do you?" she asked.

"Can we please have a conversation without a bunch of accuracy?" I asked. She grinned at me.

Alecia was, of course, late. Everyone was seated and having their first round of chocolate when she came in, twirling and laughing delightfully so everyone would know she was delightful. Her tiara looked like it had been stolen from Queen Elizabeth. The rest of her was dressed for the toga party, and she carried a scepter in one hand.

"I know," she said, "I'm still tan from my honeymoon."

"Everybody looks so great!" Valerie enthused.

"Luckily I know a costume designer," Alecia agreed.

"So why don't we go around the room and tell a little about ourselves . . ." Valerie began.

"I'll start," Alecia said promptly. "Well, my name is Alecia King . . . ohmygod I said King! My name is Alecia Hoyt, I just married Mark Hoyt last month and let me tell you, it has been a whirlwind!"

"Alecia," Valerie interrupted gently, "I mean, we should each say a little about our characters, the goddess we came as, and see if people can guess who we are."

"Oh." Alecia shrugged. "Okay, if you want to."

Valerie was dressed in flowers and eventually they figured out that she was Blodwin, goddess of the earth in bloom—probably because there wasn't such a thing as the goddess of the earth in crisis. Another woman was imaginatively wearing a white dress and carrying a briefcase—she was Hathor, goddess of women in business. Alecia was Alecia, goddess of hot air.

"Okay. About my character," Alecia said mischievously when it was her turn. "Let's just say this one is very, very appropriate for someone like me."

"Aradia?" someone guessed.

"Aradia?" Alecia echoed uncertainly.

"Goddess of witches," Sam explained with an amazingly deadpan expression.

"No, no," Alecia said. "This has to do with my recent experiences."

"Aphrodite, goddess of erotic love," suggested a woman who hadn't seen Alecia at her wedding.

"Good guess!" Alecia encouraged inaccurately. "But no. Here's another hint. I'm probably the person in the room with the most expertise in this subject."

"Was Narcissus a goddess?" I asked innocently from my place in the kitchen.

"Dad," Valerie warned.

Several of the women blinked at me: With all the estrogen flying, they had forgotten I was even there. Sarah was stifling a laugh.

"Hera!" Alecia said impatiently. "Goddess of marriage and weddings."

"Oh, right," Sam said.

"God, you guys, it was so obvious," Alecia complained. She waved her wedding rings at them. "I mean, hello."

"Well, that was fun!" Valerie said, meaning, "except for the part with Alecia."

"It's been like what, six weeks? Oh my God, my two-month anniversary is coming soon!" Alecia pressed a hand to her mouth, looking amazed. I wondered how much I would have to pay her to keep her hand there for the rest of the party.

Now that everyone's secret goddess identity had been revealed, I figured the party would hit a dead spot. The same thing usually happens when I have a few of my friends over—an initial rush of excitement, and then a lull.

TOM (EXCITED): *Do you have any beer?*

ME (EXCITED): *Yes. Want one?*

TOM (EXCITED): *Yes!*
(LULL)
(TEN MINUTES GO BY)

ME: *Want another beer?*

TOM: *Not yet.*

Not wanting to have this happen at my daughter's bridal shower, I opened my mouth to suggest some interesting topics we could discuss, such as the Yankees' pitching staff, but discovered that women don't seem to do lulls. More than one conversation ignited at once, with the topic seeming to be "What I Did, or Will Do, at My Wedding."

I have been hanging around men for all of my life, and I will tell you this is something we never, ever do. I have never once heard a man contemplate out loud where he wanted to get married, who he wanted for the ring bearer, or what flowers "would be pretty."

"Valerie's getting married, too!" Sam announced when she felt she was attracting too much of the attention.

"I look at my wedding dress every day!" Alecia said for exactly the same reason.

The ladies turned their tiaras in Valerie's direction, begging for details.

"We're sending out our save the date cards this weekend. Marty wanted them to be 'Save the date, save the whales,'" Valerie explained.

"I hope they won't be the save the date things that are refrigerator magnets, those are so tacky," Alecia interjected.

"No, they're not magnets. Those things take like a million years to biodegrade," Valerie said.

"Plus they're tacky," Alecia insisted.

"Do you have a theme picked out yet?" someone asked Valerie.

"No, not yet. Marty wants something to do with the planet."

"God, you are so smart to let your fiancé think he's involved," Alecia told my daughter. "Keeps them out of the way."

"One idea that Marty had was for the flowers," Valerie said.

"My bouquet had calla lilies, tulips, and roses," Alecia sighed.

"We thought, to make a statement, you know, we could

have nonnative plants, and then to symbolize the destruction they cause, instead of throwing the bouquet I would burn it."

"People were amazed at how far I threw the bouquet." Alecia laughed. "I told them, look out, but they didn't believe me."

"But I think I'm probably just going to go with wildflowers," Valerie said.

"Good idea," someone agreed. I could see the idea of burning the bouquet hadn't gone over real well with any of them.

"Your fiancé sounds like a very special man," someone else remarked, leading me to reflect that there was more than one way to interpret "special."

"He's great. He's kind of a geek, but, you know." Valerie shrugged.

"But you love him," Sam said, and all the women nodded firmly, as if deciding by acclamation.

"Hey, you know what?" I interjected. "Your theme could be "My Big Fat Geek Wedding!" Get it? Geek?"

"That's funny," Sam said, meaning "it's not."

"Get it?"

"We get it, Bruce," Sarah assured me. She has told me repeatedly that she doesn't think my puns are funny, which is odd because on most topics she's not usually that wrong.

Suddenly Alecia looked horror-struck. "Not that you're fat, your dad wasn't saying *that*."

"No, 'course not. Hey, let's play a game," Valerie replied.

"When I got married, I thought I was so overweight, too, but everyone said I looked just beautiful," Alecia assured my daughter. "Besides, you have plenty of time if you want to shed those extra pounds."

Valerie explained that the game they would play was going to be a variation of "pin the tail on the donkey's butt." (I sort of hoped it would be "stuff a sock in Alecia's mouth.") She unveiled a large poster of the god Zeus that featured a picture of the statue of the Greek god that stands in the National Archeological Museum in Athens.

Now, this statue is both naked and anatomically correct. However, for the game, a very critical of part of Zeus's anatomy had been removed—the "correct" part, if you get my drift. In the game, the blindfolded women would, one at a time, attempt to affix the crucial body part to the correct place, while everyone else laughed hysterically.

This is another thing that I can assure you that men never do.

The whole thing made me a bit squeamish, so I went outside for some fresh air. When I returned, someone had pinned the object to Zeus's forehead in an apparent commentary on how men think. I loftily ignored it.

They talked some more about Sam's wedding and listened some more about Alecia's wedding, and at one point Valerie told the story of How Moldy Proposed, which now had him kneeling before her at sunrise on a mountain peak and handing her a ring and uttering very romantic words, like "will you share my hybrid vehicle" or something.

"Well, but this is really all about Sam," Valerie said at one point, which I am sure came as news to Alecia. Valerie handed out paper and pens, announcing we would now play a game called "Trivia Questions About Sam." The person who got the most answers correct would win a prize.

"Might as well put my name on that prize," I chortled. "No way anyone's going to beat me at this."

TYPICAL BRIDAL SHOWER TRIVIA QUESTIONS

TRIVIA QUESTION ABOUT THE BRIDE	CORRECT ANSWER
Who was her favorite teacher?	Obviously, her father. A father teaches his children so many things through their lives, there really is no way she can ever thank him, though returning his blender would make a good start.
Who was her favorite coach?	Clearly, her father. While coaches come and go, it is always the father who offers the wisest and most important advice, even when the sport is volleyball, which is a game he never actually played and still isn't quite sure he understands.
Who had the most important impact on her life?	Simply speaking, her father. Sure, there may have been times when he seemed out of touch, when he seemed to be overreacting, when he seemed unreasonable or interfering, but in the grand scheme of things, we can now see that he wasn't.

"Okay. First question. When Sam was thirteen years old, she had her first kiss. Who was the boy she kissed?"

"What?" I sputtered. "Are you kidding me? *Thirteen?*"

"Dad," Valerie said.

"You kissed a boy when you were just thirteen years old? I'm sorry, but that's it. You're . . ." I paused, not sure what words were going to come out of my mouth next. *Grounded?*

"Dad," Valerie said again.

"That was a long time ago, Dad," Sam said, as if there were a statute of limitations on such behavior.

It turned out my daughter's first kiss came from a boy named John. I made a mental note to call his parents.

"Okay. Next question. Who was Sam on a date with when she met Geoff for the first time?"

"Wait a minute. You're on a date with one boy and you throw yourself at another?" I demanded.

"Dad," Valerie said.

"I didn't throw myself at anybody, Dad. He asked me for my phone number and I gave it to him," Sam said defensively.

"Some complete stranger asks you for your phone number and you just hand it to him like that?" I asked in disbelief. "He could have been Ted Bundy."

"This sort of thing used to happen to me all the time," Alecia tittered, "guys hitting on me even though I'm obviously on a date. Still does, even though I'm married."

Turned out the boy on the date that ended in Sam passing out her phone number like free cookies was also named John. Let me just say that it doesn't do a father's heart any good to hear that his daughter has had dates with a bunch of Johns.

"Next question. What was happening when Sam and Geoff had their first kiss?"

"Let me guess." I said. "Sam was handing her phone number to somebody else."

"Dad," Valerie said.

"Our first kiss wasn't romantic at all," Alecia said, pouting. "If I had known he was going to ask me to marry him, I would have wanted to do it somewhere instead of the front seat of his car. Like, on a boat in the moonlight, or someplace."

I couldn't understand why Alecia didn't notice that no one was reacting to anything she had to say. She could have announced she was the Green River Killer and people would have just kept talking around her.

Sam's first kiss with Geoff was at sunrise in the park.

"Sunrise? You went on a date and you were out until sunrise?"

"Dad," Valerie said.

"Come on, Dad. I have my own apartment. I went to college," Sam said gently. "What do you think?"

"I don't *want* to think," I told her. "It's not my job to think, it's my job to know, and what I know is that you shouldn't be going out with complete strangers who find your number written down somewhere and then you wind up staying out all night."

"Okay, I won't do it anymore."

This stopped me. Never in my life had Sam ever agreed to one of my rules without shouting at me and slamming her bedroom door a few times.

"Can we go on?" Valerie asked sweetly. "Okay. What is Geoff's nickname for Sam's boobs?"

"*What?* That's it, the wedding's off."

"Dad," Valerie said.

"What, Geoff runs around talking about Sam's . . . Sam's . . ." After a lifetime of denying to myself that she even had them, I found it impossible to talk about it now.

"I have to say, I agree with your father," Alecia stated, leading me to believe I was probably wrong. "I don't even like it when my husband *looks* at mine. I'm like, 'Hello, my face is up here.' Oh, wait." Alecia's eyes sparkled. "Did you hear what I just said? My *husband*. I still can't believe it's true." Alecia held up her rings for everyone to ignore.

The correct answer to this offensive question turned out to be "Hot Tamales," which is completely nonsensical and suggestive of an electrical disturbance of the brain.

After a few more questions, the scores were tallied, and I didn't do as well as one might have expected, mainly because my daughter failed to heed the lessons I had taught while raising her.

Sam opened gifts—I gave her a blender, which earned me a slightly puzzled glance since she knew that I knew she already had mine. More sugar was eaten and then the ladies departed, several of them thanking me for being such a good sport about the trivia questions, which suggested that I hadn't been as clear on the whole subject as I'd intended.

Alecia stayed behind, not to help clean, as I would have assumed, but because during the party she felt we had just not gotten enough Alecia. (I imagined she was the only person who felt this way.) She wanted to talk more about her wedding and offer more advice to Sam, which Sam absorbed the way a rock absorbs water. Valerie took down the columns, and Sarah helped me in the kitchen.

"And I have the best news," Alecia announced from the couch. The four of us stopped our cleaning and waited with dread.

"It's about the honeymoon, Sam. I called the manager at our hotel—I got to know him really well while we were there because there were so many problems at first with things not being just right. And guess what. You can have our *same room!*"

Sam and Valerie exchanged a look.

Priscilla and FDR were paying for Sam and Geoff's honeymoon as their wedding gift—a generous gesture, to be sure, but one that had Alecia assuming she now had some say in where the newlyweds would be going, where they would be staying, and even, as we learned over the next half hour, what they would be doing.

"I'll give you a list of everything we did. It's just the sort of thing I do for people," Alecia gushed. "Your second night there you'll want to go to this wonderful fish place we found, the views are fantastic, and if you make a scene they'll give you a table right by the window."

"Alecia, I need to pick up those plates," Valerie said, pointing to some dishes on the coffee table where Alecia was sitting.

"Sure," Alecia said, moving over so Valerie could get them.

Alecia revealed that the sort of things she needed to tell Sam were best discussed over lunch, but as a preview she was willing to give us a description of her honeymoon that took as long to tell as her honeymoon. The four of us started nodding, cleaning up, not really paying attention, though at one point I zeroed in when Alecia said, "And don't let him pressure you to do, you know, 'wifely duties,' or whatever. You're going to be so exhausted, you need time to chill out and enjoy yourself. Men are always, you know, they don't care that you've just had a huge wedding and now you need a vacation, they're always so insistent. I finally had to lay down the law, I mean, come on, this is my honeymoon, too."

Sam and Valerie glanced at each other with a look that I recognized from when they were teenagers and I gave them wise advice about boys. It was not, I belatedly realized, a look of admiring appreciation for the wisdom they were hearing.

By promising to have lunch with her, Sam finally managed to get Alecia out the door. She immediately whirled on me. "Oh my God, Dad! I do not want to go to the same place that she did. I want to have my own honeymoon!"

"I agree!" I said. "Anyway, after she left they probably burned the place down just to get the experience out of their minds."

"I don't want to stay in her room. And what, I'm not going to have sex?"

Whatever I was going to say next was obliterated by her

mentioning the taboo topic. Sarah comfortingly touched my shoulder.

"This is crazy!" Sam fumed.

"Dad, you've got to do something," Valerie agreed.

"I . . . what? *I* have to do something?"

"You can't let Alecia stick her nose in this!" Valerie fumed. "You need to, like, call her mom or something."

Chills went up my spine. "Call . . . Priscilla? Valerie, the woman terrifies me."

"I don't want to go to *France*, I want to go to Hawaii," Sam said.

"I thought they went to French Polynesia," I said.

"Whatever," Sam said. "I don't care. It's my honeymoon, not hers." Tears started leaking down Sam's cheeks.

Valerie turned to me in distress. "You have to do something, Dad!"

"Okay, okay, sure, I'll handle it. Don't cry, honey."

"This whole thing has just gotten so stressful," Sam said.

"I said I'll take care of it. Okay? I'll take care of it."

"Thanks, Dad," Sam said gratefully.

"Thanks, Dad," Valerie echoed.

I nodded, wondering what exactly I was going to do.

ELEVEN

❧

Countdown to Bridal Blastoff

Picture this: A herd of buffalo are standing around in a field, probably saying to one another "Hey, didn't there used to be a lot more of us before those guys showed up with the rifles?" They're munching on whatever it is that buffalo munch on, waiting for the weekend so they can relax. Suddenly, one of them hears a buzzing noise— a bug in his ear! He kicks and all of the other buffalo get nervous, and then the one buffalo panics and then they all panic and stampede into town and trample everyone there.

That's sort of how a wedding goes: We were all just minding our own business and then everyone started panicking about stuff that doesn't really seem very important, like how to decorate the horse-drawn carriage that I thought I vetoed. Next thing you know, we're all being trampled.

(By the way, the women involved in the wedding won't appreciate it if you compare them to a herd of buffalo.)

BRIDAL FITNESS: LIKE JOINING THE MARINES, ONLY WITHOUT THE GAIETY

So maybe they aren't buffalo, but listen to how brides talk about themselves:

"I ate like a pig!"

"I'm fat as a cow!"

When a daughter says these things, the best response is, "Oh, honey, stop it, you're making me crave a bacon cheeseburger."

The problem is that in many wedding ceremonies, the guests wind up with nothing to look at for half an hour but the bride's butt. (Of course, the bride's buttocks are as hidden by the dress as the bride's shoes, but she won't listen to this observation because it would mean not buying new shoes or new buttocks.)

To assist her in celebrating the commercialization of her false body image, my daughter Sam phoned a personal trainer.

"You don't need a trainer, you have me," I reminded her. "I'd be happy to put you through some cardio-vegetable workouts."

My kind offer was ignored, and one day I came home and there was a personal trainer, all teeth and triceps, in my living room talking to my daughters.

"Bruce, good to meet you," he greeted, bounding up from the couch with faux energy. His veins were popping out as he shook my hand, something I thought he should get looked at, maybe rub some of Valerie's organic body-goop into the area twice a day until the blood vessels dissolved. "My name is Smiley Underpants." (It was something like that, anyway.)

My daughters, of course, were all atwitter* that Smiley was there with his supposed muscles and good looks, but I wasn't fooled. I quickly sniffed out the three reasons why we weren't going to be hiring him for his special "Fit 2 B Wed Bridal Total Workout Program™."

1. It involved money.
2. It involved time.
3. It involved me.

"Why would *I* want to do this?" I demanded.

"Dad, you were saying you wanted to lose a few pounds," Valerie reminded me.

"No, *you* were saying that. I said I needed new trousers. Not the same thing."

"Dad, you're my father and I love you. I want you to live a long life," Sam interjected.

"Oh, sure, fight dirty," I retorted.

Smiley grinned at me. I decided that he must have several rows of teeth, like a great white shark taking a chomp out of an unsuspecting swimmer. "Bruce, do you mind if I say something here?"

"Like, good-bye?" I replied hopefully.

"Dad," Valerie said.

Smiley went into a long explanation of how his plan, combining a unique blend of diet and exercise, would make me hungry and sore all the time. "Diet and exercise," I said, nodding. "Wish I had thought of a weight loss plan with such unique elements."

"Dad," Valerie said.

---

* Women appreciate being told they are "atwitter" as much as they appreciate being told they are like buffalo. Just so you know.

"It would be really fun, Dad," Sam said. Of course, this is someone who thinks it is fun to spend all of her vacation time in volleyball tournaments.

We eventually reached a compromise: My two daughters could sign up for the "Fit 2 Wet Beds Program," or whatever it was called, as long as I didn't have to participate. They were pretty disappointed, but I stood firm, and caught them glancing at each other in a way that said "Darn, we were once again unable to manipulate our father into doing something we wanted him to do!" I handed Mr. Smiley Underpants his check and graciously accepted a free copy of his *30 Day No-Excuses Lose Weight and Be Hungry*™ booklet. Just looking at the cover made me ambitious for a buffet.

"Thanks, Dad," my daughters both said. Sometimes, in all the wedding planning and check writing, brides will forget to thank their fathers for going over budget, but my girls had so far been pretty good about it when I reminded them.

IF YOU THINK THINGS ARE UNDER CONTROL, SOMEONE'S GIVING YOU BAD INFORMATION

Six weeks or so before Sam's wedding, I felt it was important that everyone take a moment and congratulate me. Because of my guidance and direction, my oldest child had been able to meet and overcome every challenge, from napkins that couldn't be ordered in the exact right size to whether the dog, who was to be the ring bearer, should wear a garland of flowers and ribbons even though past history suggested he would react to the fancy decorations by eating them. Valerie's wedding was scheduled for May of the following year, which felt further away than the next comet, and Lindy Lou-Who the Obliterator and I had reached an agreement wherein she would keep me informed of important details at all times. (Actually, I told her I wanted to receive regular reports and she said, "We'll see," but I was encouraged.)

The napkin controversy serves as a template for how fathers and their bride-to-be daughters handle wedding emergencies, each putting forth a series of solutions until they reach a compromise.

HELPFUL TEMPLATE FOR PROBLEM SOLVING

Situation: Napkins are the wrong size

DAUGHTER'S SOLUTION	FATHER'S ALTERNATIVE ALTERNATIVE
It's not that the napkins are the wrong size, they are the wrong color! They're supposed to come in Aura, but they came in Amnesty! They don't match anything, the vendor made a mistake and says they can't get the right color here in time! This is horrible! We're going to have to go to another vendor, put in a rush order, and spend 3 times as much!	Let's cancel the wedding.
We're not going to *cancel the wedding*.	Well, look, how bad can it be? I know you wanted Oreo, but I am sure that it's still a nice color, this . . . Euthanasia?
Amnesty! No, they're the color of fungus! We can't use them! We need to get different ones!	Well, look, are you sure we even *need* napkins? Why can't people use their sleeves?

DAUGHTER SOLUTION	REASONABLE FATHER ALTERNATIVE
Oh, and what, save money on silverware, just have the guests tie their hands behind their backs like in a pie-eating contest or something?	Hey, that's not a bad . . .
The only other alternative would be to use cloth napkins, but you didn't want those because of the expense.	Right, we don't want those.
So we need to put in this rush order today!	Well, which is cheaper, the cloth napkins, or the rush order on a bunch of . . . Aural napkins? Orca?
Aura. Well, obviously, the cloth napkins are less expensive, but you said we couldn't afford those.	Honey, this is why you need me in charge of the wedding plan. Can you see how it makes more sense to order the cloth than to have the paper, once all the fees are considered? I initially vetoed cloth because of the expense, so now, logically, we should go with the cheaper alternative again, which is the cloth.
I guess that is more logical.	Of course it is. Now, how do we get our money back from the napkin vendor? We're not paying for a bunch of Appendicitis-colored napkins!
Oh, that's okay, it was only a sample that he sent, so we're not out any money.	That's good.

See how having a firm, controlling hand over all aspects of the wedding makes everyone happier? If the guests arrived at the reception and the napkins were all Oral-colored, they probably would have gone into a frenzy of outrage and looting. With a father's input, however, everything goes smoothly, and I'm sure that after the wedding we'll get lots of nice compliments on the napkins, nobody suspecting what horror might have befallen them.

With all ships sailing so smoothly, I was unprepared for a call from my younger daughter.

"Dad!" Valerie greeted. "We've got a problem."

"Let me guess: Mulchy doesn't want any of your guests exhaling carbon dioxide."

"Dad. No. We're down here at the dress shop getting fitted for the bridesmaids' dresses."

"Oh, yes, how goes the three-hour tour?" I asked. This had become something of a sore point with my daughters—their bridesmaids' fitting was scheduled to take an entire day, whereas my son and I were in and out of the tuxedo shop in half an hour, and that included new underwear. I couldn't see what the big deal was, don't we all get dressed every day?

"We're having an emergency. Can you come down?"

I went to the window and looked out at the clouds, my chest swelling and my cape flapping behind me in the breeze. "Of course," I said, my voice lower. "I'll be right there."

When I arrived at the dress shop, the women were wailing, sobbing, and rolling on the floor, chewing on their own arms. Well, not really, but there was a definite sense that something awful was going on, and that something was Alecia. "This happened at my wedding, too," she was saying to Sam. Now I understood the issue—whatever it was, if it had happened at Alecia's wedding, Sam definitely didn't want it happening at hers. "You just have to pay the extra money. It's the price of getting married," Alecia said, with a flip of her hand that indicated that additional costs of any kind were of no concern to someone like herself.

"Dad," Valerie greeted me. She grabbed my arm and pulled me into a corner to talk. She was wearing a dress in a color I guessed might be "Aura," in a style that I guessed might be "Ludicrous."

Bridesmaids' dresses are deliberately ugly so that as the groom is strolling down the aisle toward his bride, he can glance at the other women and say to himself, "Thank God I'm marrying the hot-looking one. Those other chicks look like balloon accidents."

"All of the dresses are way too big!" Valerie said. "We're going to have to pay for alterations, and that's going to be like two hundred dollars each!"

"Couldn't you all just gain weight?"

"Dad! Plus, Alecia has been here talking about the honeymoon. I thought you were going to tell her that she needed to butt out because Sam and Geoff are going where they want. How come you didn't do that yet?"

"I haven't had time, I've been really busy getting fitted for the tux," I protested.

"Well, look, some of the bridesmaids can't afford to pay another two hundred dollars. Dad, *I* can't afford it! What are we going to do?"

It turned out that the ladies had all ordered their dresses two full sizes too large because they "ran really small." Now that the dresses had arrived, they turned out to be (guess what) two full sizes too large.

I decided I needed some expert opinion on this, and phoned Sarah. I quickly explained the situation to her, then asked her what she thought of my solution, which was to have her come to the store to fix everything.

"We should have ordered the dresses from the same place we got the wedding gown," I groused.

"Which is what I said you should do," Sarah pointed out.

"I don't see how that's relevant, what's done is done."

Sarah starts every morning by drinking a full quart of Google, and even as we spoke I could hear her typing away. "This is a scam!" she pronounced after a moment.

"Weddings?"

"No, the bridesmaids' dresses. The whole thing is a big scam."

"Plus they're very unattractive," I observed.

"They tell you that the dresses run small, but they don't, so when they arrive you have no choice but to pay for alterations. Oh, and sometimes they order the dresses from a different designer, a cheap knockoff place, and not from the designer you saw in the catalogue. They rip the tags out, which is against federal law; the tags have to be in the dress." Sarah read me the regulation.

"Got it," I said, nodding. "So when you get down here . . ."

"I can't, I have a deadline."

"But, Sarah, be reasonable, this is about dresses, for heaven's sake. I mean, if it were antitank weapons or something, I'd help *you* out."

"I would never order antitank weapons in the wrong size."

"Funny."

"Have to run, darling. You can do this, you're in charge of the wedding plan, remember? You're Super Dad!"

Most the time Sarah is a very high-quality girlfriend, but in this instance I felt pretty let down. The only solutions I could see were: (a) persuade the bridesmaids to join some other wedding, (b) tell Sam she couldn't get married, or (c) write some checks to help the ladies out.

I walked around the corner and stopped. From my vantage point I could see my daughter Sam sitting on a couch, Alecia on one side, and the owner of the shop on the other. The woman who owned the shop was thin enough to call Paris Hilton "that fat girl," and she carried with her an air of contempt. Her face was very pretty but cold, her manicured nails the color of the blood she extracted from unsuspecting brides and their friends. Sam's was flushed from upset as the shop owner shook a check at her.

"We can't take a postdated check," she was saying sternly. "It's against policy."

I instantly discerned what had happened: One of Sam's bridesmaids, a girl she'd known since grade school, had been pressed for time and left while the alterations dispute was still going on. She'd bravely left behind her own check to cover the cost of altering her Aura-colored dress, but had requested they not cash it until payday. These were kids, just starting out in life, and their budgets were taking a major whack just paying for the dresses. Another two hundred dollars might break them.

Alecia was nodding in agreement. "It's not done, Sam, it's really tacky, your friend should never have done that to you."

The way Alecia pronounced the word "friend" it sounded like a bad stain, and for some reason, that's what did it for me. I strode forward as if propelled by all the Fathers of All the Brides in history.

"What's your name, again?" I asked bluntly. The shop owner blinked at me.

"I'm Mrs. Mann," she said.

"Why did you advise them to order their dresses so big?"

Mrs. Mann narrowed her eyes. "They run small. You can't alter a dress to make it bigger."

"That's true," Alecia confirmed. "For my own wedding,

we ordered all of the dresses three sizes larger, just to be safe."

"But these dresses aren't small. They're too big. You gave them bad advice." I picked up the dress and looked inside. No tags.

"They can either wear them as is or have them altered. Their choice." Mrs. Mann shrugged. "Not my problem."

"No, you gave them bad advice. You'll have to pay for the alterations yourself."

She looked amused. "Oh, no, that would be against policy."

"It *is* against policy, that's well known," Alecia said.

"You own the store, Mrs. Mann. It's your policy," I stated.

Mrs. Mann glared at me as if wondering how I'd so cleverly figured that out.

"Where are the tags, Mrs. Mann?" I asked.

"What?"

"The tags. There are no tags inside this garment. You're supposed to have tags stating the country of origin, the manufacturer, the fabric, and the cleaning instructions. Removing those tags prior to sale is against federal law."

My daughters were regarding me as if I were performing a magic trick.

"We always remove the tags," Mrs. Mann said. "It's a courtesy to the bride."

"In my wedding . . ." Alecia started to say.

"Shut up, Alecia," I said kindly. Her mouth dropped open. I turned to the shop owner. "You know what, Mrs. Mann? Your store is going to be famous."

She glanced from me to my daughters and their friends, not sure.

"See, I write a newspaper column. And I'm going to write

about how you and your store have a *policy* that brides will be misinformed about the size of the dresses they buy purely as a means of getting them to pay for alterations. And then I'm going to go to the manufacturer listed in the catalogue and ask them if they made this dress, or if it is a cheap knockoff. And then I'm going to call the Federal Trade Commission about your store's *policy* of removing tags that are legally required to be intact. By the time I've run a series of articles about you, Mrs. Mann, everyone in the city will know where *not* to buy their bridesmaids' dresses."

We stood in absolute silence while I fantasized about winning the Pulitzer for blowing the lid off of Mrs. Mann's scam, and Mrs. Mann fantasized about using a gun to blow the lid off me. When she opened her mouth, you could hear the hinges squeak. "I suppose we could do the alterations at a reduced . . ." She saw my baleful expression and revised herself, "At no cost to the bridesmaids. No charge." She swallowed.

"And you're what?" I prompted.

"What?" she asked, puzzled.

I nodded to my daughter. "Tell her."

"Oh." She turned to Sam. "I am very sorry for the misunderstanding."

Out in the parking lot my daughters hugged me as if I'd just invented a cure for split ends. "Dad, that was great!" Valerie told me.

"Where did you get that thing about the tags?" Sam wanted to know.

"Just something I picked up," I explained, shrugging.

"Sarah," Sam guessed.

"Right."

Alecia swung around the corner in her car and pulled up to where we were standing. She drove a convertible because she enjoyed the free and easy access it gave to a view of her. "Sam, let's do lunch soon, we've got stuff we have to talk about!" she called. Valerie and I glanced at each other, realizing we had somehow become invisible to Alecia and that we were grateful for that. Alecia sped away.

"Dad, you have to do something about her," Sam told me.

"Couldn't we just bask in the victory over the Mann woman for a minute before talking about another war?" I asked.

"Dad," Valerie said.

LAST-MINUTE EXPENSES

There are two types of wedding expenses: (1) those you can forecast and plan on and include in your budget, and (2) last-minute expenses you didn't see coming. Both types of expenses will run you over your budget.

For example, the wedding gown isn't the only dress the bride needs to make it through the entire event. She needs:

- The rehearsal dinner dress
- The go to the chapel to get dressed in the wedding dress dress
- The wedding dress
- The wedding reception dress
- The leaving the wedding reception dress
- The visit Dad in debtor's prison dress

The reason you need a rehearsal dinner dress is because it is a very special affair that happens only once in a woman's lifetime, and the reason you need a rehearsal dinner is that the in-laws are paying for it. You need to look your best, so you need a new dress.

A reasonable father might point out that yes, the rehearsal dinner happens only once in a lifetime, but so does everything else. For example, Wednesday, June 11, 2008, happens only once in a lifetime, so do you need a special dress for that?

If you say this to a woman in full bridal mode, she'll respond yes, she needs a special dress for that.

The reason you need a special dress to go to put on your wedding dress is that several informal pictures will be taken of you arriving and you want to look your best.

A reasonable father might respond that the whole point of "informal" pictures is that you not look your best, and anyway I thought you were at your best at the rehearsal dinner, so why not just wear *that* dress?

Because there will also be photographs taken at the rehearsal dinner, and you don't want it to look like you had on the same dress both times!

The reasonable father might then say, okay, so you look your best in some outfit that you wear to put on your wedding dress, which means, logically, that when wearing the wedding dress, you look *less* than your best.

At this point the bride will burst into tears, run from the room, and slam a door somewhere in the house. Congratulations, you've won the battle and lost the war.

What this proves is that when it comes to last-minute expenses, the father is not suppose to ask reasonable questions or make logical statements, because reason and logic are very upsetting to a woman planning a wedding.

REVENGE OF THE FLOWER CHILDREN

Like most men, what I know about flowers comes from the miniseries *Band of Brothers*, based on the book by Stephen E. Ambrose. At one point, an edelweiss flower is found on the uniform of a fallen enemy soldier, and it is explained that the flower is a symbol of bravery—it blooms only above the tree line in the Alps, so any soldier wearing one must have made that mighty climb.*

In a wedding, it's just as hard to find the right flowers as it was for that soldier to retrieve the edelweiss, though in some ways he's to be envied because when he got there, he only had to pick *one* flower, and when he got back from the trip to get it, somebody put him out of his misery with artillery.

"Why don't you pick the flowers from the top of the Alps?" the father will ask sarcastically as he trudges from florist to florist, increasing his allergies with every step.

"Oh, Daddy," he'll be told, "don't be silly, of course we don't want flowers from the top of the Alps. We want flowers from the top of the Himalayas."

My daughter's theme of Neil Diamond meant that all of her flowers needed to be flowers that bloomed in August. (When her reasonable father pointed out that there was this recent invention called the hothouse, he was ignored.) So she was wrestling with breeds of flowers I'd never heard of, like "euphorbia," which sounded like a country in Africa, and "freesia," which sounded like a movement to save the people of Euphorbia.

The ladies' room would be decorated with a flower called "ravioli," which sounded like stuffed pasta.

"Dad," Valerie said. "It's not ravioli, it's gladioli, and anyway we might not do that because it could interfere with the fragrance of the sachets."

"Unless we use scented candles in the ladies' room instead of the sachets," Sam reminded her.

---

* It turns out that the whole edelweiss flower thing is made up, but don't worry, the Second World War itself is still true.

"Right," Valerie said.

"Flowers, sachets, candles?" I sputtered. "What do you women do in there? In the men's room, we feel lucky to have running water!"

Sam took a cell phone call, and her expression went from her normal, "I'm so happy to be getting married it's giving me an ulcer" look to one that said, "I'm getting really bad news from my dentist/doctor/undertaker."

"Uh-huh," Sam said several times. "We haven't decided yet," she said more than once. She also said, "Yellow roses" once, which set off about ten minutes of "uh-huhs." She snapped her cell phone shut and gave us a bright smile. "That was Alecia, reminding me that we agreed that I wouldn't use any of the same flowers from her wedding in mine."

"Why would you agree to that?" Valerie demanded.

"I didn't," Sam responded simply.

"Dad!" Valerie said sternly.

"What? What do you mean, *Dad*. I don't even know what kind of flowers Alecia had in her wedding! I assumed they were fly traps."

"You have to do something about her, Dad," Valerie said.

"Have you told her Geoff and I are going to Hawaii on our honeymoon?"

"Of course! Well, no, not completely. Not yet," I admitted. "I thought I'd wait until, you know . . ."

"Until when?" Valerie demanded.

"Until the honeymoon."

"Dad!"

"Well, I don't see what the hurry is," I said defensively. "We have plenty of time."

"Dad, as soon as Geoff buys the tickets, his mom is going to know," Sam warned, "and Geoff is booking the trip *tomorrow*."

"See? Plenty of time," I said weakly.

I was spared more inquisition by the timely arrival of Mulchy, who was joining us so he and Valerie could go to a meeting with the Lindinator. He looked unhappy to be in a flower shop, a feeling he shared with my wallet. Valerie and Sam both gave him a hug and a kiss, but I elected to pass.

"Sorry I'm late," he apologized. "The station's having a pledge drive."

Valerie relayed the exciting news that lily lived in the valley and that euphorbia had been liberated. "It's a hot pink bloom, perfect for Hot August Nights," she said. I decided I didn't know what she was talking about but that didn't make me a bad father, I just hadn't watched *Band of Brothers* enough to become a total expert in flowers.

"Did you know that a lot of flowers are grown in Southeast Asia by nonunion workers?" Mulchy asked Sam.

Valerie slid her arm through his and laughed lightly. "Come on, Marty. We're off to see Lindy!"

WHY MOLDY IS IN A BAD MOOD

Good Old Moldy's face seemed trapped in such a scowl, I was afraid his expression wouldn't improve until someone gave him a shot of Botox. Apparently he'd promised Valerie that he wouldn't say anything about Sam's nuptials, which he viewed to be a crass waste of money better spent on things like public radio. He had strong views about how his wedding to Valerie was going to be different, which was unusual because normally the groom offers very few opinions for the bride to ignore. Most of his opinions I was able to glean from his occasional remarks, and for the most part they seemed to be less about what he wanted than what he didn't want, and why.

MULCHY OR MOLDY'S REASONS TO BE AGAINST THINGS NORMALLY FOUND IN A WEDDING

WEDDING ITEM	MOLDY'S REASONS FOR BEING AGAINST IT	FATHER'S REASONABLE RESPONSE
Flowers	A flower is a plant performing reproduction. Why cut it off in the middle of such a wonderful act?	If you never buy Valerie flowers, it's you who's going to be cut off from "wonderful acts."
Food	It's wrong to kill living things for our own use.	Aren't plants living things? Don't we kill vegetables all the time? When was the last time a bunch of carrots were used in a salad and *survived*?
Joy	With so many things going wrong in the world, it is hypocritical for us to be celebrating anything.	Hey, what gave you the idea I was celebrating? I'd be happy to call the whole thing off. Besides, it's probably best for you and Valerie not to leave town; we still haven't found a babysitter for your highway.
Appliances	Washers, dryers, dishwashers, and the like were all bad for the environment. Moldy lived with his parents and was angry that his mother used these appliances. When he got married, he and Valerie would move into their own place and do without them.	Sure you will.

After they walked out the door, I turned to face Sam. "If he's so against humans, why is he marrying one?"

"Dad, he's only twenty-four years old," Sam responded. "Remember being that age?"

"No, actually, I don't," I said frankly. "Do you think they're right for each other?"

"What? Of course!" Sam responded indignantly.

"Okay," I replied in retreat. There are some subjects that are taboo around a wedding between two people, like, the two people.

Sam's cell phone rang. She looked at the caller ID, then at me. "Alecia," she said.

I knew what she was going to ask before she asked it.

"When are you going to do something about her?"

TWELVE

The Calm Before the Storm Is Not So Calm

The days leading up to a wedding can put a lot of strain on relationships. For example, the same day that we decided to purchase the nonunion Southeast Asian flowers with names like perturbia and glad-a-roni, I phoned my friend Tom and asked him if he would do me the small favor of calling Priscilla and informing her that my daughter and her son would not be going to French Polynesia and sleeping in the Alecia King-Hoyt Memorial Bedroom. His response was to decline, which I felt put a strain on our friendship.

"This puts a strain on our friendship," I informed him icily. "I thought you told me you'd do anything for me, even take a bullet for me."

"Yeah, but not this."

"What are you afraid of?" I challenged.

"Nothing. I just don't like the way she looks. She reminds me of W. C. Fields."

"That's no reason not to call her!" I snapped. "W. C.

219

Fields was a *comedian.* He never hurt anybody. And anyway, it's Winston Churchill."

"Then why don't you call her? Churchill was on our side."

"Like that makes any sense at all," I fumed. I rang off, took a deep breath, and dialed the number Sam had given me.

Priscilla answered and, once I had reminded her of who I was, seemed glad I'd called. While we exchanged pleasantries, I heard an extension pick up, but the mystery person remained unidentified and was probably just the FBI listening in because they suspected Priscilla was a hit man for the mob.

"I assume you're calling about the flowers," she said.

This stopped me. "The flowers?"

"This was discussed back when Sam changed the wedding date. You understand Alecia's concern, I'm sure—she's worried that some of the same flowers will be in Sam's wedding."

"Sam and Geoff's," I said for clarification, wondering if this woman remembered it was also her son's wedding.

"Of course," Priscilla growled.

"Actually, I don't remember much about the flowers that were picked except that they had weird names," I admitted to Priscilla. "Anyway, I don't see what the big deal will be, so what if the flowers are the same?"

At that moment I knew who was on the extension: Alecia. I could somehow identify her by her silent indignation.

"Well, Bruce," Priscilla answered darkly, "our children deserve to have distinct weddings, with distinct themes, colors, and flowers. Due to the change in schedule—"

"I'm sorry, that's not why I'm calling," I interrupted. Normally I'm willing to get into an argument over something I know nothing about, but the truth was I didn't care about the flowers—if Priscilla insisted on discussing the matter, I would give her Moldy's number. "It's the honeymoon. Sam and Geoff have elected to go to Hawaii instead of Bora-Bora.

That's where they want to go, plus it turns out the trip will be less expensive that way." At least, I hoped this last part was true. "So, well, good talking to you, Priscilla."

The telephone wire was positively vibrating with Alecia's outrage.

"Mr. Cameron," Priscilla replied, "I don't understand. Alecia has already made arrangements. This was all settled weeks ago."

"I'm not sure if I understand why it is not okay for my daughter to have the same flowers, but it is okay for her to have the same honeymoon. It doesn't make any sense."

There was a long pause, during which Alecia left the call with an aggressive click. Seconds later I could hear her whispering furiously to her mother in the background.

"Mr. Cameron, when my husband and I agreed to pay for the honeymoon, we naturally assumed . . ."

Assumed what, that it would be yet another opportunity to indulge their daughter? I'd had it. "Then we'll have to decline your kind offer. I'll pay for their honeymoon myself."

I heard my credit cards gasp in shock.

For a moment Priscilla was silent. "I am so sick of you people," she finally said, ending the call with a slam. I stared at the phone in disbelief. "She just hung up on me," I told it.

I wasn't sure what this meant for the future of my relationship with the King family.

What it meant was that a few hours later Geoff called me to apologize. "I didn't know this thing with my mom and Alecia. Sam tries to keep me out of stuff like this because she's afraid I'll kill my sister. I've been dealing with my dad about it the whole time. *He* knew we were going to Hawaii."

"Don't worry about it," I replied, reflecting on the fact that FDR hadn't informed his wife about the change in plans. He must be as afraid of her as I was.

"Thanks for offering to pay for it, that was really classy. You've done so much for us. I really appreciate it."

"You're welcome, Geoff," I said sincerely. I hung up, thinking that while he and my daughters had repeatedly thanked me for spending MasterCard's money and for all my work in Wedding Crisis Central, Moldy or Mulchy had never done anything but act petulant that I wasn't doing more to overthrow capitalism. Though they were only four or five years apart, Geoff seemed to be a generation ahead of Valerie's fiancé in maturity. And that wasn't good.

OFFICE OF AL & TIPPER GORE

July 18, 2007

W. Bruce Cameron

Dear Bruce:

Thank you for inviting Former Vice President Gore to be an officiant at your daughter's wedding.

As you may know, Mr. Gore has recently finished writing a book called "The Assault on Reason," released in May 2007. He is also engaged in a campaign to educate people about the climate crisis facing our nation, and indeed, our world. He continues to travel extensively in this endeavor, recently surpassing the 1,000 mark of individuals being trained all over the world to help in the mission and learn how to present his climate change slideshow in their own voices.

As a result of the related demands on his time, Mr. Gore will unfortunately be unable to participate.

Again, thank you for thinking of Mr. Gore and best of luck with the wedding!

Sincerely,

Stacy Schumaker

P.S. Please note that our office is not offering comments, letters or endorsements for events at this time.

2100 WEST END AVENUE • SUITE 620 • NASHVILLE, TN • 37203 • PHONE: 615-327-2227 • FAX: 615-327-1323

PRINTED ON RECYCLED PAPER

Do Not Talk About Fight Club

I knew that Tom and I would eventually repair the damage done to our friendship by him being such a coward. I'm not the sort of person to hold a grudge, particularly against a long-time friend like Tom, in whom I trusted to always have a flat-screen television.

Sam and Geoff had fought over her perception that he didn't seem to care about the many critical details of the wedding that were keeping her awake at night, but he calmed her down by assuring her he did care, very, very much, and we all felt better that even though they weren't yet married, he had already learned that when it comes to disputes like this, the best thing a man can do is lie. When I asked, Sam denied that she and Geoff had been fighting. Marty and Valerie were fighting because apparently they had agreed that he wouldn't try to inject his political opinions into Sam's wedding, and he felt that commenting on the origins of Sam's flowers was not political but socioeconomic. When I asked, Valerie denied they had been fighting. Finally, Alecia was refusing to speak to Geoff, which everyone agreed was as wonderful a wedding gift as she could have given him. When I asked, everyone agreed they were fighting.

In the final days before a wedding, the bride carries around lists of things to do, to which she keeps adding tasks but never seems to cross any off. The list is ordered in priority and looks like this:

To Do

1. Panic
2. Freak out
3. Have an anxiety attack
4. Repeat

THE OLD MAN TURNS OUT NOT TO BE COMPLETELY USELESS AFTER ALL . . . JUST SORT OF USELESS

There are several things a father can do during the final days before the wedding that will assist the daughter so she can concentrate her energies on her mental breakdown.

Marriage License. It's easier to get a license to marry than it is to get a license to catch walleye. Apparently the government doesn't care who gets married and has children, but they are very particular about who catches their fish! At any rate, the father can contact the local county clerk to find out the exact requirements and endear his family to the government by complaining about the fishing license, all in one phone call. Then the father can assemble the documents—birth certificates, etc.—place them together in a manila envelope, and then forget where he put the thing. (That's what I did, anyway. Hint to fathers: Check your car's glove box.) There's also a blood test and, of course, fees for everything, none of which were in the original budget because who equates "the happiest day of my life" with "paying money to the government." Fathers usually take the position that if an item was included in the original budget, they'll pay for it, but if an item wasn't budgeted, they'll refuse to pay for it and then pay for it.

Pack for the Honeymoon. Chances are that your daughter thinks of Hawaii as being a tropical paradise, but doesn't realize that in August the temperature can sometimes dip down to a chilly 74°F. The father can make sure she packs plenty of bulky sweaters and jackets to cover the ridiculously tiny bikini that no daughter of his is going to wear and I don't care if she *is* married. (Hint to fathers: Don't try to hide the bikini in the glove box in your car; they'll find it while looking for the marriage license paperwork.)

Seating Chart. Nothing is more aggravating than trying to arrange for a hundred people to sit down in such a fashion that none of them is next to Alecia. It's also vexing that an exact body count seems to elude everyone—this is a wedding, you should know how many people are going to show up! Does NASA say, "We're going to launch in ten minutes with somewhere between three and six astronauts?" (Sarah pointed out to me that whenever I spoke about this wedding, I compared it to a military operation or a moon mission. "Well, duh," I said.)

At any rate, the father can help because men don't get emotionally mixed up in personalities when they don't know any of the people involved. So putting two former roommates next to each other even though they've each vowed to kill the other causes no particular concern for the father. Ultimately, people are going to get up and sit where they want as soon as dinner's over anyway, right? (Hint to fathers: Don't say this out loud to your daughter; it's like telling Green Bay that Congress has outlawed football.)

Phone Everyone in the World. That's what it will seem like, anyway. It turns out that other people have been living normal lives and not spending every waking and sleeping moment thinking about your daughter's wedding. Does the chair vendor remember he's supposed to deliver chairs? Of course he does, but your daughter will feel a lot better knowing that you bugged the guy with a phone call. Are the flowers "okay?" ("Some of the flowers are nervous," I reported. Nobody laughed.) Is the caterer prepared to cater? How about the minister, is he still religious?

Handle the Invasion. Incoming relatives will get scattered like paratroopers on W-Day. Most of them will prove so

incapable of following even the most rudimentary direc-
tions you'll question the wisdom of anyone with your last
name ever reproducing again. They'll also feel it necessary
to call you with updates, what I decided to call "lack-of-
progress reports."

"Your father is still getting dressed. We have to leave for
the airport," my mother calls to report in a tone that suggests that most of the blame falls on me for having done
such a poor job of picking a father.

"Your mother isn't even packed!" my father roars, picking up the extension.

"Don't come," I suggest.

"I *am* packed, I just need your father to put some things
of mine in his suitcase. He has plenty of room."

I picture that when my parents introduce themselves
to other people for the first time, they'll say, "I am Bruce's
mother, and this is Bruce's father."

They eventually decide that arguing with each other on
the phone with me listening in makes no sense because if
they can just get to the airport they can have arguments in
front of the whole family.

Rally the Troops. The good thing about a family is that
when a crisis hits, they tend to face the challenge together,
and, under the father's leadership, can handle nearly any
difficulty. The bad thing is that no one sees it this way
except for the father. In fact, the only conscript in my personal army turned out to be my son, who tended to drift to
a halt unless I was watching him.

"Your job is to go to the store and get last-minute stuff for
the women," I told him.

"Not feminine products!" he responded, horrified.

"No, not those. I mean, they wouldn't ask us to do that."
I swallowed. What if they did?

"The stuff they want doesn't even make sense, it's like powder to make them look flushed, and masks for their eye. I'll take Terri with me, she'll know what they want."

"I think Terri will probably want to gather with the rest of the women in a big freak-out session," I speculated.

"What I'll do is just go to the store and buy something at complete random, and then they'll be all, 'men are stupid' and they'll ask Terri to help me."

"I can see that you're getting a good education at that college of yours," I said admiringly. "Okay, also I need you to pick up Cousin Tina at the airport."

"Who?"

"Cousin Tina. You'll recognize her, she looks a lot like Cousin Ted."

THE FATHER IS TOAST

At some point, the father of the bride is supposed to say a few words, and "Can anyone here loan me some money?" is not considered appropriate. The bride depends upon him to put into loving prose some glowing things about his daughter's marriage, with emphasis placed on how fantastic it is to enlarge the family so that it includes people who hang up on you.

For some men, standing up in front of a group of people and being engaging and delightful comes naturally, and we call these men "Jay Leno." For those of us on a different channel, we need to carefully prepare for the toast by writing out what we will say and then reading our words in a halting, stilted voice, as if they are part of an indictment.

With Geoff, I had to think of what I knew about him, which was, well, that his name was Geoff. Also he'd been hanging around the house for a long time, and wasn't he the guy who mowed the lawn for me once, or was that good old Mulchy? I decided to make my toast as meaningful as I could without getting into a lot of details.

TOAST FOR MY DAUGHTER SAM'S WEDDING— FIRST DRAFT

Geoff, when I first met you, I thought
[stay away from my daughter]
that you were a fine young man
[probably were a model prisoner]
who came from a good family
[because I hadn't met any of them yet].
I decided you
[should go away]
were welcome into my home
[where you promptly ate all my food].

(Next I would turn and address my daughter.)
And Sam, like most fathers of such a beautiful girl, I've always wanted
[you to be a nun]
for you to have the very best
[of all the appliances in my home, which is good because you took them]
in life, and have done everything in my power
[not to kill you when you were a teenager]
to raise you to appreciate a good thing when you saw it, and Geoff is certainly a good thing!

(Pause for lots of laughter.)
This wedding is really

[more than I can afford]

about the coming together of two people who love each other, and of two families

[who don't]

joining to help celebrate that love. Everyone, would you please

[contribute cash]

raise your glasses to the wonderful young couple, my daughter and my new

[gulp]

son-in-law!

LET FREEDOM RING, ONE LAST TIME

A few days before the wedding, the groom will have a bachelor party, a ritual that makes as much sense as spending the night before a dog show letting the dog roll in dead fish. You're in the final countdown to a ceremony celebrating your love for one woman, so why not imperil the whole thing with some drunken debauchery? The notion seems to be that since you have thought about it long and hard and made the commitment to get married, you should have a party and give your friends one last shot at talking you out of it.

That's not the stated purpose, of course—this is a bunch of men we're talking about here, they don't really *have* a purpose. But sooner or later the conversation will inevitably turn to something like this:

FRIEND: *So you're getting married.*

GROOM: *Yep.*

FRIEND: *The old ball and chain! No more fun nights for you, no sir.*

GROOM: *Yep.*

FRIEND: *Tied down to one woman. Got to do everything she says from now on. Drive a minivan. Do the dishes. No more ball games, now you'll be at the opera, or at a garden party. It's yes, dear, what can I do for you, dear, from now on.*

GROOM: *Yep.*

FRIEND: *So long manhood! Pee sitting down! Dress like a little girl!*

The married men who are at the party will object, saying it is not that bad, their wives aren't in control of what they do, and then they'll check their watches and realize they said they'd be home by now, so they'll run out the door.

The reason that the single men will deride the decision to settle down with one woman is that males want to be free to pursue as many relationships with as many women as we possibly can, which for the vast majority of us is nearly none. We'll warn the soon-to-be-married man that he is giving up his *freedom.*

The Seven Sacred Freedoms of the Single Man

1. The freedom to spend any night alone, safe from bothersome female companionship.
2. The freedom to treat every day as a special, unique opportunity to have a gloriously fun time watching the game with your buddies exactly as you've done a million times before.
3. The freedom to be sick, to endure problems, to make mistakes, and to encounter hardships without the added encumbrance of someone caring about you.

4. The freedom from the distracting and irritating things women do, like have sex with you.
5. The freedom from having to share your stuff with someone else, stuff like the laundry and cooking and balancing the checkbook.
6. The freedom to be irresponsible and carefree and spend your money however you (and only you!) see fit and wind up at age forty with your most valuable assets a six-year-old Porsche and a snowboard.
7. The freedom from getting all caught in that deadly emotional trap of having a woman adore you and want you to be happy for the rest of your life.

SOME ENCHANTED EVENING

Geoff's bachelor party was scheduled to take place at the exact same time as an event that I thought would probably tame any excessive wildness on the groom's part: Sam's bachelorette party. It wasn't lost on him that he was marrying a woman who was at least as competitive as Lance Armstrong—anything he did, she would seek to outdo. But when I heard that his send-off was going to be held at a "gentlemen's club," I decided that perhaps, as an added precaution, Geoff could use a little dose of future father-in-law. I announced that I would be delighted to attend the party, responding to an invitation that was uttered by no one.

Apparently the "gentlemen" who normally attended the club were taking the night off, because when we arrived I didn't see anyone at the bar who didn't look like he was violating his parole. Geoff's friends were a boisterous group of young men, many of them fellow employees at the Internal Revenue Service (you know how fun-loving *those* guys can be!). They shuffled into the dimly lit, loud, humid room, all of them pasting grins on their faces as if by collective force of will they could make the place less depressing.

A woman pounced on us the moment we sat down, a woman with missing clothing. Her inadequate outfit was built of flashy metals and thin straps, as if she were an alien from a planet where the residents breathed through their skins. I frowned at the science-fiction skank of it, wanting to phone her father.

She offered us drinks at a price that reflected the establishment's determination to use only the best of profit margins. "This one's getting married in a few days!" chirped the guy sitting next to Geoff. The waitress gave Geoff a cool appraisal.

"We'll see about making your evening extra special, then," she leered.

"I'm the bride's father," I felt it was time to say. The men sitting around Geoff deflated as if I'd just declared a ban on tax audits.

There is simply no better feeling than using the Power of Dad to hose the testosterone off of a bunch of young men.

Glumly, the men turned to watch the entertainment, which consisted of a nearly naked woman trying to bend a large brass pole. Music thumped into the room, rattling us like depth charges. Neon lights suggested gaiety and fun were being had at that very moment somewhere in the place, though most of the fellows at the bar merely looked morose. One man stared at the label on his beer bottle as if his fortunes depended on him finding the hidden meaning of the word "Budweiser," while the guy next to him watched the woman dancing, gazing at her without expression or movement or pulse.

"To great times!" one of Geoff's friends called when the drinks arrived. I guess that since he didn't specifically suggest that the great times were being had *here*, the auditors at the table decided to allow the statement. Glass clinked.

Another woman, wearing an outfit that I gave a 4 on the 1-to-5 Father Disapproval Scale, approached our table and beamed at all of us as if she found us all irresistibly attractive.

"Buy me a drink?" she suggested.

The men gaped at her—perhaps this sort of thing didn't happen as often as you'd think in their line of work. "Sure," one of them finally responded weakly.

"I'll have a Champagne surprise," the woman told our waitress, who nodded—perhaps this woman had ordered this drink before. "I'm Tawny," she introduced herself. "Thanks for the drink!" (It cost twelve dollars.)

Her drink arrived. It had no Champagne in it—surprise!

"So, would you guys like a private dance?" Tawny asked seductively.

Everyone swiveled to look at me as if I were the mob leader. "Hey." I shrugged. "It's up to Geoff, the man who will be marrying my daughter and becoming a permanent member of my family in less than three days."

A small smile played across Geoff's lips. "We'll just stick with the show on the stage," he said.

Tawny pouted, disappointed that all she'd been able to frisk from us was twelve dollars for a one-ounce glass of watery orange juice. She flounced off.

I noticed that above the bar, a flat-screen TV displayed a NASCAR race. I wondered at the logic: Men who found naked women boring but were excited by the sight of a bunch of cars zooming around in circles would come to this place and spend six bucks a beer to hang out?

A couple of hours later, though, I noticed that the guys around the table, when they weren't all excited about the deductible nature of Roth IRAs or whatever it was that they were talking about, tended to spend more time watching NASCAR than they did the dancing women. There is something about a woman acting seductive when she is actually completely uninterested that is less than captivating.

I took stock of the ennui settling in at the table and decided that my work was done. I announced I was clearing out, the young men perking up as if this would change *everything*.

"Thanks for coming," Geoff told me, the small smile still on his face. Though he wasn't the designated driver for his group, he looked as sober as I was. "I'm right behind you, this was . . . well, the guys pretty much insisted on it."

"Just be good," I told him, giving him one more blast of Dad Power as I shook his hand.

In the car I called my daughter. "If you're calling to report on Geoff about something, I don't want to hear it," she warned me when she heard my voice.

"I wasn't going to say anything," I protested mildly.

"Why," she said suspiciously, "did something happen? Never mind! I don't want to know."

"What about you, how did your thing go, your bachelorette party."

"It was fun. We had a good time."

"But not too good a time," I replied, switching my Dad Power voice back on.

"Dad, Alecia was there. How much fun could we have?"

"You invited Alecia?" I asked, surprised.

"No. Geoff just sort of announced she was going."

"Ah," I said. We said good-bye and hung up. "Touché, Geoff," I said aloud.

THE FINAL INSOMNIA

In Charles Dickens's famous novella about insomnia—*A Christmas Carol*—Scrooge is visited during the night by a bunch of ghosts and forced to contemplate the very nature of his own existence. Then he goes out and spends all his money on other people.

This is exactly what it is like to be the father of the bride on the eve of her rehearsal dinner: You're trying to sleep, but the ghost of MasterCard Future keeps rattling your chains. Wide awake, you stare into the darkness and ask yourself just what the heck you think you are doing.

Your daughter can't get *married*. Just a few years ago she was learning to drive, running around town doing errands for you, dropping things off at different places, things like the transmission. Didn't you have to kiss all of her dolls before she would go to sleep at night, when was the last time you did that, six months ago?

And who is this Geoff? He said he worked for the IRS, but didn't men often lie about having glamorous jobs in order to snare desirable women? Weren't there bands of roving con artists who would pretend to be from solid families in order to lure in unsuspecting daughters and then kidnap them and force them to work in shoe factories? Wasn't the planet being watched by alien beings who coveted the beauty of your daughter and who could create an android to get her to fall in love and then whisk her off to their ship for gruesome experiments?

In forty-eight hours she won't be in your family anymore, she'll be in her own family, a family with Geoff, a virtual stranger! What if she has a daughter like Alecia? What if he gets a job transfer to a remote arctic weather station? (Okay, maybe the IRS doesn't do that very often.) What if your daughter needs you and Geoff won't let her call you?

That's the one that stabs you right in the heart. What if she needs you? How could a daughter *not* need her father? But now it will be up to Geoff to help her when she's in trouble, and he's not up to the job, no one is up to the job but you, you're the father!

When the sun rises you'll be as awake as you were when it set. You'll drain the coffee from the pot (no more instant coffee; Sam got a coffeemaker at her bridal shower) and pour your concerns out to your dog, who will listen attentively, hoping your rant will eventually lead to toast.

You're twenty-four hours away from the wedding day.

Burying the Hatchet With (Not in) Your In-Laws

The most false confidence-building moment in the entire wedding process is the wedding rehearsal—basically, a group of people practice walking in a straight line, as if preparing themselves for a sobriety checkpoint. Then they practice standing, or, in the father's case, sitting. I've seen quilting videos with more drama.

Everyone tensely concentrates on their movements as if learning the opening number for *Hairspray*. "Too fast!" the minister warns as the bridesmaids come up from the back of the church. "Too slow!" he says a minute later. "Okay, just right," he finally says.

What my daughter has always wanted, a wedding officiated by Goldilocks.

I'd been dreading the rehearsal because it meant coming face-to-face with Priscilla, and I don't have a concealed weapons permit. Surprisingly, though, she was dour, grumpy, and cold toward me, so I guess I was forgiven.

The seating arrangements took some thought, because ours, like so many families, had been reassembled using inferior parts like the Fop. Obviously I'd sit next to Sarah and Judy would sit next to her husband, but should we be in the same pew? I was the last to sit, so should I sit in the aisle across from Priscilla, or should I slide down so the two mothers were on the aisle? Should the Fop wear a suit that cost more than the wedding gown? Issues like this were discussed at length, even though the minister had encountered situations like ours a million times before, because everything about a wedding has to be discussed at length or it's not a real wedding.

Once that issue was settled, all eyes turned toward my daughter's Labrador, Duke. The dog had a satin saddle tied to his back and was to trot down the aisle, moving neither too slow nor too fast, and take the ring to Geoff. Sam always claims that Duke is a lot smarter than my own dog, which is a bit like saying a hamster is smarter than a carrot.

"Duke brought the engagement ring, so it's only right that he brings the wedding ring," Sam explained to me in what I supposed passed for logic in her wedding-fevered brain.

After the bridesmaids moved at precisely the correct place down the aisle to take up position, Duke was brought up and positioned at the back of the church.

"Come easy, Duke! Come easy!" Geoff called softly. In my opinion, "Come easy," as commands go, was probably two words too long, but apparently they'd been working on this. His ears dropping in concentration, Duke moved toward Geoff at a sedate pace, and he mounted the steps and stood next to the groom without hesitation.

"Good boy," Geoff praised. I thought about my own dog, who instead of executing complicated tasks was, at that moment, probably at home pawing through my trash can.

The ring was handed to Geoff's best man, whom I recognized from what I had come to think of as the Night of Nudity and Tax Law. My son Chris stepped forward and led Duke away from the pulpit, shooting me a look to let me know he was burdened with a lot of important jobs and didn't have time to do the things I'd instructed via voice mail. (I've known my son all his life and can easily read his expression when he's trying to get out of doing chores.)

Then it was my turn.

"Ready?" Sam whispered. She clutched my arm with strong confidence. We stepped forward, hesitated, then stepped forward again in a stuttering gait that made us look like we were picking our way through messes made by Duke. It's what Sam wanted, though, step pause step.

"I've been trying to reach you, your voice mail is full," I whispered sideways to her.

"I know, I keep getting messages from Alecia," she replied through clenched teeth.

"*That's* why this is so enjoyable, Alecia's not here!" I exclaimed.

"Well, she'll be at the dinner." I gave Sam a look. "Her parents are paying for it, so what choice do I have." She shrugged.

"How about you and I just go out for a burger, instead?" I suggested lightly. But as soon as I said it, the funny dropped right out of it for me—what if we could do that, just my daughter and me, out for a burger? I could remember when the two of us would run errands together on Saturday afternoons, Sam lecturing me from her car seat. For a long time she had no front teeth and it took her an hour to chew through a hamburger, chatting the whole time, while I nodded and stole her french fries. But now look at her, my little girl, getting *married*.

Then, God help me, when the minister asked "Who gives this woman in marriage," I was supposed to answer with a firm "Her mother and I do," but instead my voice quavered and tears filled my eyes. Everyone smiled at me as if I hadn't lost my mind, and Sam patted my arm in a way that choked me up even more.

How was I going to make it through this? I slumped into my

seat, relieved to at least have my part in the rehearsal over.

"Let's do that again!" the minister said brightly.

ANOTHER LAST SUPPER

The rehearsal dinner brings together the families of the bride and groom, letting everyone establish the foundation for the relationships that will characterize the next half century of grudges and resentments. There's an overall tension in the room, which a lot of families address with alcohol.

Alecia and her husband were, of course, late. "I know, I know!" Alecia called as she burst into the room, the doors flying open as if she were leading an assault (which, in some ways, I felt she was). She modestly dipped her eyes and ran her hands over her dress so we'd all know it was something special. "This is going to be so much fun!" she told us, clapping her hands.

With Alecia there, the conversation shifted from Sam's wedding to hers, which was fine by me. My emotions needed a break.

Finally, Geoff's father stood, clinking his glass. "Today," he said sonorously, "in a day that will live in infamy . . ."

Actually, that's not what he said. He said, "We have nothing to fear but fear itself, though my wife gives some people the willies," or maybe just something pleasant about how our two families were coming together so nicely except Alecia. (Maybe I added the "except Alecia" part in my own head.)

We drank a toast, the party wound down, and I left, kissing both my daughters on their cheeks. "Get to bed early," I told Sam.

"I will," she promised, her eyes sparkling. "Tomorrow at this time, I'll be married!"

Of course, it wasn't as easy as all that.

THIRTEEN

≈

Cold Feet on a Hot August Night

Abride's wedding day begins like any other day except for the throwing up. She'll look in the mirror to see what a night of sleeplessness does to the female face, and realize that in just a few hours, she's going to throw up again.

The groom, of course, has a pretty tense day ahead of him as well.

WEDDING DAY FINAL TASK LIST	
BRIDE'S LIST	GROOM'S LIST
Wake up to early alarm.	Wake up, unsure what woke you.
Bathe, fret over blemish.	
Meet maid of honor, go over *her* task list.	
Call church, make sure everything is okay.	

BRIDE'S LIST	GROOM'S LIST
Try to eat something.	Have breakfast.
Call florist, check on status of flowers.	
Call mother, make sure she has dress ready to go.	
Call father, make sure he's awake and stressed out.	Watch the game.
Double-check something old, new, borrowed, blue.	
Handle last-minute caterer question.	
Call to make sure horse survived the night and will be there.	
Receive call from florist; no one at church to let him in.	
Call minister, get someone to let in florist.	
Call reception hall, make sure someone is there to let in florist.	Bathe, shave.
Do hair and makeup to get ready to go have your hair and makeup done.	Get dressed.
Make sure best man has rings.	
Have hair done.	
Put on church arrival dress.	
Give directions to lost relatives.	
Have makeup applied.	
Arrive at church	Arrive at church.
Call mother, where is dress?	
Help bridesmaids with their dresses.	
Put on wedding dress.	

BRIDE'S LIST	GROOM'S LIST
Take call from Tom, curious about quality of cake. Point out it wouldn't be right for you to have eaten any yet.	
Get married.	Get married.

THE BRIDE LETS HER HAIR DOWN

With nothing better to do (the father of the bride's schedule is only slightly more active than the groom's) I wandered over to see how the bridal hair and makeup show was going.

Sam's apartment looked as if some people had wanted to have a food fight but had wound up tossing clothing at one another instead. Her mother Judy was attempting to pick up some of the clothes while talking on a cell phone to someone about adding a few last-minute people to the reception dinner guest list, though a quick glance at my own phone confirmed she wasn't talking to *me*, the person I felt should have been consulted first. Sam was sitting in a chair in the living room, a large mirror propped up before her. A woman hairdresser was holding Sam's long, thick hair on top of her head. "Are you sure?" the woman was asking.

Alecia stood by with her hands on her hips. "Of course she wants it up. Sam, don't you remember my wedding?" Alecia turned to the hairdresser. "My stylist cost a *fortune*. He does all the local celebrities."

"I see," said Sam's stylist.

I decided to sit this one out. Valerie leaned forward so she could see her own face in the mirror, as if that helped. Judy hung up and came over to see what the controversy was, meeting my eyes curiously. I shrugged, indicating with silent hand gestures that either Sam didn't want her hair up or that her brain had just exploded with the force of a grenade, depending on how you interpreted it. Judy frowned at me.

"Are you sure, Sam?" Valerie asked doubtfully.

"You don't have your hair down on your *wedding day*," Alecia pronounced scornfully.

"Geoff fell in love with a girl with long hair. The only time I wore it up, he didn't like it," Sam declared.

"Geoff's not here," Alecia pointed out.

"Yes, but he'll be at the wedding, though, don't you think?" Sam asked sweetly.

The stylist stood passively by, waiting for Sam to make a decision. Alecia, however, had made hers.

"Don't listen to her," Alecia told the stylist. "It's a wedding. She has to have her hair up. I'm going to have my hair up, and I'm not even the one getting married!"

"That's right, Alecia. You're not the one getting married," Sam said, an edge in her voice.

"Sam," Valerie said.

"God, Sam, you're not even *thinking*," Alecia snapped. "What about your pictures? Ten years from now do you want to be looking at your wedding album and there your hair is down like you're some trailer trash who had to get married because she got pregnant? I'm trying to help you."

Judy, having her first full-on Alecia Moment, could only gape. I tried to indicate with hand gestures that now *my* brain was exploding, and Valerie turned and stared at Alecia in disbelief.

Sam stood up.

Now, I've been watching Sam stand up for all her life. I

was there the first time she did it, in fact. But I've never seen her rise with such resolute power, the female athlete inside her suddenly the dominant force in the room. "I don't want your help, Alecia."

"Oh, Sam," Alecia started to say.

"I don't want your help, I don't want your advice. I don't want to hear your voice or see you for the rest of the day. In fact, I don't want you at my wedding, Alecia."

"What?"

"You are not invited to my wedding."

"You can't . . ."

Sam didn't say another word, but she took a step forward, and Alecia couldn't help herself, she took a step back. Furious, she glanced at each of us, not seeing an ally in any quarter. When Alecia's look fell on me, her eyes narrowed, and I knew my relationship with her was over, and the relief I felt was tinged with gladness.

"You *people*," Alecia hissed. Her face flushed with rage, she whirled and stomped from the room, closing the door to Sam's apartment with enough impact to wake up the seismographs at the U.S. Geological Survey. After the echoes died down, I lifted my hands to applaud, but before I could do so, Sam burst into tears.

Judy and Valerie rushed forward to comfort her, while all I could do was shrug at the hairstylist, making hand gestures that she couldn't interpret, either.

For a second there, I thought I'd understood what was going on.

SAVING FACE

Caller ID advised Sam that Priscilla phoned four times over the next fifteen minutes, so Sam didn't answer. When Geoff called, though, she took the cell phone with her into her bedroom and closed the door.

"Oh my God, Dad," Valerie said to me when Sam was out of the room.

"In my experience, sometimes when your leg is in a trap, you have to gnaw it off," I replied simply.

Valerie blinked at me. "When was your leg ever in a trap?"

"Well, not my leg."

"So you chewed off someone *else's* leg?" she demanded.

"I'm not saying that, I'm just saying that Sam did the right thing. Valerie, the important thing here is that we finally stood up to Alecia."

"Right. *We* did. That's the important thing," Valerie said, trying to make her voice sound sarcastic or something. "What's Sam going to do now? Alecia's going to be her sister-in-law!"

"Well, that's why God gave us the witness protection program."

"Dad."

When Sam returned, her tears were dry. "Geoff said if I say Alecia's not invited, then she's not invited. Geoff's calling his parents to tell them."

"Thank God," I said. They both looked at me. "I mean, I would have called them, of course."

"Of course," Valerie said, still attempting the sarcasm thing.

Sam slumped into the chair. "I just . . . the thought of Alecia all day long, telling me what to do, and then afterward, telling me all the things I did wrong and how much better her wedding was than mine, I realized I couldn't do it. I've been thinking about it for days, like, having a fantasy where I told her she wasn't invited, and then today I just blew. Geoff says this sort of thing happens to her all the time and that she'll get over it because we're practically the only people still talking to Alecia after *her* wedding."

"Well, but I do feel that so much damage was done to my relationship with her, she'll probably never talk to *me* again," I said hopefully.

"So, hair down?" the stylist clarified.

"Absolutely," Sam affirmed.

Even though her hair was mostly dry, the stylist took about an hour to blow it out with a dryer—pretty easy work, if you ask me. Next she applied makeup, which comes in several "looks." A woman needs to decide what her look is ahead of time, so the makeup person doesn't do it wrong and have the bride wind up resembling Bill O'Reilly. To assist fathers everywhere in understanding that makeup isn't just makeup, it's a *look*, I went over to Tom's house and helped him watch the movie *Rocky* for the tenth time and utilized his computer to Google the various makeup looks I'd heard my daughters talking about. Here are the results of my scientific findings.

Bridal Makeup Looks

Luminous

Picture what a face would look like with a bunch of beads of moisture on it—sort of like Sylvester Stallone's face at the end of the fight in the first *Rocky*. If you were to shine a spotlight on it, a luminous face would glow like a pair of raccoon eyes in the headlights. So if your daughter says she wants a "luminous" look, it means she wants to look like Rocky Balboa after he lost to Apollo Creed.

Dewy

Thomas E. Dewey ran for president in 1948. He had a mustache and said famously stupid things like "Our rivers are full of fish" and "You know your future is still ahead of you." If your daughter says she wants a "dewy" look, it means she wants to wear a mustache and lose an election to Harry Truman.

Matte

According to experts (Tom and myself), "matte" is just a fancy-pants spelling of the word "mat." A mat is a canvas-covered pad, like the one on which Sylvester Stallone kept getting knocked down by Apollo Creed in the first *Rocky*. So if your daughter wants to look "matte," it means she wants to look flat and soft and as if Rocky Balboa has been rolling around on top of her.

Creamy

I suppose you could say that Rocky got creamed by Apollo Creed. I mean, by the end of the fight, the poor guy sure did look luminous. The difference, though, at least according to Google, is that California now exports more cream than Wisconsin. So if she wants to look "creamy," she wants to look like Rocky Balboa, only if he were from California instead of Philadelphia.

In the end, I'm not entirely sure which look Sam went for, because by the time the makeup was on, she sure didn't look anything like Rocky, at least as far as I could remember. I may need to watch the movie again. She was, however, even more beautiful than Adrian Balboa in *Rocky III*, when Rocky was rich and could afford expensive makeup and hair for his wife.

When my daughters first started wearing makeup, I didn't like it because I thought they looked like they were enrolled in prostitute school. They pretty much ignored me until they turned sixteen, and then started to realize that their father's "Less is More" philosophy toward mascara and rouge made sense because he could deny them the car keys.

Now, though, I could see that the stylist had found ways to emphasize the natural beauty in Sam's face, and when my daughter turned to me, she was positively glowing with luminous, creamy dew.

"Okay, do we have something borrowed, something blue?" Judy asked.

MORE STUFF YOU MUST HAVE

As a way to enhance the purchase requirements of the wedding, every bride is informed she must have something old, something new, something borrowed, and something blue. None of these items are in the budget because they fall under the "of course" exclusion—you don't have to include them in the total expenditures because *of course* you must have them, it's tradition. When I heard about this, I naturally had some ideas.

A FATHER'S REASONABLE IDEAS FOR THIS WHOLE SOMETHING OLD, SOMETHING NEW TRADITION

TRADITION	FATHER'S REASONABLE IDEA	DAUGHTER'S IDEA
Something old	Seems to me that your diamond is about the oldest thing in the whole wedding. We've got that covered.	No, it has to be something new old, not something I already have old. I was thinking of buying antique pearl earrings.
	New earrings? How is that something old?	Dad, they're antique. Antique means old, even if they're new.
Something new	Okay, well, I guess the earrings also qualify as something new.	Dad. It can't be the same thing. It has to be something else.
	Okay, well, the dress is new.	I found the cutest pearl ankle bracelet. It is a single pearl on a gold chain. It's very pretty.
	But no one will be able to see that.	You don't have to be able to see it, the tradition is about the bride, not other people.
Something borrowed	I just got my credit card bill—this whole wedding is borrowed.	Jennifer let me have her pearl necklace for $300. It's the whole reason I bought the pearl earrings.

TRADITION	FATHER'S REASONABLE IDEA	DAUGHTER'S IDEA
	That's not borrowed, that's *rented*. Tell her forget it.	I can't do that, she is one of my dearest friends.
	Some friend! What else does she charge you for?	The $300 is for the insurance. It's a really expensive necklace, so the only way I could borrow it was to pay for the insurance. It means a lot to her.
	I thought this was about the bride and not other people.	I want to wear the necklace.
Something blue	How about I hold my breath until I win a single argument with you on this stuff? I ought to turn pretty blue doing that.	Dad, we're not arguing. I really appreciate everything you've done for me. The something blue part I've got covered, it's something that only Geoff will see.
	Hey, I thought this wasn't supposed to be about other people!	It's not. Geoff's not other people, he's my fiancé.

On Time and Behind Schedule

I changed into my tuxedo and admired myself for a few or ten minutes, saying "I'll have mine shaken, not stirred," then drove to the church. There were four interconnecting rooms off of the main hall, and the bridesmaids had captured three of them, while the groomsmen were ensconced in the remaining one. To ensure that the groomsmen didn't accidentally breach security, the women had piled suitcases in front of the door that would have given the men access.

That's right, the women had brought suitcases. It looked as if they thought that at some point the wedding party might morph into a dance troupe and take the whole show on the road.

The bridesmaids who were nearly finished being dressed were in the outermost room, and I stopped in to say hello. They were all frantically racing around, sticking pins in one another, brushing hair, putting on makeup, and taking cell phone calls. "We're behind schedule!" Valerie told me anxiously as she raced past to the inner rooms, slamming the door behind her. While the door was momentarily open, I caught a brief glimpse of Judy doing something appropriately maniacal, like pulling down the curtains to sew some last-minute bridesmaids's outfits.

I left the chaos and went to check to see if the men were in a similar state. They were lounging around playing cards.

I decided to stay with the men.

My phone rang—before cell phones, weddings were not even possible.

"I'm doing all the work," my son complained without preamble.

"Is that so?"

"I can't find Cousin Tina, but I did pick up Aunt Lucy, she was wandering around the airport. She claims there *is* no Cousin Tina."

"Well, she's in for a shock."

"I got two uncles and a second cousin located and inbound. I got Grandma and Grandpa to their hotel— they're mad at each other for some reason."

"They're mad at each other for *every* reason," I corrected.

"Terri's been to the store to buy stuff for the bridesmaids like five times—haven't we been planning this for over a year?"

"I'm not sure about the 'we,'" I replied, "but yes, you have the time frame right. You'd better get back here, we start the show in half an hour."

"I'm ten minutes out. Hey, are we having swans?"

"We're not even having *Alecia*."

"Awesome!" He hung up.

There was a knock on the door. Sarah was standing there, looking lovely in a dress that, as something of an expert on what is worn to weddings, I could immediately identify as being of some sort of color. "Okay," she said. "The problem with the caterer is fixed, the bartender was found, the band's drummer got out of rehab, and a babysitter was located for little Kenny."

"We reached Aunt Claudia's doctor and got a replacement prescription for her medication. The airline found Cousin Dean's suitcase and is delivering it here. Somehow somebody fixed Valerie's shoe," I replied in clipped tones. This is what a wedding does, turn a conversation between two people who love each other into what sounds like coded messages. "Oh, and a new horse was found, since the old one got sick."

"I didn't know horses even got sick, what did it have?"

I shrugged. "Hay fever?"

"Funny. What are you guys doing in there?"

I blocked her view of the men languidly playing cards. "Oh, we're appropriately frantic," I assured her.

"We're less than half an hour away, anything else I can do?"

"We've lost Cousin Tina, but I haven't got a clue how to even start looking for her. You look great, by the way."

"Thanks." Her eyes sparkled. "See you out there."

"Roger, over and out."

About half an hour later, my watch revealed we were five minutes overdue for a wedding, and I knew that in another few minutes I would start to pace. The other guys looked worried too, but only because they thought Geoff was holding a straight flush. I knew he was bluffing. Valerie knocked on the door and stuck her head in. She was in full bridesmaid mode and looked, well, silly. "Honey, you look like a bridesmaid," I said, which all the men had agreed ahead of time was both an honest and safe compliment.

Her face was ashen. "Dad, could you come out for a minute, please?"

I tossed down my cards. "Sure, honey," I said. There was something about her expression that made me willing to get up even though I was holding a pair of kings. "Everything okay?" I asked once we were out in the hallway.

"Sam needs to talk to you," she said. I followed her into the inner sanctum of the bridesmaids' rooms. The ladies were all dressed like Valerie and were oddly silent, watching me pensively as I passed through to the middle room. "Where's your mother?" I asked, hesitating.

"She had to go get Terri, somebody rear-ended her at the store. She's okay, but her car can't drive. And anyway, this is kind of a . . . father thing."

"A what?"

"She needs her dad." Giving me an unreadable look, Valerie pushed open the door to the innermost room. My pulse ticked up in alarm as I passed through to where Sam was sitting in her wedding gown. Valerie closed the door behind me.

It was on my mind that I should react to and say something about the dress, but I didn't get a chance to. Sam was weeping in a way I hadn't seen since she was an emotional little girl. I sat and she plowed her face into my shoulder.

"Oh my God, Dad," she moaned.

"What is it? Sam? What's the matter?" I asked urgently.

Between sobs, it came out. "I don't know . . . I don't know if I can do this. I don't know if I can get married!"

Wow.

I held her and felt the quakes traveling up and down her body. "I'm . . . so . . . sorry," she choked out, her voice muffled.

I took a deep breath. Now what? I had invested a considerable amount of my bank's money in this event, and there were a lot of people out there getting restless in the church. But that didn't matter, did it? What mattered was right here in front of me, drenching my tuxedo.

I said to Sam what all fathers need to say to their daughters on their wedding day, because nothing is more important to us than their happiness.

"It's okay, Sam," I told her. "Right up to the moment you walk down the aisle, we can cancel. It doesn't matter."

"You've spent all that money," she wailed, anguished.

"I don't care about that. What I care about is that you're sure you want to get married. If you want to call it off, we call it off."

"I just don't know if I'm getting married because I want to get married, or because I want to have a wedding, you know?"

I didn't know. To me, getting married in order to have a wedding would be like giving birth in order to have the pain. But I could understand how a bride could get so completely caught up in planning her perfect day that she would lose sight of the fact that the whole thing was about being so in love with a man that she was willing to be married to him for the rest of her life.

"I don't know what to think anymore. I keep thinking

this is a huge mistake. I mean, the past month I've barely even talked to Geoff except to fight with him about really stupid stuff."

"Okay. It's okay," I assured her.

"But I do love him, don't I? I mean, when he proposed I was so excited and I knew then that I wanted to be his wife, what happened to *that*?"

"Well . . ." I started to say.

"Then I had to plan the wedding all by myself, practically, and the thing with Alecia, he wasn't exactly a huge help with that, it's like the men in his family are afraid of the women and I don't want that kind of relationship, do I? What if that's the only way he knows how to relate to me, once we're living together? I mean, are people born to be just like their family members?"

I thought about Cousin Tina. Not always, I decided. Sometimes people aren't even born to be like themselves.

"I don't want to live like that," she lamented.

"Well . . ." I started to say.

"But that's not how he is with me, he's never been like that with me! I don't know, what does Alecia have to do with anything?"

"Well . . ."

"Alecia's like this curse, she keeps showing up even though I kicked her out! God! I don't know what to do!"

I decided not to say anything, since I wasn't going to be allowed to, anyway.

"I just don't know what I'm feeling anymore. It's like planning the wedding crowded everything else out. I feel all squeezed."

Her eyes were dry, now, and she looked less confused and more relieved. "It's really okay with you? If we don't go through with this?"

"It's really okay."

"I love you, Dad," she said simply.

"I love you too, Sam."

She sighed, exhaustion creeping into her eyes. "What a mess *this* is going to be," she murmured.

We sat in companionable silence. "One thing, though," I said after a bit. She looked at me expectantly. "I think maybe you should tell Geoff about this yourself."

"You mean . . . like right now?"

"Well, yeah. He's conveniently located nearby."

"But he'd see me in my dress. It's bad luck."

"I'd say calling off the wedding is pretty much the worst luck possible, wouldn't you?" I asked dryly.

She searched my face, and then, to her credit, she laughed. "Okay. Okay." She nodded. "You're right. Oh God." She turned to the mirror and gasped. "Give me a few minutes, and tell Valerie I need the stylist back in here, okay?"

"I'll go get him, then," I said. She nodded again, and I stepped out of the inner chamber. Valerie was waiting for me.

"What do we do, Dad?" my daughter asked me.

"Go in and help her. She needs makeup, her eyes look like Rocky's after round six."

"Dad," Valerie said.

"I'm going to go get Geoff."

Valerie's eyes widened, but she went in to be with her sister. I stepped into the Room of Bridesmaids. They all stared at me in mute horror. "It will be just one more minute," I said pleasantly. I walked out and was unfortunately in full view of the entire congregation, which started to murmur as if we were in a courtroom drama and the witness had just admitted having an affair with the defendant.

The boys were still playing cards, oblivious to the fact that the wedding was now officially fifteen minutes behind schedule. "Geoff, could I speak to you for a second, please?"

Geoff came across the room, his eyes on mine. "Is she okay?" he asked worriedly.

"She needs to talk to you."

"Why? What's wrong?"

"I just want you to come with me and talk to Sam, Geoff," I said steadily, turning on my Dad Power beams so that he had no choice but to obey. His face grim, he nodded.

We walked out together. More murmuring, especially when we entered the Bridesmaid Chamber. The women inside all gasped as if I'd just brought in Frankenstein's Monster.

"We're going to suspend the rules here for a minute," I told them.

When I opened the door into Sam's dressing room, she was standing in the middle of the floor, Judy and Valerie each holding an arm for support. Geoff took in the sight of her in her gown.

"Whoa," he said slowly.

Sam blushed at the reaction. A tremulous smile flitted across her face. I nodded at Valerie and her mother, and the three of us discreetly left the room.

"Why don't the two of you go explain to the bridesmaids why having the groom see Sam isn't the same as the mummy's curse, and I'll wait here," I suggested. Judy and Valerie agreed and went into the other room, where the women were gathered as if awaiting news of the birth of the new prince.

I took up a Secret Service stance outside the door, my arms crossed and a "nobody gets past me" look on my face.

I couldn't hear what they were saying, at first, until Geoff raised his voice.

"I don't care about that, Sam!" he said sharply.

I decided that in the role of protector of my daughter I should slide over to where the voices were coming from, by the vent. If I needed to burst in and punch Geoff in the nose, I was willing.

"I just want to be married to you," Geoff was saying. "I never cared about the wedding. Look, why don't we take the tickets and just leave, go to Hawaii. Elope, get married there."

I found myself sort of wishing he'd come up with this idea a few thousand dollars ago.

Sam asked him something I didn't hear.

"No! None of that is important. It's you, Sam, don't you see? I love you. I want to be with you. That is all I care about."

I unclenched my fists. Who a woman marries is her choice, not her father's, though clearly we could use some legislation to fix that. So ultimately, whether there was a wedding today was Sam's decision, but were it up to me, I felt that Geoff had earned the right to be her husband.

There was a lot of murmuring, which I couldn't quite make out even with my ear pressed against the vent. Then suddenly the door banged open and they were both looking at me. I jerked up, whacking my forehead on the vent knob.

"Ah . . . something wrong with the air conditioner, I was thinking I should maybe go tell somebody, you know, it could be dangerous," I stammered out.

They obviously felt this was plausible. "Dad," Sam said, "are you ready to have a wedding?"

"Sure, it's sort of last minute, but I could probably arrange that."

"Dad," Geoff said, concerned. "You're bleeding."

I pulled out a handkerchief and pressed it to my head. Sure enough, a tiny bit of blood was in evidence. Then I stopped dead.

Geoff had just called me "Dad."

IT'S NOT A WEDDING UNTIL SOMEBODY GETS INJURED

I half expected that the church would be empty, but the drama had kept everyone glued to their seats. There was more buzz when Geoff came back out. I held up my hand. "It's okay," I announced. "We just had, you know, an air conditioning problem." I pulled the handkerchief away from my forehead so they could see how serious it was.

The cover story didn't work so well on a larger group, but that didn't matter because the men were assembling at the front of the church as if Geoff were a kicker and the groomsmen were the specialty team, ready to race downfield and tackle the receiver. (Analogies like this help men stay alert during weddings.) Sarah was seated, then my son led his mother and then Priscilla to their seats, then stood off to the side, ready to escort Duke the dog off the playing field once there'd been a successful ring handoff. The bridesmaids were doing their slow, broken-toe walk down the aisle.

Valerie stepped up next to me, holding Duke by the collar. The dog was panting, and I stared at him. His lips were fire engine red, as was his tongue.

"You put lipstick on the *dog*?" I whispered.

"Dad!" Valerie whispered back. "No, he got into the red hots."

As part of the Hot August Nights theme, bowls of red hots, the little red candies that taste like pain, were going to be set out by the bar. Dogs, with their amazing sense of smell, can instantly identify the pungent spices as making the candies inedible, but Duke decided to eat them anyway. He frequently made the same decision with coffee grounds and deflated balloons. Valerie handed the dog to me. "Good boy, Duke," she lied.

Valerie went down the aisle. Step, stop, step, stop. All this preparation to get to this point, why were we dragging this out *now*? If it had been up to me I'd have put everyone in Nikes and made them sprint to the finish line.

Valerie was in position. The room grew quiet, heads turning to see the bride. Instead, they saw me with the tarted-up canine, as if I had decided to give away the dog instead.

"Come easy, Duke! Come easy!" Geoff called out. I released the dog's collar.

Duke barked.

"Come easy!" Geoff called again.

Duke backed up, barking, then shook his head as if there were water in his ears. Everyone in the place laughed.

Well, that was it, the wedding was off. I shrugged at Geoff.

And then Sam was at my side. "Okay, Duke. Come here," she said. Duke lowered his ears and trotted up to her, tail wagging.

My daughter looked up at me. Her face was radiant, her gaze clear, the doubt gone like a vanishing storm. Her dress was the one I really didn't like, the sexy flowing one, but she made it look both womanly and elegant.

Any other bride might have had a psychotic episode over Duke's failure to deliver the ring, but my daughter just took it in stride, laughing with everyone else.

The organist hit several keys as if warming up for the opening day of baseball, then launched into the wedding march. I escorted my child and her stupid dog together down the aisle, step, stop, step, though at each stop Duke looked up at us in bewilderment, fooled every single time.

Amid more laughter, Geoff wrestled the ring off Duke's back, and then Chris hauled the animal off to the side.

There'd been some discussion over whether we should go with the old fashioned father-gives-away-the-bride (and dog) thing, because Sam thought it was maybe a little sexist. She was not, after all, my property. ("No," I shot back, indicating the place on my kitchen counter where I used to have a toaster, "you *own* my property.") She was an independent person, not mine to give away. I explained, though, that the whole process is symbolic of an agreement that I'm making that Geoff can take my daughter away from me and I won't kill him. Geoff was really in favor of the not killing him part, so the ritual was included, which meant it was now time for my speaking role.

"Who gives this bride, this little girl, who just last month wouldn't sleep without her blanky, who just last week needed a push on the swing set, who just yesterday was running over the mailbox?" the minister asked—or at least, that's what I heard.

"Her mother and I do," I replied in a voice that was as strong and firm as a baby bird's. I found my way to my seat and grabbed Sarah's hand and held on so I wouldn't fall to the floor.

I numbly listened to the sermon, hearing nothing but the sound of my own heart thudding away in my chest. Words were exchanged.

"Do you, Geoffrey, take this woman, Samantha, to be your wife, ripping her from her father's home, taking her away from her father's protection, and exposing her to dangers such as job transfers and other unacceptable conditions that might make it even harder for her father to continue to watch over her?

"I do."

"And did you, Samantha, spend all of your father's money?"

"I did."

"Then by the power invested in me to extract a small fee that wasn't included in the original budget, I now pronounce you husband and wife."

Sam and Geoff kissed each other as if they meant it-when Alecia got married, it was more like Carter kissing Brezhnev. They turned and faced the crowd.

"Ladies and gentlemen, may I present to you, Mr. and Mrs. Geoffrey King."

Who? Wait, what? The organist was playing and people were fleeing. Sarah tapped me on the back as if the red light had turned green and now I had to parachute into occupied France. "Go!" she whispered. I stood and numbly followed my daughter, Mrs. Geoffrey King, out the door.

FOURTEEN

～

Last Dance

It is very important to have lots of pictures taken immediately following the actual ceremony so that years later the bride and groom can look through their wedding album and say, "This is what we were doing while everyone else was having a good time at the reception."

The wedding photographer will act as if he is documenting the proceedings for the Warren Commission. Everyone will change positions according to his commands—you might as well pick a bossy and unpleasant person to be the official wedding photographer, because by the end of the evening you'd hate him even if he were Santa Claus.

One wedding magazine I read contained a list of fifty recommended poses—in other words, you should miss the reception entirely! In my view, there are only five poses you need.

1. Bride in the middle looking happy, groom next to her looking happy, father behind them looking broke.
2. The entire wedding party standing around looking happy, except at this point it is less a "wedding party"

than a "wedding full of people getting really hot in uncomfortable clothing."

3. The dog lifting his leg on Priscilla's purse.
4. The bride looking happy, the maid of honor standing next to her looking happy because *her* wedding comes next and she can force her sister to wear an even more ridiculous outfit.
5. The bride and groom standing there looking happy, the father looking at his watch.

A really, really good wedding photographer will sense when the people are getting ready to riot, because that's when he can hit the father up for a gratuity to move things along. "Well, I still want one with the dog and the dog's parents looking rapturously at the wedding bouquet," he'll say when the father approaches him and says he wants to get to the open bar before Uncle Bob drains it. "Or maybe, maybe I could just go with the maid of honor handing a flower to the minister and wrap it up."

Little does the photographer know, the gratuities (for which there was no budget because, in the words of my daughter, "everyone knows gratuities are considered *extra*") have already been parsed out into little envelopes. A father might very reasonably point out that it makes no sense to decide how much to tip before you've benefited from a service—the tip is a reward for good service, right?

"If the waiter comes and dumps a bowl of soup on my head, do you still think I should tip him the full amount?" I demanded of my daughter.

"Of course not. We're not having soup."

"Okay, well, let's say it is a pitcher of water, then."

"Then I'd say no."

"Aha!"

"You'd tip the caterer. Give him the envelope; he takes care of the individual waiters."

There were so many people getting little envelopes they would have qualified for their own zip code. I scanned the list. "What about the chickens that are giving their lives for this dinner, shouldn't we tip them?" I asked sarcastically.

"Dad," Valerie said. "Don't let Marty hear you talk about that, he's angry enough that they aren't organic free-range chickens."

"He's a vegetarian! He's not even going to eat them, why does he care?"

"If you have to ask, there's no use explaining it," Valerie sniffed.

After the photographer has burned through more film than it took to film the Harry Potter movies and everyone is feeling really cranky, the bride and groom depart for the reception in a special conveyance. Good ideas for this are:

- A limousine, like maybe the one that once belonged to Puff Daddy.*
- An old, classic car, like maybe a 1931 Bugatti Royale (worth 8.7 million dollars, but that's okay, you're only *renting* it).†
- The *Queen Mary* (if you don't live by the ocean, be sure to budget for an extra large trailer).
- A horse-drawn carriage, like maybe the one that Cinderella took to the ball (best for October weddings when there are plenty of pumpkins available).

---

* Aka Pampy D, P. Diddy, Puff, and Diddy.

† Only six were ever built, so call Hertz extra early to make a reservation.

In the end, my daughter settled for the carriage. Since this was her wedding day and rain was forbidden, it was open in the back, which was good because we couldn't have gotten that dress into an enclosed space without a pitchfork. As it was, by the time she and Geoff settled in, it looked like they were in a bubble bath.

Clopping to the reception hall a half dozen blocks away, Sam and Geoff waved like newly coronated royalty as every car honked at them, the drivers of the automobiles celebrating their joy over not paying for any of this. The horse figured all the honking was for him, and tossed his head proudly, lifting his legs like a Lipizzaner.

Naturally, we had to have ten minutes of photographs as we arrived at the reception, which was okay because that's how long it took to help Sam out of the carriage.

Next came the reception line, which is where you line up and people come up to you and ask who you are. You explain that you're the father of the bride and are therefore irrelevant to the proceedings, unless of course they happen to be one of the dozens of people expecting you to hand over an envelope of cash that night. I tried to get the attention of several of these people, figuring I could at least get a drink of water from them, but I was universally ignored—probably they knew that their tip amount was already in the envelope no matter what kind of service they provided.

Standing next to my daughter, I learned a lot about reception line etiquette. Apparently, it is as important that your compliments be as excessive as the photographs.

RECEPTION LINE ETIQUETTE

DON'T SAY	SAY
You look pretty.	You look ethereal, mystical, phosphorous.
The ceremony was meaningful.	The ceremony cured my athlete's foot.
I am so happy for you.	I am so happy, I don't care who dies tonight.
Your wedding vows moved me to tears.	Your wedding vows gave me a seizure.
You two make a beautiful couple.	Compared to you, all other married couples are like corpses rotting in the sun.
When I saw you in that dress, I couldn't help it, I cried.	When I saw you in that dress, I couldn't help it, I threw a blood clot.

"You must be very proud," Sarah told me during a brief lull in her reception line social obligations. (Sarah wasn't being ignored by anybody, especially the men, who seemed very interested in standing close and peering down her neckline. I tried to glare them into backing off, but it turns out that Boyfriend Power is significantly less potent than Dad Power.)

"I *am* proud," I admitted, surprising myself. We still had a reception to get through, but my daughter was married, nobody but me had gotten a flesh wound, and we'd found Cousin Tina/Ted (she'd been in the back, flirting with one of Geoff's less-observant male coworkers). "This was really hard to do, but Sam pulled it off, and we didn't have to hire Lindy Looney Tunes."

Sarah laughed, then turned to greet the next person in

line, who turned out to be one of those guys who thinks he's good looking just because he's all handsome. He shook Sarah's hand and then held it, asking if she were Sam's sister. Sarah dutifully laughed, but the line had been tossed at her about six times already and I knew that the fish weren't biting.

"I'm the father of the bride, plus Sarah's long-time, very serious boyfriend and her karate instructor," I told the guy, holding out my hand so he'd have to release hers. Reluctantly, he took it, and Sarah went on to the next man in line.

"My! You're the prettiest sister of the bride yet!" the next guy gushed.

THE HOT AUGUST NIGHT

Upon entering the reception hall, wedding guests were treated to the spectacle of several round tables filled with flowers and candles, a "ticket booth" greeting area, and Uncle Bob at the bar.

The ticket booth was Sam's invention. Acting on some crazy impulse, she did something brides almost never do-she asked her fiancé his opinion about the wedding. Specifically, she asked Geoff what it was about August nights that he liked the best, and he told her that when he was young, he and his father would go to an amusement park and ride the roller coasters. It was a special time, because both his mother and his sister were afraid of rides, so it meant that it was just Geoff and his father together. (I agreed that any time spent away from Priscilla and Alecia was probably special.)

At the wedding ticket booth, guests received a roller coaster ride ticket that doubled as their escort cards—by matching their ticket number to their seat number, they could find their chairs. Then they stood in front of a fixed digital camera, where a quick shot was taken of them and any guests they'd brought along. Within seconds, the photograph was printed on a page that had space for comments and a signature—it was a guest sign-in book with photographs, so that as we squinted at the signatures we would have a better chance at figuring out who some of these people were.

I didn't read about any of these ideas in any of the bridal magazines that were stacking up in my bathroom; they were all Sam's innovations. My daughter is a very special woman.

The wedding favor was a small thermometer—Hot August Nights, get it? And the flowers were, I assumed, all August flowers, like protubria and narcolepsy. I went over to the bar to get a glass of wine and say hello to Uncle Bob, who introduced me to the bartenders and told me their life stories.

Tom was standing by the cake, his expression one of studied innocence, as if he'd been drifting around the room at random and just happened to wind up there, of all places.

"I'll make sure you get a slice, you don't have to guard it," I assured him.

"Oh no, I was just admiring it," he replied. "I mean . . . you're sure I'll get a piece?"

"It's going to be fine."

He surveyed the room. Sam and Geoff had left—she was putting on her reception dress so that everyone would know the clothing budget had gone over. "Hard to believe, just a few months ago, you were planning this thing, all by yourself," he said. (I may have given him a somewhat one-sided impression of how the whole thing came together.) He sighed. "Wow. And to think, probably won't be too long before I'm where you are, watching my own daughter walk down the aisle."

"Probably not too long," I agreed. "Well, except, you don't have any children, Tom."

He looked at me in horror.

"You mean you didn't know that?" I asked, truly concerned.

"No, it's just that . . . Well, I blew it."

"You sure did," I said. "Blew what?"

"Cat's out of the bag now," he lamented.

"Would you please tell me what the heck you're talking about?"

"Emily's expecting."

"Really? Wow, Tom, that's fantastic!"

"Expecting a baby, I mean."

"I knew that's what you meant. Well, congratulations!"

We moved as if to hug, thought better of it, and stiffly shook hands as if he'd just sold me a car. "I wasn't supposed to say anything. You know, because of the wedding, didn't want to steal any thunder."

"That was really considerate, Tom," I told him, meaning it. "But it doesn't steal from Sam's thunder, it adds to it!"

"Right," Tom replied uncertainly.

I looked over to where Sam and Geoff, beaming, were coming back into the reception hall, cameras flashing and people cheering. Sam looked even happier than when her volleyball team won a national title, and Geoff actually sought out my eyes and waved at me. When I swallowed, my throat was tight. "Wow," I said.

I went over to talk to Emily and congratulate her on her pregnancy. Tom elected to remain by the cake. Emily was flushed with excitement. "I knew he wouldn't be able to keep the secret," she said, but it was less a complaint than an acknowledgment that Tom tended to get a little overenthusiastic about things.

I laughed in agreement. "I remember
bass boat, he ran right over to tell me abo
"Sure. Exactly the same thing," Emi
suppose was a touch of irony. I went to
her the good news.

THE FATHER GETS HIS SAY

Duke made an appearance during dinner and seemed very,
very glad that everyone was having chicken. Unlike Alecia's
wedding, where she and her husband were up on the stage
and she acted like she was doing a one-woman show (*The Alecia Monologues*), Sam and Geoff sat at a round table as if they
were mere mortals. Every few minutes someone would clink
his water glass, and Sam and Geoff would oblige with a kiss.

Dessert was homemade ice cream, either in an ice cream
cone or with the wedding cake. Sam explained to me that
one of the things she remembered from childhood August
nights was me making homemade ice cream that wound up
as the consistency of soup. I marveled that she could remember something from so long ago and yet get it so wrong about
the consistency.

Tom had several pieces of cake, which was okay, he was
eating for two, now.

Geoff's best man stood and made a long rambling toast
about how there are some inconsistencies in the instructions
for filing jointly instead of separately, or some such, which
the groomsmen found hilarious and everyone else found as
incomprehensible as the rest of the tax code. After about ten
minutes of this kind of levity, he settled down and proposed
that Geoff and Sam should always be as happy as they were
right now, provided they filed the right form. We clinked
glasses, drank, and then everyone looked expectantly at me.

I stood and gazed around the reception hall, which was completely quiet except for the sound of Duke lapping up someone's chicken. Sarah was giving me an encouraging smile. Tom was eyeing my unguarded cake. Chris was making goofy faces at me, which was only fair, because when he was a little kid performing in school assemblies I did the same thing to him. Valerie looked as if she were already composing the sarcastic things she'd say to me when I was finished. Their mother looked proud, the Fop looked foppish, and Sam looked radiant, so grown up next to her new husband that I almost didn't recognize her.

The crowd had already been warmed up with Internal Revenue humor, so I figured I could skip the jokes I'd planned. Instead, I cut to what I wanted to say.

"I remember when Sam was born. She looked a little ticked off, and I swear she tried to take a swing at the doctor for disturbing her nap."

People who knew just how competitive my daughter could be were laughing at this.

"But the memory I will treasure the most takes me back to when she was in second grade. I went up to the elementary school to walk her home—we were moving to a new house across the country, so it was a special day, her last day in that particular school. The teacher let her go five minutes ahead of everyone to recognize the occasion, so as I stood there at the edge of the playground, I saw the doors pop open and Sam emerge out into the sunshine. All by herself, she went to the middle of the playground, spread her arms wide, raised her face to the sun, and twirled. I remember . . . I remember how my heart soared, seeing my little girl, how she could celebrate life, take such joy out of such a simple thing as a sunny moment on a warm October day."

I turned and focused on my oldest child. She gave me an encouraging smile, and for a moment it was as if it were just the two of us again, standing there on the playground together.

"Sam, you've always looked toward the future with the same optimism and joyful disposition as I saw in your smile that afternoon. Looking at you now, I still see it—you're moving into your future with your arms wide open and your face turned up to the light. Geoff, you are marrying a true genius in the art of living. Learn from her, and you'll be happy, too."

I knocked back my Champagne like it was a hit of whiskey and I was Wyatt Earp. Sarah reached up and took my hand, her eyes moist as they smiled up into mine.

"Let's dance!" Valerie called out.

A SLOW START

The band seemed surprised that the people at the wedding expected them to do something with their instruments besides display them. Valerie's shout caught them with ice cream halfway to their mouths, and they hastily assembled into a huddle. I sure hoped that they were not asking one another if any of them knew any songs.

Valerie, as maid of honor, was the first to decide something must be wrong. I saw her listen to the four men talking at once, her face in a frown. She gestured over to me. I stood up.

"Tom, that's my cake. And tell Duke that's my chicken." I went over to the band. "I've had only one guitar lesson in my whole life, but if you really want me to, I suppose I could start off with 'House of the Rising Sun,'" I said.

"It's a money thing," Valerie said.

"Ah." Of course. I faced the band, addressing all of them. "You didn't get your check?"

"We did, but it's supposed to be cash. See, that was the agreement," a young man told me. He looked more somber and darker than the others, so I assumed he was the bass player. "It's how we always do it. It's how we did the other one."

"The other one? Geoff's first wedding?" I replied, perplexed.

"They were the band at Alecia's wedding. She sort of insisted we use them," Valerie explained.

"Okay. Well, I suppose I can find an ATM, but can you start playing now, while I go get the cash?"

This seemed reasonable. They looked at one another, exchanging a few words. "No," the bass player told me.

"Dad!" Valerie said urgently, looking distressed.

I reached into my pocket, where I had a thick wad of envelopes of cash. "Okay," I said, "how much to get you to start playing?"

It turns out you can buy the first hour of a cash band for the cost of a minister, a caterer, the florist, and a valet. I handed over the envelopes, telling Valerie I'd find an ATM and raise the rest of the money before our time ran out. "Just keep Tom away from my cake," I said. She vowed to guard it with her life.

Geoff caught me as I was heading out. He thanked me for the toast, and asked if there was a problem with the band. "None at all," I said, clapping him on the shoulder.

Hey, it was his wedding day, why get him upset?

Of course, the whole situation would resurface again before the end of the evening, but I had no way of knowing that.

LAST DANCE

By the time I returned, the band had taken a break and Sam had tossed her stunt bouquet over her shoulder, aiming with sniperlike accuracy at her sister. Valerie had no choice but to catch the thing. The open bar had lubricated conversations, and the room was full of loud and happy noise. I pulled the bass player aside and slipped him a thick wad of bills from my anorexic bank account. He hastily stuffed them into his jacket pocket.

We were off stage and half hidden by a curtain, putting us in a perfect position to hear someone, I couldn't tell whom, ask to be called up on stage.

The vocalist said something I couldn't hear.

"Just say that you've heard that a family member is a really good singer and then call me up on stage. Like it was a suggestion from the crowd, you know?"

I stuck my head around the curtain in time to see Cousin Tina/Ted handing a twenty over to the vocalist, who nodded agreeably at this turn in the conversation.

When the band cranked up again, I grabbed Valerie and dragged her out on the dance floor. Judy took the floor with her husband, who danced, unsurprisingly, like a Fop. I smiled indulgently.

I'm a pretty good dancer and often get a lot of compliments about the way I can move. Tonight was no exception.

"Wow, you really . . . I've never seen anyone dance like you, Dad," Valerie said.

"I know, honey. I was born with it."

"Glad you didn't pass it on to me."

To make her eat my words, I did a quick and elegant twirl. "Sorry, sorry," I said to the woman I'd collided with. "Did I hurt you? Sorry."

"What was that, a triple axel?" Valerie asked.

I ignored the question. "So why aren't you and Good Old Moldy out here?"

Marty was sitting by himself at a table, pointedly not having any fun so people would know he was serious about all the problems facing the world. Valerie shrugged.

"Some people just don't dance," I suggested.

"And some people just shouldn't," she agreed. I looked around to see who she was talking about. "Sorry, sorry," I said to the guy I sort of punched by accident. "So, Valerie, ten months or so and we'll be doing this at your wedding, right?"

The tempo of the music slowed, and I stepped in to show off the fact that I can do a simple box step if I have to. "Sorry, sorry," I said. "Are your toes all right?"

"It's okay, Dad. Dad. You know how you made me watch *The Godfather,* like, a hundred times?"

"Wow, now there's a movie I haven't seen this year." I looked around for Tom.

"Dad," Valerie said, "you know that part where the Godfather can't get mad at anyone on his daughter's wedding day?"

"Actually, it's that he can't refuse a request. Why, you have somebody you need rubbed out?"

She took a deep breath. She stopped dancing, and I stopped too, so that we were facing each other from just two feet away. I could see every nuance of her expression, but emotions were flickering across it like lightning in dark clouds. I waited, and she bit her lip, looked away, forced herself with visible effort to look back, and finally met my eyes. "Dad, I kinda decided to call off the wedding."

I kept my face completely blank. "Seriously?" I said after a minute.

"Yeah, for real."

"Wow." I tried to look casual, but I was searching her face for signs of devastation. Her gaze was now clear and steady. "Does Marty know?"

"Of course he does."

"Honey, was it hard?"

"No, it was . . . he's my best friend since high school. We just decided that it wasn't meant to be. I mean, we look at Sam and Geoff." Valerie and I both glanced over to where the newlyweds were clutched together in a slow dance, their eyes smiling into each other's.

I frowned. "I'm not sure they should be kissing on the dance floor."

"Dad," Valerie said. She sighed again. "It's just that Marty and I don't have that, you know? We're not all wild for each other. I want the man I marry to care more about me than he does about sea otters."

"I understand."

"You're not mad?"

We started dancing again, my arm back around her. "Of course not. You can cancel any time, right up until the minister pronounces you married. That's my official policy."

"Thanks, Dad." She gave me a quick kiss on the cheek.

"Are you honestly okay?"

"Well, I guess I'd be lying if I didn't say I wanted a wedding," she admitted.

"I guess I'd be lying if I said that I did," I answered.

"But a wedding leads to marriage, and Marty and I shouldn't be married, we decided."

"What about Lindy Land Rover, how does she feel about it?"

"She paid extra so that all of our deposits were refundable, and held off doing anything that cost money. She said she just had a feeling it wouldn't work out."

I marveled that someone like the Obliterator could divine something I hadn't seen coming. "What about her fee?"

"Well, no, that's not refundable."

"Ah." I glanced over at the Fop, who smiled at me affably.

The song ended. I tried to organize my thoughts, but to tell you the truth, after all that had happened that day, I wasn't thinking very clearly. I gave her a hug. "I'm proud you made such a difficult decision, Valerie," I finally said, "and I think it's for the best. You deserve a man who loves you as much as Geoff loves Sam."

She kissed my cheek again and went back over to sit with Marty. I gave him a little wave and he nodded back at me—he was an okay guy.

"Whoa, Bruce, I wish I could dance like that," Tom told me when I returned to the table. "I guess I'm just too afraid of people making jokes about me while I'm out there."

"Come on, Tom, you should take Emily for a whirl. Nobody's going to make jokes about your dancing."

"I dunno, they sure made jokes about *your* dancing."

"I understand," the vocalist boomed at us, "that we've got a family member who is a really, really good singer!"

I stood back up. My children regarded me with sick dread. *"Please no,"* Sam mouthed at me.

"Cousin Tina, would you please come up here?"

"What? Who told you?" Tina demanded, while several members of my family stared without recognition at the muscular woman in the short skirt who stood up. Cousin *Who?*

"Come on, come up here and show us how it's done," the vocalist insisted, to absolutely no encouragement from the crowd.

Tina took the microphone and started singing "Brother Love's Traveling Salvation Show," the Neil Diamond song whose opening line is "Hot August Night." And you know what? She could really sing! (Later I was to find out that she actually makes a living as a singer now, and has been touring the country under the name, "Ted and Tina Turner.")

At the next break, I noticed Geoff making his way over to the band, and I followed him, wondering if he was going to ask them to have Tina do another set. "Hey," Geoff said pleasantly. "You guys are really good."

"The groom!" the bass player greeted. "Glad you're happy. Congrats, man."

"I heard about the mix-up at the start, with the cash and everything."

"Oh, yeah." The bass player eyed him, wondering if Geoff was going to start an argument, but Geoff just looked blandly affable.

"Sorry about that. You did my sister's wedding a few months ago, but nobody told me about the cash thing."

"Oh, hey, it's cool, don't worry about it." The bass player nodded. His fellow band members, glad there wouldn't be a scene, smiled in relief.

"I imagine that's for taxes?" Geoff asked.

"Right, yeah, it's amazing, I mean, we all have day jobs, so if we reported this income we'd be royally screwed."

Geoff nodded thoughtfully. "Uh-huh."

"Appreciate your understanding," another band member said.

"Oh, I understand," Geoff agreed. He pulled out his business cards and passed them out. I took one, curious.

Geoffrey King

Special Auditor

INTERNAL REVENUE SERVICE

The band members looked as if he'd handed them live hand grenades.

"I'm going on my honeymoon, but when I'm back, I sure would like to get together with you guys. We have a lot of catching up to do, I'd really like to find out what you've been up to the past several years," Geoff said with equal bland-ness. His smile stayed friendly as he nodded at each of the stricken musicians. "See you later."

Time to Close the Door and Turn Out the Lights

I danced with several more people as the evening wore on, though only Sarah didn't make a bunch of snide comments about it.

"You okay? You seem distracted," she asked as I taught her some of my smoother moves in a slow dance.

"Oh, I was just wondering what to do with the leftover booze when it's over, do I take it with me or just pour it into Uncle Bob?"

"Tell me really," she urged.

"Oh. Well, I'm just thinking, in a few more minutes she's going to be leaving, and then that's it, she'll be gone." I gave Sarah a tremulous smile.

"But not forever. People do come back from Hawaii, you know. Not willingly, but they come back."

"I know, but then it will be totally different. She'll be mar-ried. I'll be making loans to the both of them now. It'll never just be me and Sam, it'll be me and Sam and Geoff."

"And me sometimes?" she suggested playfully. "Or is that what you meant by 'totally different.' "

"No, of course you'll be there. I mean, someone has to make us dinner."

"Funny man." She gave me a squeeze. "Well, talk to her, then. Go ask her to dance."

Sam was watching and laughing at a video taken earlier that seemed to consist of her girlfriends sobbing. "We'll be friends forever!" one of them was saying as I walked up and tapped Sam on the shoulder.

"Have time for a dance with the president of the Bank of Dad?"

"Sure! I've been watching you, looks like you've made up a lot of new steps!"

I'd taken a page from Tina's book and handed a twenty to the vocalist—I'd have to be sure I reported it to Geoff. As Sam and I went onto the dance floor, there was no big announcement or spotlight (oddly, even before I'd mentioned it, the band advised that Sam had requested in very strong terms that no one pay any special attention to her when she danced with her father). They did, however, strike up a special song: "Color My World," the song I used to sing to Sam when she was a baby and I wanted her to sleep.

"I remember trying to sleep when you were singing this," Sam joked.

"Ha. Funny. Oh, sorry about your foot, there."

"It's okay. Dad, thanks for everything, especially there at the end, you know, when you said it would be okay to cancel at the last second. Knowing I had that option, it took all the pressure off."

"I'm a very wise father," I agreed.

"This has been the happiest day of my life."

"Mine too, sweetheart."

"Really?" She looked into my eyes.

"No, not really. I mean, I'm happy to have my blender back, but all in all—it's a hard thing, knowing that your little girl is all grown up, *married*."

Her eyes were wet. "But I will always be your little girl, Dad."

"And I'll always be your father, Sam. Don't ever forget that."

"I won't."

"Don't let Geoff forget it, either."

"He won't."

"I mean it."

"Dad."

We danced in silence for a minute, then. Once when Sam was four years old we went to a wedding and I picked her up and danced with her in front of the band. She was so thrilled with the lights and her fancy dress and all the cake I thought she'd be awake for three days, but as we rocked together her head magically fell on my shoulder, and soon she was fast asleep. I held her little frame, so light and insubstantial, and vowed for the thousandth time that I would always be there to protect her.

So I did it again, right there, holding her on the dance floor, telling myself that no matter what happened, I would always be there for her.

The song ended, and there must have been some sort of fog machine going because my vision was clouded, my eyes stinging and leaking. "I'm going to go now, Dad. It's time for Geoff and me to go."

"Okay, Sam." I gave her a shaky smile.

"I love you, Dad."

"I love you too, honey."

At Marty's suggestion, the guests were to throw birdseed instead of rice. I grabbed a handful and lined up, but when my daughter and her new husband swept by, my eyes were so wet I couldn't see anyone, and probably wound up tossing the seeds in Priscilla's face, where they would take root and sprout thorny thistle plants.

"Bye, Sam!" I croaked out in a voice so quiet I couldn't even hear it myself. And then the limo took off, driving down the street with Sam and Geoff waving out the back window. I felt like running after it shouting, "Wait, I'm not ready!" Instead I forced myself to just remain rooted to the spot. "Bye, Sam," I said again, even quieter.

After a moment, the crowd went back inside for more dancing, but I stood there and watched the taillights of the limo grow smaller and farther away until at last they completely vanished from view. It was like watching the sun drop below the horizon, signaling the end of a long, glorious day.

I turned and Sarah was standing there, smiling at me.

"Take me home," I said to her.

FINAL THOUGHTS

W hen my book *8 Simple Rules for Dating My Teen-age Daughter** was published, my daughters both declared that they would never speak to me again, which was ironic because they'd already told me this several times before—each time by *speaking*. (They really appreciated it when I pointed this out.) It didn't help matters when the book went on to become a television show on ABC and once a week my children would have to answer questions about things like "How did you feel when your mom came to school to teach sex education?" (It never happened.)

Now, I've always believed that one of the most important functions of a father is to embarrass his children, but even I can see that when it gets to the point where your children's exploits are famous in places like France, Belgium, and the Middle East (where the sitcom is currently airing), and in Indonesia, Japan, and Spain (just three of the places where the book has been published), I may have taken the embarrassment thing just a little too far.

So, for the sake of my children, let me address a ques-

---

* Workman Publishing, 2001

tion you might have about the book you just read, namely: "Did all of this really happen?"

I've often said a humorist is a real person who lives in a fictional world. Thus, while it is true I've owned many dogs in my lifetime, none of them has actually written me a letter complaining about the cat, as I once claimed in a newspaper column. I tend to exaggerate things sometimes, for humorous effect.

(*He tells lies*, my children would advise you.)

(*He doesn't feed me enough*, my dog would add.)

One of the greatest humorists of all time—Dave Barry— famously says "I'm not making this up" precisely because otherwise the assumption would be that what he's written must be fiction.

So what's true, and what's not, about *8 Simple Rules for Marrying my Daughter*? Well, I'm pretty sure the Apollo Space Program really happened, for one. And I do, like many people, have two biological parents. But are the characters of Tom, Moldy, Sam, Valerie, Chris, Judy, Priscilla, and so on all actual human beings, truly represented in these pages? Did my daughter really get engaged next to the porta-potties? Is my Cousin Ted really well on his way to becoming my Cousin Tina?

As I said, I often exaggerate for comedic effect. I have real people in my life, but I wouldn't reveal their insecurities, mistakes, personalities, or lives in a humor book. If I did, it would hurt them, and I'd probably get a nasty letter from my dog.

Writers are often told "write what you know." Ian Fleming was a spy* who went on to write the James Bond series, which became one of the most successful movie franchises of all time. (If that sort of thing happens to me, well, so be it.) Undoubtedly he drew from his experiences to create the

---

* Ian Fleming worked in Naval Intelligence in the aforementioned Second World War. His code name was 17F.

plots and characters of his novels, but I've never thought 007 was *real*, even though lots of people think of me as being rather James Bond–like, myself, and thus it could be argued that the character is based on me and I should be paid a small amount of the revenues from the next five movies.

Of course, no one ever accused Ian Fleming of being a humorist (though the lyrics to the *Goldfinger* theme song are arguably hilarious. I mean, "he loves *too much*?" Have you even *met* Goldfinger?) Fleming was, however, accused by other spies of writing the truth, yet he was crafting works of fiction—it was all supposed to be made up. So there's some danger in writing what you know—how much of your fiction is based on fact?

Here's what I know. I love my children and want for them the very best in life, though I'm hoping not to have to pay for all of it. I protected them from worldly dangers when they were growing up (using some of my Bond-like skills), and my fatherly duties involve protecting them today, including shielding them from intrusions into their personal lives. I can't think of anything more intrusive than if their father were to write an accurate accounting of something so private as their real-life relationships.

So what really happened?

I think it would be best for everyone if you regard every single thing you just read as complete fiction. That's certainly how I see it, anyway.

W. Bruce Cameron,
August 2007